ARK CODE

Searching for the Ark of the Covenant using ELS Maps from the Bible Code

Barry Steven Roffman

published by Green Shoelace Books

ARK CODE
IBSN 0-9616306-4-7
Copyright © 2004 by Barry Steven Roffman

Scripture quotations from the Torah are from the Stone Artscroll Chumash, Artscroll Series; and scripture quotations from the Tanach are from the Soncino Books of the Bible.

ARK CODE CONTAINS THE HEBREW NAMES OF GOD. AS SUCH, IT IS A HOLY TEXT. PLEASE TREAT IT IN THIS MANNER.

First Edition, first printing April 2004

Library of Congress Control Number (LCCN): 2004100997

Published in the United States by
Green Shoelace Books
PO Box 5179
Alameda, CA 94501
e-mail: ArkHunt@juno.com
     [an imprint of Windstar Books]

Quantity discounts are available for books. Write to attn: Sales Manager, at the address shown above for terms and discounts, or e-mail the address above.

Manufactured in the United States of America

Cover Design by Peri Poloni, Knockout Design
http://www.knockoutbooks.com

CONTENTS

Special Thanks To:

Doctor Robert Haralick, Distinguished Professor, City University of New York and Chairman of the International Torah Codes Society, Research Mentor

Roy Reinhold, Editor and Codes Researcher

Kevin Acres, *CodeFinder: Millennium Edition* Software Programmer

Blake Lindsey, Graphics Designer

Rabbi Robert (Moshe) Roffman, Chaplain, United States Air Force Reserve, Son, Talmudic and Mathematical Assistant

Dr. Martin Roffman, Editorial assistance

Walter Keith York, Codes Researcher, Editorial assistance

Captain Glenn Killam, USNR-Retired, Editorial assistance

Moshe Aharon Shak, Research Associate and Hebrew language consultant

Dr. Eliyahu Rips, Hebrew University, Jerusalem, Research Associate

Harold Gans, Military Code Breaker and ITCS Member, Research Associate

Dr. Brendan McKay, Australia National University, Research Associate

Royal Caribbean Cruise Lines, First expedition voyage donor

Michael Drosnin, Author of *THE BIBLE CODE* and *BIBLE CODE II* – source of inspiration for *ARK CODE*

Yochanan Spielberg, *Bible Search Pro* Programmer

Kathy Roffman, Beloved wife and partner

David Alexander Roffman, Youngest son – who put his toys in storage to make my first site survey expedition a reality.

Satellite Photo of Northern Egypt (prime suspect site)

Dedicated to my family and all seekers of truth.

FOREWORD

by Dr. Robert Haralick
January 4, 2004

The first written reference to any Torah code was from Rabbi Bachya in the thirteenth century. He cryptically wrote that the code that begins with the first *Bet* of the book of *Genesis,* and skips 42 letters between each successive letter of the four letter code *Bet Hey Resh Dalet,* indicates the average length of the lunar cycle. Indeed it does so to five decimal place accuracy. Jeffrey Satinover in his book, *Cracking the Bible Codes,* gives a full discussion of this code.

Rabbi Weissmandel in a book, *Torat Chemed,* published in his name by his students, gives an account of many interesting codes that he found by manual discovery. Until the work of Witztum and Rips, who began systematic work with computers in the mid 1980's, Torah codes were a curiosity.

In 1994, Witztum, Rips, and Rosenberg published a paper in *Statistical Science.* This work described a formal statistical Torah Code experiment in which the equidistant letter sequences of the names or titles (appellations) and death/birth dates of an *a priori* set of famous rabbis formed unusually compact formations in the *Genesis* text. By a Monte Carlo experiment they showed that the probability had to be less than 16/1,000,000 that this would have happened by chance. Therefore, they concluded that this was not a chance event. Their paper began the controversy on Torah codes.

The controversy

Can it really be true that there is a text dating over 3,300 years old that has in it a code of certain events that would happen thousands of years later? Such a text could not be written then by an earthly being. Either a time traveler wrote it, or God (simultaneously present in past, present and future time) authored it. Those who hold the naturalist hypothesis, that every observable event has a natural cause, can be expected to assert that both the time traveler and God are out of the box of natural causes. This conclusion may even lead them to reject the evidence for Torah codes with an emotional commitment that may make them knowingly mislead others.

In 1999, McKay et al. argued in their *Statistical Science* paper that the Torah code experiments of Witztum, Rips, and Rosenberg on the *Genesis* text succeeded because in one way or another they selectively omitted certain names to make the experiment produce a seemingly statistically significant result. To demonstrate this, they cooked an experiment using a Hebrew text of *War and Peace.* They showed that by *non a priori* selective omissions (and some spelling stretches), their Monte Carlo experiment yielded a comparably small probability. In essence, they argued that had there been no stretches and that had a full *a priori* set of appellations been used, neither the WRR experiment in the *Genesis* text nor their experiment in the *War and Peace* text would have had statistically significant results.

Their paper does not openly stress that the experiment with the *War and Peace* text was cooked; that it was a *non a priori* experiment; and therefore the low probability their experiment yielded should not be accepted as a real probability. So like a magician who performs tricks of illusion, the McKay paper is the product of a magician, an illusion. The problem is that most people will not have enough technical background to understand the difference between something that is real and something that is deliberate illusion.

My own experiments in the past year combined the *a priori* appellation lists of Witztum, Rips, and Rosenberg with the cooked appellation lists of McKay et al. We redid the *Famous Rabbis* experiment with an improved protocol and statistical methodology. We tested the Null hypothesis of "no Torah code effect" against four different alternative hypotheses. Our experiments show that the combined list of appellations has the same or a slightly stronger effect in the *Genesis* text than the original list for three out of the four alternative hypotheses, and a slightly weaker effect for the fourth alternative hypothesis. For the McKay list in the *War and Peace* text there was a significant decrease in the effect for all four alternative hypotheses. With the improved protocol, the combined list had a statistically insignificant effect in the *War and Peace* text for all four alternative hypotheses. Statistical significance was measured at the $\alpha=.001$ level.

These results provide evidence of the fallaciousness of McKay et al.'s assertion that had a more full *a priori* list of appellations been used, the Null hypothesis of "no Torah code effect" would not have been rejected in both the *Genesis* text and the *War and Peace* text. We conclude that the Torah code effect is real for the *Famous Rabbis* experiment using the *Genesis* text. We also conclude that as expected there is no Torah code effect in the *War and Peace* text.

Our further experiments showed something even more amazing. With respect to the *Great Rabbis* experiment, what is encoded is multiply encoded. It is not just one Torah code matrix that contains the encoding of an appellation date pair, but many matrices do. To determine this, we found many matrices for each appellation-date pair and arranged the matrices from best to worst according to a compactness measure. Then we compared the best matrix from the Torah with the best matrices from ELS (equidistant letter sequence) random placement model monkey texts (scrambled letter texts used for statistical comparisons). When there was an encoding it was not just that the best matrix was better than most all of the monkey text matrices, but the next to best was too, and the next to the next to best was also better, etc. When this pattern was taken into account in an appropriate combined statistic, we found that the pattern was statistically significant at the α=.001 level.

The import of the multiple encoding result is that the big picture is missed when only one matrix or table is shown. When one is shown, it is typically the best one. But basing an experiment on the best matrix alone means that it is easier to counterfeit the result. Each test of the Null hypothesis of "no Torah code effect" has a probability of error. There is the probability of accepting the Null hypothesis when it is not true; and the probability of rejecting the Null hypothesis when the Null hypothesis is true. Experiments based on best matrix alone will have higher probabilities of rejecting the Null hypothesis when the Null hypothesis is true.

Barry Roffman's experiments

In 1998, I first became acquainted with Barry Roffman's experiments which employed Torah codes in a novel way: there was a sketch of a Torah Codes ELS map with course angle directions to designate a location. I can testify that from his early work to all the evidence he provides in this book, his hypothesis has not changed; and he has been working with and developing the same idea. In other words, from 1998 on there was public knowledge that he did *not* do thousands of different kinds of experiments and reject those that did not succeed, so that in this book he would only tell about those that did succeed. At Barry's request in 2002, I wrote programs that would perform a proper Monte Carlo experiment on his matrices. Without going into all the technical details, the experiments showed that his matrices are statistically significant. It was not likely that they would occur by chance.

There is one more thing that needs to be understood about Barry's hypothesis about the Ark and Torah codes. The Torah code hypothesis, that most of the Torah code researchers hold, is that key words that relate to logically historically related events tend to have ELSs that form more compact relationships in the Torah text than would be expected by chance. Put in symbolic form, this statement is *A* implies *B* where *A* is "key words that relate to a logically historically related events'' and *B* is "tend to have ELSs that form more compact relationships in the Torah text than would be expected by chance.'' The hypothesis says nothing about compact formations of ELSs that are associated with key words not related to any historical event.

At this time, we do not know where the Ark of the Covenant is hidden. It may be where Barry hypothesizes it, or it may not. If it is not where he hypothesizes, then we do not have an historical event corresponding to his key words. If an archaeological exploration at the site he hypothesizes does not yield any evidence about the ark, this would *not* provide any negative evidence against the Torah code hypothesis. The truth of the proposition that *A* implies *B* is not affected by negative evidence against the proposition that *B* implies *A*. However, if an expedition yields evidence of the ark where he hypothesizes, then that evidence will be supportive for the Torah code hypothesis. This is because the archaeological evidence establishes the historical event so that we can assert *A: The Ark of the Covenant is buried near Lake Bardawil at El Zuqba, Egypt.* His book provides the evidence for *B* – that at least in the case of the Ark of the Covenant, geographic site names are encoded in such manner as to lead us to something very precious that has been lost for at least 2,590 years.

Dr. Robert Haralick is the Distinguished Professor in the Computer Science Graduate Center at the City University of New York (New York, NY 10016). He is also chairman of the International Torah Code Society (ITCS), a worldwide association of top codes researchers.

Ark Code

Searching for the Ark of the Covenant

You shall place in the Ark the Testimonial tablets that I shall give you. It is there that I will meet with you, and I shall speak with you from atop the Cover, from between the two cherubim that are on the Ark of the Testimonial tablets, everything that I shall command you to the Children of Israel.

Exodus 25:16 & 22

Chapter 1

ELS MAPS IN THE TORAH

The Torah (first five books of the Bible) contains a series of Equidistant Letter Spaced (ELS) maps pointing to the long-hidden location of the Ark of the Covenant. Key site names are encoded in such manner as to have the angles between each of them and the Ark site correspond to actual course headings on real world maps. While I could begin by telling the story of how these maps were found and what they may mean, I choose to present the maps first and then set forth their derivation and significance for the sake of those predisposed to reject such encoding out of hand. The story itself, supporting matrices, methods, and analysis will follow in succeeding chapters.

After reading Mr. Drosnin's *BIBLE CODE* book in 1997, I hypothesized that the Torah Code, if real, would likely contain the specific location of that which was most central to the worship of God during the existence of the First Temple in Jerusalem: the Ark of the Covenant. Recovery of the actual physical Ark (believed to have disappeared between 925 and 586 BCE) would probably prove the ELS encoding of the Torah, if the Torah Codes computer software and area charts were the sole sources of data used to find the Ark. Two tests were required to support the hypothesis:

(1) Statistically significant data collection worthy of actual field investigation, and...
(2) Recovery of the Ark by means of actual expedition should the first test be met.

The first test was more than met. Data found resulted in my invitation to speak at the first meeting of the International Torah Codes Society (ITCS) in Jerusalem in 1999. However, funding is required to properly complete the second phase of the investigation (begun with a brief trip to Egypt after my 1999 ITCS presentation).

By the time I had arrived in Jerusalem, it was clear that many simplistic Bible Code or Torah Code plots can be replicated in non-religious texts. This especially applies to material aimed at convincing individuals to switch from one religion to another. In short, while I have seen many significant matrices developed by other researchers, there are some who use *cheap shots* out there in the world of Bible Code research. Further, I haven't seen many substantiated statistically significant, specific predictions made based upon the Code that have actually been verified with the passage of time. Perhaps this is because people have asked the Code for too much. While it is possible to encode many events into a text of 304,805 letters, my own research seems to indicate a greater probability for a more limited encoding scheme, one that primarily (but not exclusively) maps out the location of the Ark of the Covenant.

Primary resources employed include CodeFinder: Millennium Edition Bible code software, BA Chart 56100, Biblical atlases, and a vintage 1935 map of the Northern Sinai (1:100,000 scale for the Qatia area) found in Cairo, Egypt in 1999. The term, *Ark of the Covenant* (ארון ברית, pronounced *Aron Brit*), is encoded seven times in a single reading of the Torah at skips (ELS) of -306, +3,102, +3,621, -8,752, +9,698, -15,677 and -24,926 letters (+ means the encoding is in a forward direction, - means it's backwards). It's customary by some researchers to place greatest emphasis on what can be found encoded at the minimum ELS. Here this minimum ELS equates to a skip of -306.

Upon examining the open text material of the encoding at a skip of -306, it became apparent that there was sufficient meaningful material to justify further pursuit of the investigation. At Numbers 33:4, *Ark of the Covenant* intersects the phrase מצרים מקברים את (*Egyptians were burying*). Further, although the verse speaks of the burying the Egyptian dead, we may presume that the Ark was also buried. The chapter and verse, 33:4, correspond to a longitude that goes through the Sinai Peninsula of Egypt (33 degrees 4 minutes East). A Hebrew term for *longitude* is קו ארכ (*kav aroch*, or line of length). A short form of it, ארכ, is next to *Ark of the Covenant* at a skip of +2 in Figure 1A.

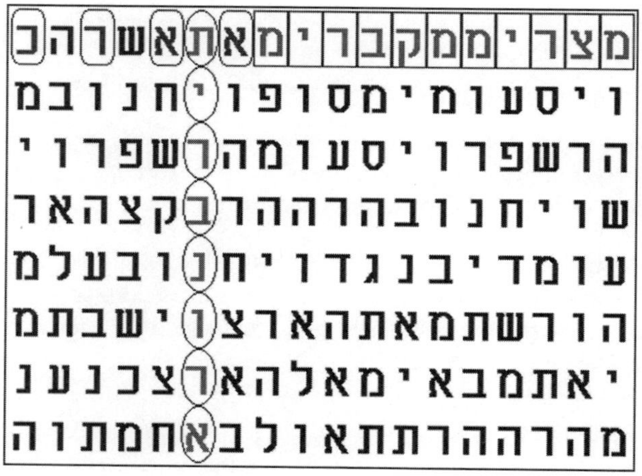

Figure 1A
Initial Findings from October 1997

Terms on Figure 1A	Translation	Symbol	Skip	Start	End
ארון ברית	Ark of Covenant	◯	-306	Numbers 34 V8 L13	Numbers 33 V4 L14
מצרים מקברים את	Egyptians were burying	▢	1	Numbers 33 V4 L2	Numbers 33 V4 L12
ארכ	Longitude	▢	2	Numbers 33 V4 L15	Numbers 33 V4 L19

Using the same hunch about coordinates equal to chapter and verse, *Ark of the Covenant* was sought in the open text and found three times in Deuteronomy 31; but only one verse corresponded to a Middle East minute of latitude on land: 31° 9'. Although this was not very statistically significant, Figure 2 showed the word for *latitude* (רחב) was encoded there, so I searched for map site names near the coordinates of 31 degrees 9 minutes North, 33 degrees 4 minutes East.

Figure 2 – The Ark in Deuteronomy 31:9

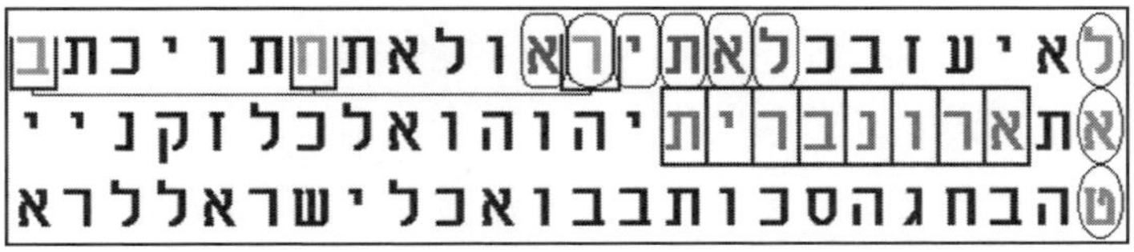

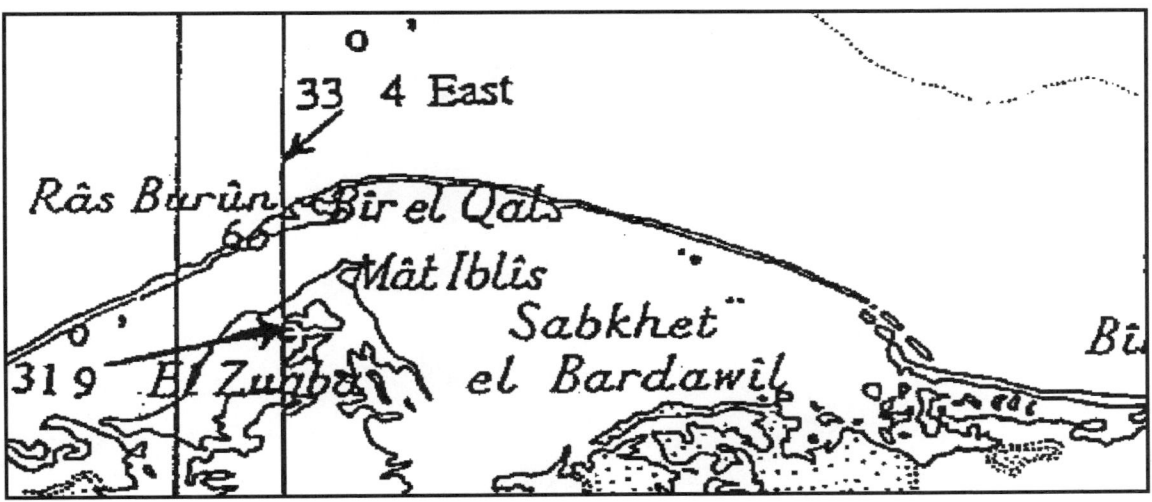

Terms	Translation	Symbol	Skip	Start	End
לא-ט	31-9	◯	63	Deuteronomy 31 V8 L35	Deuteronomy 31 V10 L36
ארון ברית	Ark of Covenant	▢	1	Deuteronomy 31 V9 L47	Deuteronomy 31 V9 L54
רחב	Latitude	⊔	6	Deuteronomy 31 V8 L46	Deuteronomy 31 V9 L5
לא תירא	Do not fear	◯	1	Deuteronomy 31 V8 L42	Deuteronomy 31 V8 L46

Map 1 - The Pre-Expedition Map of Bardawil

Important nearby geographic sites included *Zuqba* (צקב) and *Bardawil* (ברדול), shown with a diagonal line through it on Figure 1B in Egypt. On Figure 1B, *Zuqba* (at skip -1) intersects and shares a *bet* (ב) with *Ark of the Covenant* (ארון ברית). *Bardawil* is encoded at skip -303, and it starts at the same letter (ב) in ארון ברית. Lake Bardawil surrounds the initial 31° 9' North, 33° 4' East site on the El Zuqba peninsula.

**Figure 1B
Bardawil, Zuqba, and the Ark of the Covenant**

Terms on 1B	Translation	Symbol	Skip	Start	End
ארון ברית	Ark of Covenant	◯	-306	Numbers 34 V8 L13	Numbers 33 V4 L14
ברדול	Bardawil	☐	-303	Numbers 33 V37 L21	Numbers 32 V40 L12
צקב	Zuqba	▢	-1	Numbers 33 V37 L23	Numbers 33 V37 L21

There were many other position-related terms found near the axis term, *Ark of the Covenant* (at skip –306). To avoid confusion by showing them all on a single matrix, a series of additional matrices will be shown with one or two terms displayed in an addition to the identical axis term. The combined are results are shown in their entirety as Figure 1 in Appendix A.

Terms on 1C	Translation	Symbol	Skip	Start	End
ארון ברית	Ark of Covenant	◯	-306	Numbers 34 V8 L13	Numbers 33 V4 L14
ברדול	Bardawil	☐	-303	Numbers 33 V37 L21	Numbers 32 V40 L12
ים סוף	Yam Suf*	▢	1	Numbers 33 V11 L7	Numbers 33 V11 L11
* Lake Bardawil is believed to be the Yam Suf, that is, the Sea of Reeds.					

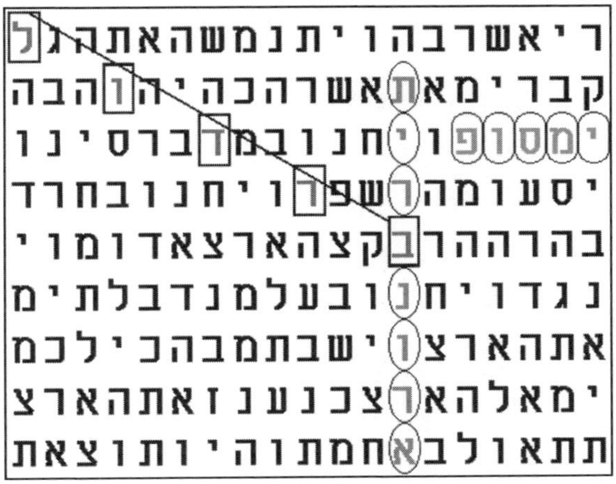

Figure 1C

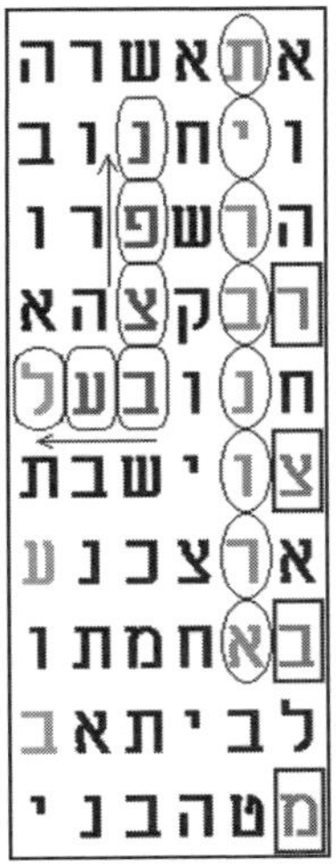

Figure 1D

Terms on 1D	Translation	Symbol	Skip	Start	End
ארון ברית	Ark of Covenant	◯	-306	Numbers 34 V8 L13	Numbers 33 V4 L14
מבצר	Fortress	▢	-612	Numbers 34 V23 L10	Numbers 33 V37 L20
בעל	Baal	▢	1	Numbers 33 V46 L18	Numbers 33 V46 L20
צפן	Zephon	◯	-306	Numbers 33 V37 L23	Numbers 33 V11 L15

Baal Zephon is a fortress passed by the Israelites during the early phase of the Exodus.

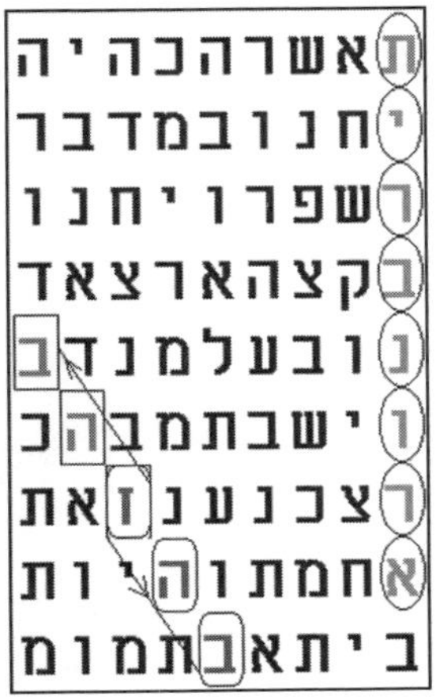

Figure 1E

Terms on 1E	Translation	Symbol	Skip	Start	End
ארון ברית	Ark of Covenant	◯	-306	Numbers 34 V8 L13	Numbers 33 V4 L14
זהב	Gold	▢	305	Numbers 34 V2 L41	Numbers 34 V14 L25
זהב	Gold	▢	-305	Numbers 34 V2 L41	Numbers 33 V6 L24

The Ark was made of gold. Figure 1E shows gold appears encoded twice sharing the same letter zayin near the Ark.

מצרימממקברימאתאשרהכהיהוהבה
ויסעוממסופויחנובמדברסינו
הרשפרויסעומהשפרויחנובחרד
שויחנובההרההקצהארצאדומי
עומדיבנגדויחנובעלמנדבלתים
הורשתמאתהארצוישבתמבהכילכמ
יאתמבאימאלהאצכנענזאתהארצ
מהרההרתההאולבאחמתהייותצאת

Figure 1F

Terms on 1F	Translation	Symbol	Skip	Start	End
ארון ברית	Ark of Covenant	○	-306	Numbers 34 V8 L13	Numbers 33 V4 L14
מצרים	Egypt	□	1	Numbers 33 V4 L2	Numbers 33 V4 L6
מצרים	Egypt	▢	-312	Numbers 33 V46 L28	Numbers 33 V4 L2

Figure 1F shows that an encoded Egypt runs through the axis term. Egypt also appears in the open text.

מומצרימממקברימאת
ופויסעומימסופוי
ובהרשפרויסעומה
קדשוייחנובההרההר
יסעומדיבנגדויחנ
ווהורשתמאתהארצו
מכיאתמבאימאלהא
הרמהרההרתההאולבא

Figure 1G

Terms on 1G	Translation	Symbol	Skip	Start	End
ארון ברית	Ark of Covenant	○	-306	Numbers 34 V8 L13	Numbers 33 V4 L14
מפה	Chart	□	307	Numbers 33 V3 L81	Numbers 33 V23 L18

ק ו נ	56100*	☐	–3	Numbers 33 V37 L13	Numbers 33 V37 L7

British Admiralty Chart 56100 covers the El Zuqba/Bardawil area where the Ark is believed to be. Encoding on Figure 1G is probably just due to chance, but if not – then the Author had foreknowledge of which chart would cover the area.

Originally there was some question about the name of the peninsula jutting into Lake Bardawil. When I went to Israel in 1999, I thought it was *Zuaba* rather than *Zuqba* because of the poor quality of a photocopy of Map 1 that I was working with. As will be explained later, there remains a slight chance that the name really is Zuaba, but my current map evidence indicates Zuqba. For the record, the original Zuaba spelling was based on Figure 1H below:

Figure 1H – Zuaba with Ark of the Covenant

Terms on 1H	Translation	Symbol	Skip	Start	End
ארון ברית	Ark of the Covenant	○	-306	Numbers 34 V8 L13	Numbers 33 V4 L14
זאבה	Zuaba	☐	-7	Numbers 34 V2 L41	Numbers 34 V2 L20

With the Zuqba spelling found on Figures 1B, we see that this name is crossed twice by the word for *position* in Figure1I:

FIGURE 1I

On Figure 1I the word *Position* is encoded twice. The two words share one letter, a kuf, which is also shared by Zuqba, the suspect position of the Ark.

Terms on 1I	Translation	Symbol	Skip	Start	End
ארון ברית	Ark of Covenant	○	-306	Numbers 34 V8 L13	Numbers 33 V4 L14
מקום	Position	□	-310	Numbers 33 V46 L21	Numbers 33 V11 L6
מקום	Position	□	-616	Numbers 33 V53 L19	Numbers 32 V39 L39
צקב	Zuqba	▭	-1	Numbers 33 V7 L23	Numbers 33 V37 L21

Is the Torah really a map? When Dr. Rips expressed his belief that the Ark remains hidden in Jerusalem, I sought *Jerusalem* (Biblical spelling of ירושלם) and found it at skip +303 starting 22 letters right, and seven rows up from Zuqba's first letter (צ). The Temple Mount in Jerusalem serves as one vertex of most ELS Ark Code map triangles. The Temple coordinates used were 31 degrees 46 minutes 39.72 seconds North, 35 degrees 14 minutes, 4.38 seconds East. On ELS Map Figure 1, if we focus on the first letter of Jerusalem (י), the angle from this letter to the first letter of צקב (Zuqba) corresponds to a course of 252.35°. The course from Jerusalem to Zuqba at 31° 9' North, 33° 4' East by the on-line Java Applet *Coordinate Calculator* ™ is 251.9° True. Further, the angle from the last letter of *Temple* (מקדש) to the first letter of *Ark of the Covenant* corresponds to a course of 251.565° True, an even better match to Java's 251.9°. The 251.565° course is seen later on six more maps. The difference between 251.565 and 251.9 degrees over this distance from Jerusalem is about 3,110 feet. The calculator assumes a perfectly spherical Earth. The Earth is actually an oblate spheroid with an equatorial diameter 26.872 statute miles greater than the polar diameter. The Java Applet doesn't handle hundredths of seconds for coordinate entry arguments, only tenths of seconds. ***Note: ELS course calculations are <u>not</u> based on line or letter spacing. They are based only on number of rows (Y) and columns (X) between terms.***

For the two courses derived from ELS Map Figure 1 (252.35° and 251.565°), the average course is 251.9575°, quite close to Java Applet's course of 251.9°. The distance from the Temple Mount to the coordinates in question is about 135 statute miles. Over this distance a difference of .0575° between for the Java Applet course of 251.9° and the average course of 251.9575° is about 715 feet.

There was 1 chance in 881 for *Temple* to be on Figure 1 (in Appendix A) in a position equivalent to the 251.565° course to the suspect coordinates, but on a larger ELS Map 1 below, it was 1 chance in 363. The logic behind these probabilities is given in Appendix A.

ELS Map 1 – Zuqba, Bardawil and Jerusalem

```
יהוהעדהודישואתאבי ומפני ונכבשהארצלפני יהוהואחדתש
מהכאשראדני דבר יצולהממשהאתאלעזרהכהנ ואת יהושעבנ נונו
מעברלי רדנ יתנלהממשהלבנ י גדולבנ י ראובנ ולחצי שבטמנשהב
ירבנמנ הגלעדהו ילכדהו י ורשאתהאמר י אשרבהו י תנמשהאתהגל
שראלבי דרמהלעינ י כלמצר י ומצקבר י מאשרהאשרהכה יה ההבה
מ ויסעומאילמו יחנו ועלי מסוף וי סעומ ימסוף ויחנ ובמברס ינ ו
בקהלתה ו י סעומקהלתה ו יחנ ובהרשפרו י סעומהרשפ רו יחנ ובחרד
נ ובמדברצנ ואהקדשו יחנ ובהרההרב יצעומקדשו יסעו יחנ והאראדו מו י
סעומע י ימו יחנ ובד י בנגד י סעומ ד י בנגד יח ובעלמנדבלת ימ
מתאבד ו ואתכלכבמותמשמ י ד ו והרשתמאתהארצ י שבתמבהכ ילכמ
רצואתבנ י י שראלואמרתאלהמכ יאתמבא י מאלהאצכנענ ו זאתהארצ
וננמ נה ימ הגדלתתאול באחמתו ה י ותוצאת
```

Terms on ELS Map 1	Translation	Symbol	Skip	Start	End
ארון ברית	Ark of Covenant	(filled oval)	-306	Numbers 34 V8 L13	Numbers 33 V4 L14
ירושלמ	Jerusalem	(filled square)	303	Numbers 32 V21 L40	Numbers 33 V9 L58
ברדול	Bardawil (Lake)	(filled square)	-303	Numbers 33 V37 L21	Numbers 32 V40 L12
מקדש	Temple/Sanctuary	(open oval)	1	Numbers 33 V37 L6	Numbers 33 V37 L9
צקב	Zuqba	(open rectangle)	-1	Numbers 33 V37 L23	Numbers 33 V37 L21

DESCRIPTIVE REPORT AND CALCULATIONS FOR ELS MAP 1

The ELS reference is 306 characters between rows. There are 5 displayed terms in the matrix. The matrix starts at Numbers 32 V21 L25 and ends at Numbers 34 V8 L25. The matrix spans 3414 characters of the surface text. The matrix has 12 rows, is 48 columns wide and contains a total of 576 characters.

JERUSALEM – ZUQBA COURSE CALCULATION: X = 22 COLUMNS, Y = 7 ROWS. TAN = Y/X = 0.318181818. ARCTAN = 17.65012422°. 90° - 17.65° = 72.35° FROM ZUQBA TO JERUSALEM. THE RECIPROCAL COURSE = **252.35°**. **TEMPLE-ARK CALCULATION**: X = 12 COLUMNS, Y = 4 ROWS. TAN = Y/X = 0.33333. ARCTAN = 18.435°. 90°-18.435° = 71.565° FROM ARK TO TEMPLE. THE RECIPROCAL COURSE = **251.565°**.

ELS Map 1 indicates an angle from Jerusalem's letter *yud* (י) to the first letter of Bardawil (ב) that equates to a course of 248.6 degrees True. While there are many angles from Jerusalem to Bardawil's wide lake that are correct, this particular course would in fact pass through the eastern part of the lake, i.e., the part closest to Jerusalem. Using crude charts indicates this course line from Jerusalem would intersect Bardawil where Lake Zaraniq meets it. There are, by the way, a number of ancient ruins in this area.

Map 2: Where the Encoded Course from Jerusalem Intersects with Lake Bardawil

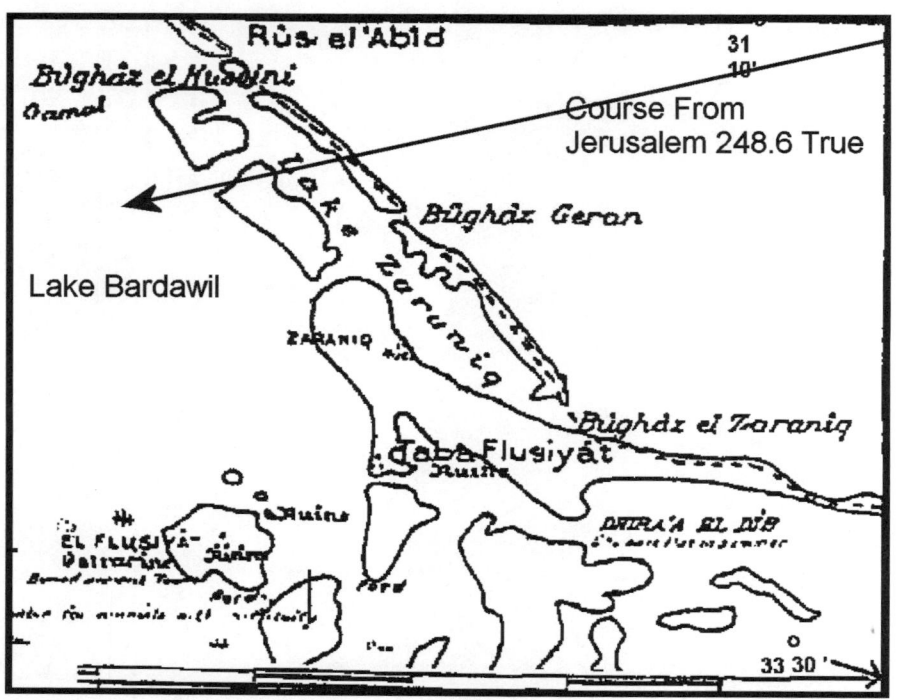

A look at this area from 162 miles up in orbit reveals that the bottom of Lake Bardawil is so shallow in most areas that it appears almost the same color as the surrounding desert sands. Exodus 14:21 states that God *"moved the sea with a strong east wind all the night."* Chaim Potok (*Wanderings,* pg 91) states that he has *"seen Bardawil and watched the narrow strip that separates the lake from the sea vanish as east winds sent the Mediterranean rolling across it."* The peninsula that juts into this sea is covered with huge sand dunes. The water to the west of this peninsula is obviously very shallow. In one place, the color photo from space even seems to show a sandbar that extends across the lake from the peninsula to the barrier island that might be shallow enough to walk across. As such, a really strong east wind might be sufficient to blow enough sand into the lake to allow for a dry path across. It would part the *Sea of Reeds.* However, neither sand fill, nor the arrival of a tsunami would explain the presence of a wall of water on the right and left when the Israelites crossed over (Exodus 14:22). Such an event (if not allegory)

10

could only be explained by a force field or a miracle.

There is some geological evidence to suggest a link of Bardawil to the Exodus. Pumice, a volcanic rock that floats, has been found at Tell el-Dab'a in the eastern Nile delta and along a Mediterranean beach near Bardawil. The rock matches pumice from Thira, an island destroyed by a huge eruption between 1628 BCE and the time of the Exodus. It apparently floated there behind a tsunami emanating from Thira. Such a wave, if due to another tsunami at the time of the Exodus, may have played a role in drowning the Egyptians when it entered the lake via two openings to the sea. Indeed, an eruption may have played a role in the 9th plague of darkness. The Bible speaks of a thick darkness that could be felt (Exodus 10:21-22). This may have been volcanic ash blown there by the winds.

More Maps From The Codes

ELS Map 2 – Found by Dr. Robert Haralick

Terms on ELS Map 2	Translation	Skip	Symbol	Start	End
ירושלם	Jerusalem	-30	◯	Numbers 11 V4 L40	Numbers 11 V1 L30
ארון ברית	Ark of Covenant	1	▢	Numbers 10 V33 L25	Numbers 10 V33 L32
צקב	Zuqba	-1	◗	Numbers 11 V1 L63	Numbers 11 V1 L61
המקום	The position	1	◖	Numbers 11 V3 L8	Numbers 11 V3 L12
מפה	Map or Chart	-31	◠	Numbers 11 V3 L12	Numbers 11 V1 L55
מפה	Map or Chart	-29	∪	Numbers 11 V4 L36	Numbers 11 V3 L13
קבר	Bury	-1	∩	Numbers 11 V4 L12	Numbers 11 V4 L10

DESCRIPTIVE REPORT AND CALCULATIONS FOR ELS MAP 2

The ELS reference is 30 characters between rows. There are 7 displayed terms in the matrix. The matrix starts at Numbers 10 V33 L25 and ends at Numbers 11 V4 L43. The matrix spans 341 characters of the surface text. The matrix has 12 rows, is 11 columns wide and contains a total of 132 characters.

COURSE CALCULATION: X = 3 COLUMNS, Y = 1 ROW. TAN = .33333333. ARCTAN = 18.4349488229 DEG. TRUE. ZUQBA TO JERUSALEM = 90-18.435 = 71.565 DEGREES TRUE.

JERUSALEM TO ZUQBA = **251.565 DEGREES.**

There are at least *nine to eleven* additional ELS maps (depending upon how we define the term *map*). ELS Map 2 was found by Dr. Robert Haralick. It shows that where *Jerusalem* (ירושלם) appears at its third shortest skip in the Torah (-30), *Zuqba* (צקב) at skip –1 touches its next to last letter, *lamed* (ל). *Ark of the Covenant* (ארון ברית) is six letters above Jerusalem, but the angle from Jerusalem's last letter, *mem* (מ) to the first letter of Zuqba (צ) corresponds to a course of 251.565°, like the match between Temple and Ark of the Covenant on ELS Map 1. This precise angle of 251.565° also appears on five other ELS map figures. On ELS Map 1, *Ark of the Covenant* and *Zuqba* (at skip –1) fit together in a 3 column by 8 row, 24-letter matrix. On ELS Map 2, *Jerusalem* and *Zuqba* (at skip –1 again) fit together in 24-letter matrix again (4 columns by 6 rows).

While Dr. Haralick was finding ELS Map Figure 2, it became obvious that the axis term in such plots should either have at least seven letters; or, in the case of a six-letter term like Jerusalem, it must be one of the shortest existing ELS finds for the term. This is because between skips 60,961 and –60,961 there are 3,479 occurrences of Jerusalem (more than nine per degree).

With ELS Map 3, the axis term is *Position of Ark* (מקום ארון). *Jerusalem* (ירושלם) is at skip -875. The angle from the first letter of *Jerusalem* (י) to the first letter of *Position Ark* (מ) again equals a course of 251.565°. The first letter of *Position (of) Ark* (מ) is the last letter of *Land of Egypt* (ארץ מצרים). The axis term is at its second lowest ELS in Torah (-2,628).

It's always preferable to work with the lowest ELS of a term. The lowest ELS of *Position (of) THE Ark* (מקום הארן) is at skip +3,373. When I sought *Jerusalem* on the plot (ELS Map 4), it was there at skip +843. The angle from the first letter of *Jerusalem* (י) to the last letter of *Position (of) The Ark* (ן) corresponds to a course of 253.5°. While this is close to the Java Calculator heading of 251.9° from Jerusalem to Zuqba, it is outside the one-degree margin of error I normally allow (it's 1.6° off), and it's 1.935° off from the 251.565° course seen above. However, the letter immediately above the first letter of Jerusalem is *mem* (מ). This letter is Hebrew for the word *from*. Thus we are really looking at a 7-letter ELS that is translated as *From Jerusalem* (מירושלם). When the course line is drawn from the *mem* in question, then we again arrive at a course of 251.565°. Further, one row below and three columns to the left of this same *mem* begins the open text word for *gold* (זהב). The Ark was made of gold, and the angle from the start of *From Jerusalem* to *gold* again equals a course of 251.565° True.

אבאשישרפואתוואתהנולאתהיהזמ
הנימבניאהרנואמרתאלהמלכנפשלא
נלאיגשלהקריבאתאשייהוהמומבו
כלקדשבשנגההייספחמשיתועליוון
ארצמצרימלהיותלכמלאלהימאניי
ימסלתתהייונהחמצתאהפינהבכורים
לאמרבחמשהעשריומלחדשהשביעיה
יההחלההאאחתושמתאותתמשתימעמרכ
כיתבאואלהארצאשראניונתנלכמוש
הארצפריהואבלתמלשבעויישבתמל
כאתכספכלאתתנלובנשכובמרביתל
וצאתיאותתמצרמיאנייהוה
יכמונסתמואינרדפאתכמואמעדאל
אשבתהבשבתתייכמבשבתבכמעליהוהן
כהזכרעשרימשקלימולנבהעשרתש
כהנתהיהאחזתוואמאתשדהמקנתוא
בנאליצורבנשדיאורדלשמעונשלמי
מספרשמתמבנעשרימשנההימעלהכלי
קדימשמאותתאלפושלשתאלפימוחמ
אותוהחונעמליומטהשמעונונשיא
לשתאלפימוחמשמאותתוחמשימוהלו
מתמגרשוונוקהתוהמדרייואלהשמותב
החצרסביבואדנייהמויתדתמומיתר
שנהכלבלבאלצבאלעשותמלכהבאהלמ
אמראלתכריתואתשבטמשפחתהקהת
קהתילמשפחתמולביתאבתמבנשלש
אותמאלמחוצלמחנהכאשורדבריהוה
שטיתטמאההתחתאישכהנקימיהמרי
פנהייינמחרצנימועדזנגלאיאכלכל
קדשהואלכהנגהעלחלזההההתנפההועלשו
יומהראשואנאתקרבנונחשונבנעמי
מנלמנחהנהכפאחתעשרהזהבמלאהקטר
שימבניישנהחמשהזההקרבנזאלישמעב

ELS Map 3

ELS MAP 3 COURSE CALCULATION FROM JERUSALEM TO FIRST LETTER OF POSITION OF ARK:

X = 18 COLUMNS, Y = 6 ROWS. TANGENT = Y/X = 0.3333333333333. ARC TANGENT = 18.4349489 DEGREES. SUBTRACT THE ABOVE ANGLE FROM 90 DEGREES. THIS IS THE COURSE TO JERUSALEM. 90 – 18.435 = 71.565 DEGREES. THE RECIPROCAL COURSE REQUIRES ADDING 180 TO THE ABOVE: 71.565 + 180 = **251.565 DEGREES TRUE**

Terms	Translation	Symbol	Skip	Start
מקום ארון	Position of Ark	●	2628	Leviticus 25 V55 L45
ירושלם	Jerusalem	☐	-871	Leviticus 23 V17 L34
ארץ מצרים	Land of Egypt	▭	1	Leviticus 25 V55 L38

13

**ELS Map 4
Course of Ark from Jerusalem**

Terms on ELS Map 4	Translation	Skip	Start
מקום הארן	Position of the Ark	3373	Exodus 15 V3 L18
מירושלם	From Jerusalem	843	Exodus 26 V14 L42
זהב	Gold	1	Exodus 26 V32 L38

DESCRIPTIVE REPORT AND CALCULATIONS FOR ELS MAP 4

The ELS reference is 843 characters between rows. There are 3 displayed terms in the matrix. The matrix starts at Exodus 15 V2 L46 and ends at Exodus 30 V 12 L63. The matrix spans 23632 characters of the surface text. The matrix has 29 rows, is 28 columns wide and contains a total of 812 characters.

X = 27, Y = 8. The angle corresponds to a course of 253.4956 degrees from the first letter of Jerusalem to the last letter of Position (of) the Ark. HOWEVER, THE LETTER ABOVE JERUSALEM IS *MEM*. THIS MEANS "FROM." IF THE COURSE IS TAKEN FROM THERE, THEN X = 27, Y = 9, AND **THE COURSE = 251.565 AS WAS SEEN ON 5 OTHER MAP PLOTS.**

Most of my significant ELS map figures were found after I visited Cairo in 1999, where I located the following map:

Map 3 - 1:100,000 Scale Map for the Qatia Area (Northern Sinai)

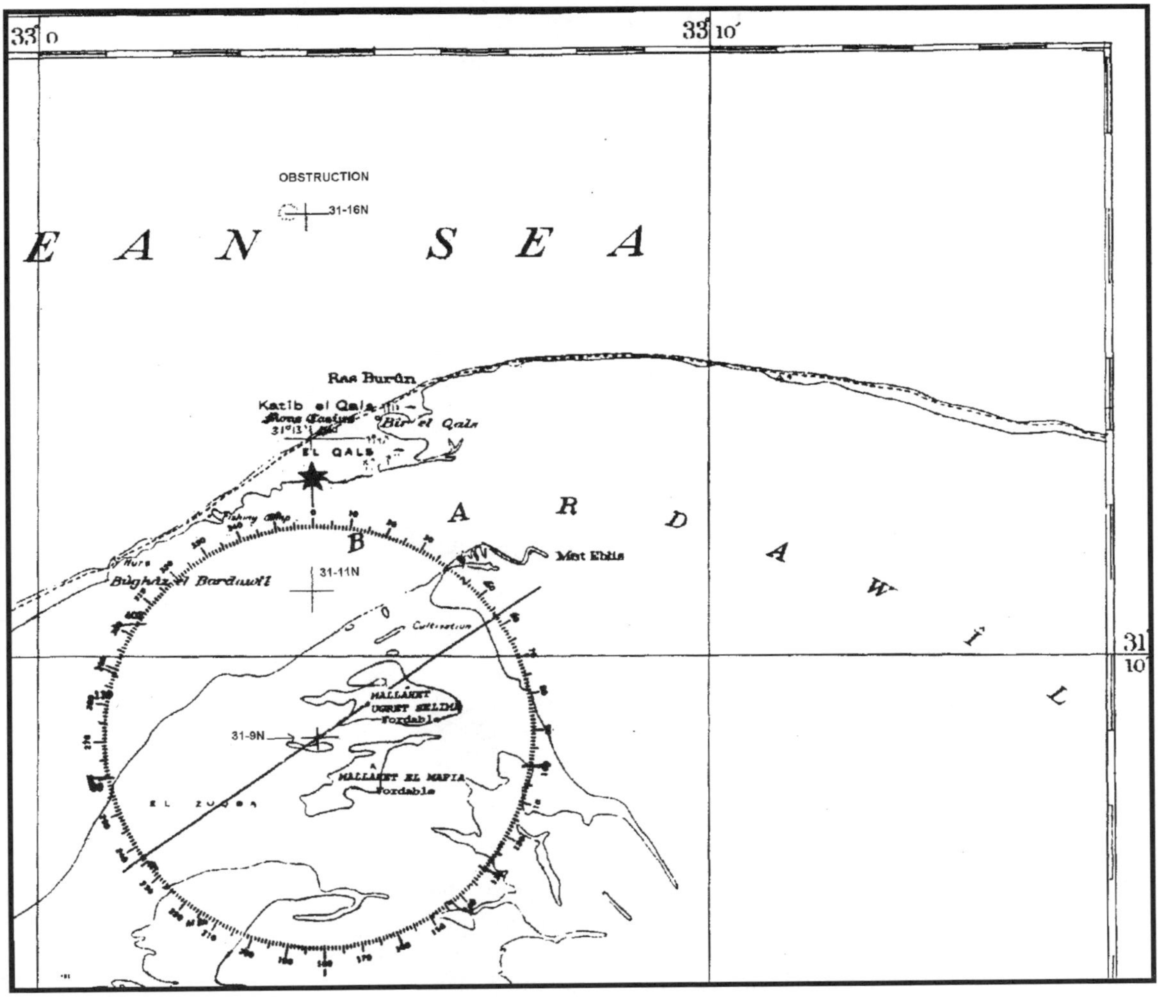

On Map 3, the named feature closest to the primary suspect site at 31° 9'N, 33° 4'E is the salt marsh *Mallahet **Ugret Selima***. As it is within 600 meters of the primary site, the GPS course to it from Jerusalem is still about 251.9°T. On ELS Map 5 below, the decision was made to search for *Mallahet Ugret Selima*. The full term wasn't found, however *Mallahet* means *often dried up salt marsh*. It's used for three sites on the full map found in Cairo. The distinguishing name here is *Ugret Selima* (עגרת שלימה). This term was found only on a *wrapped* plot (discussed later), where the program makes more than one pass through the Torah at skip +37,187. Once again when we search for Jerusalem (ירושלם), the city pops up

15

עתובת**י**מטב**י**מת
האלהה**נ**הסכתע
מחתבבלהטובאש
יכמיקומווי עז
עודשבעתימימא
צאשמשלשימויא
ויהירעבבאצצמ
בלקראתכואדבע
ויאמ**ה**ואלי וחל
ריוויבכעלצוא
מנוכינרפימהמ
לשמדימהואליה
אתדעהובאבנאו
היתדתעלהכבדי
לעלהמשכנעשתי
מעלזבחהשלמים
נאת** בי**ומהשבי
טעלתשכיראתכ
עדאלהלאתשמעו
ובראשוו**ח**מישת
להמאמאתכבלד**ן**י
מכלמעשדתימכא
רממשפחתהאחיר
גדדיסעומה**ה**נ
מא**ש**דחלקיהוהא
מוירשתמנוומנ
לכנחלהלא**ח**תאיה
דבקובבכנמכלחל
נהרהשלישיחדק
ויאמראל**ש**דיאש
שראמדאליכויש
אידעתיוירדאו
בלההפי.**ג**נשאבי
וילכומשמוו יפת
עבדיואתהרפאי
הויעש**ם**והובכנ וו
משנהעלאשרילק
יטבעתעלצלעוה
פיבה**ם**אכלמוא
תשתיקצותשתיה
מ**ד**יתנעליואתה
צל**ה**הכבהנוחלצו

once in the matrix with this site. The last letter of Jerusalem (**ם**) is the closest letter to *Ugret Selima*. It's three letters to the right and one letter above the last letter of *Ugret Selima* (**ה**). This corresponds exactly to the course from Jerusalem or the Temple in Jerusalem to the suspect Ark area indicated so far on ELS Maps 1, 2, 3 and 4: **251.565° True.**

ELS Map 5– Ugret Selima and Jerusalem

Terms on ELS Map 5	Translation	Symbol	Skip	Start	End
עגרת שלימה	Ugret Selima	●	37187	Leviticus 19 V13 L36	Leviticus 14 V40 L5
ירושלם	Jerusalem	▮	99167	Deuteronomy 8 V12 L15	Leviticus 8 V6 L33

DESCRIPTIVE REPORT AND CALCULATIONS FOR ELS MAP 5

The ELS reference is 12396 characters between rows. There are 2 displayed terms in the matrix. The matrix starts at Deuteronomy 8 V12 L10 and ends at Leviticus 14 V40 L13. The matrix spans 508248 characters of the surface text. The matrix has 42 rows, is 12 columns wide and contains a total of 504 characters.

COURSE CALCULATION: X = 3 COLUMNS, Y = 1 ROW. TAN = .33333333. ARCTAN = 18.4349488229 DEG. TRUE. UGRET SELIMA TO JERUSALEM = 90-18.4349488229 = 71.5650511 DEGREES TRUE. **JERUSALEM TO UGRET SELIMA = 251.565 DEGREES.** ESTIMATED COURSE TO 31-9 N, 33-4 E IS 251.9 BY JAVA COURSE CALCULATOR.

Ugret Selima was a breakthrough in the search to distinguish which suspect site should be given highest priority. Up until the production of ELS Map 5, my inclination had been to view 31° 9' North, 33° 4' East as the starting point in a trek that would finish at an undersea obstruction located at 31° 16' North, 33° 4' East. However, with so many maps pointing to the 31° 9' North latitude coordinate, it became necessary to reevaluate my earlier conclusion. Now consider ELS Map 6 below. On it we see the same (singular) ELS of *Ugret Selima* displayed with CodeFinder's row split function disabled. On Map 3 above (the Qatia Map), a compass rose inserted over the primary Ark site at 31° 9' N, 33° 4' E revealed that the course to this site from the nearest point of Mallahet Ugret Selima is 237 ° True. ELS Map 6 has *Ark of the Covenant* on it 11 rows below and 17 columns to the left of *Ugret Selima.* This equals a course of 237.095° from the last letter of *Ugret*

Selima to the first letter of *Ark of the Covenant*. With about 600 meters between the two sites in question, an error of .095 degrees equates to an error of about one meter (less than the length of the Ark of the Covenant itself)!

There is one last ELS map figure with an angle of 251.565, however, it is probably not in the class of those presented above. Note on Map 3 that there is an Egyptian Army fort named Katib El Qals located at 31° 13' N, 33° 4.5' E (about four nautical miles north of the primary suspect Ark site at 31° 9' N, 33° 4' E).

Is the fortress of Katib El Qals encoded? Yes, though there is a question of transliteration spelling. El Qals on my Hebrew map was spelled *alef lamed kof lamed samech* (קלס אל). On ELS Map 7, Katib El Qals is spelled *kof tav bet alef lamed caf lamed sin* (כלש אל קתב). The plot is of interest because of the placement of Jerusalem (ירושלם) and Ark of the Covenant (ארון ברית). When a course angle is drawn from the closest letter of Jerusalem (י) to the closest letter of Katib El Qals (א), the 3 columns and one row between the two translate again to a course of 251.565° True. While this is the expected course from Jerusalem to the Zuqba Ark site, the actual course from Jerusalem to Katib El Qals is 253.7 degrees by Java Calculator (a 1.8° error). So this ELS Map is suggestive of the fact that the Ark is not at Katib El Qals, but it is on the nearby bearing seen so many times before. However, when one looks at this ELS Map, the Ark of the Covenant is there on the figure where I expect it to be, south of (directly below) Katib El Qals – which corresponds to a correct course of 180° True from the fort to the suspect Ark site. Further, this particular encoding of Katib El Qals is discussed again in Chapter 17 where it is shown to be crossed on Figure 38 by an extremely accurate description of what is found at the fort (sweet water that defies geological common sense).

Terms on ELS Map 6	Translation	Symbol	Skip	Start	End
עגרת שלימה	Ugret Selima	○	37187	Leviticus 19 V13 L36	Leviticus 14 V40 L5
ארון ברית	Ark of Covenant	□	1	Deuteronomy 10 V8 L32	Deuteronomy 10 V8 L39
זהב	Gold	▭	1	Exodus 28 V14 L10	Exodus 28 V14 L12

DESCRIPTIVE REPORT AND CALCULATIONS FOR ELS MAP 6
The ELS reference is 37187 characters between rows. There are 2 main displayed terms in the matrix, though the word for gold is shown in a horizontal box. The matrix starts at Leviticus 19 V13 L36 and ends at Deuteronomy 10 V8 L39. The matrix spans 706578 characters of the surface text. The matrix has 20 rows, is

25 columns wide and contains a total of 500 characters.

COURSE CALCULATION FROM UGRET SELIMA TO ARK OF COVENANT: TAN = Y (11 ROWS)/X (17 COLUMNS) = 0.6470588. ARCTAN = 32.905 DEGREES. 90 - 32.905 = 57.095 DEGREES. THIS IS THE COURSE FROM THE ARK'S FIRST LETTER (א) TO UGRET SELIMA'S LAST LETTER, ה (CLOSEST TO ARK OF THE COVENANT). TO GET THE COURSE FROM UGRET SELIMA'S ה TO ARK OF THE COVENANT ADD 180 DEGREES. THIS EQUALS A COURSE OF 237.095 TRUE. THE ACTUAL COURSE TO THE SUSPECT ARK SITE AT 31-9 NORTH, 33-4 EAST IS 237.

ELS Map 6
Ugret Selima to Ark
of the Covenant

ELS Map 7
Katib El Qals and Jerusalem

Term ELS Map 7	Translation	Symbol	Skip	Start
קתב אל כלש	Katib El Qals	●	-10560	Leviticus 9 V17 L3
ירושלם	Jerusalem	■	18474	Exodus 28 V23 L42
ארון ברית	Ark of Covenant	▭	1	Numbers 10 V33 L25

DESCRIPTIVE REPORT AND CALCULATIONS FOR ELS MAP 7

The ELS reference is 2640 characters between rows. There are 3 displayed terms in the matrix. The matrix starts at Exodus 2 V14 L67 and ends at Numbers 14 V16 L12. The matrix spans 132037 characters of the surface text. The matrix has 51 rows, is 37 columns wide and contains a total of 1887 characters.

COURSE CALCULATION: X = 3 COLUMNS, Y = 1 ROW. TAN = 0.33333333. ARCTAN = 18.4349488229 DEG. TRUE. KATIB EL QALS TO JERUSALEM = 90-18.4349488229 = 71.565 DEGREES TRUE. JERUSALEM TO KATIB EL QALS = **251.565 DEGREES.** ACTUAL COURSE TO KATIB EL QALS IS 253.7 DEGREES. COURSE TO 31-9 N, 33-4 E IS 251.9 BY JAVA CALCULATOR.

It is believed that sites near the primary suspect site will be encoded with Jerusalem, but that the angles will not be as close or precise as they will be for the actual Ark site. Katib El Qals is such a nearby site. So is Bir El Abd, a town of about 50,000 people located close to nine nautical miles south of the Ark site. With respect to Katib El Qals, on ELS Map 8 an interesting result arises when a transliteration of *caf tav bet alef lamed caf lamed sin* (כתב אל כלש) is used. Jerusalem (ירושלם) popped up at the same interval as Katib El Qals. The angle from the first letter of Jerusalem (י) to the first letter of Katib El Qals (כ) corresponded to a course of 250° True. Once again, the actual course from Jerusalem to Katib El Qals is estimated to be 253.7 ° True. Also, four letters before the beginning of Katib El Qals we find the *Tablets of the Covenant* (which, of course, were placed in the Ark of the Covenant). This is close, but it does not intersect Katib El Qals. Therefore it may be read as a clue that the Ark is near, but not at the modern Egyptian Army fort.

On ELS Map 9, the angle from the first letter of Jerusalem (י) to the closest letter of Bir El Abd – בר אל אבד (א) equals a course of about 249.4°. The actual course by the on-line Java Applet Coordinate Calculator course is 248.8° T, an error of only 0.6°!

Terms on ELS Map 8	Translation	Symbol	Skip	Start	End
כתב אל כלש	Katib El Qals	○	18833	Deuteronomy 9 V9 L36	Exodus 10 V23 L30
לוחת הברית	Tablets of the Covenant	▭	1	Deuteronomy 9 V9 L24	Deuteronomy 9 V9 L32
ירושלם	Jerusalem	☐	-18833	Exodus 26 V2 L22	Genesis 18 V13 L37

DESCRIPTIVE REPORT AND CALCULATIONS FOR ELS MAP 8

The ELS reference is 18833 characters between rows. There are 3 displayed terms in the matrix. The matrix starts at Genesis 18 V13 L37 and ends at Exodus 10 V23 L30. The matrix spans 376683 characters of the surface text. The matrix has 21 rows, is 23 columns wide and contains a total of 483 characters.

COURSE CALCULATION. X = 22 Y = 8. TAN = 8/22 = .3636363636363636. ARC TAN = 19.983 DEGREES. SUBTRACT THIS FROM 90 DEGREES AND IT EQUALS A COURSE OF 70.017 DEGREES TRUE TO JERUSALEM. **THE RECIPROCAL COURSE FROM JERUSALEM EQUALS 250.017 DEGREES TRUE.**

ELS Map 8 – Katib El Qals and Jerusalem

```
מנמאלדואניזקנתיהיפלאמיה
לואתהאבנמעלפיהבארוהשקוא
שרביתהסהרדראהאתכלמאומהבי
וילכונגמאחיוויפלולפניוו
תתמויאמריהוהאלמשהואהרנז
ימבאמהורחבארבעבאמהידיע
ימוארבעימאדניהמכספשניאד
בניוולזקנייישראלויאמראלא
ורהמאזניצדקאבניצדקאיפתצ
אהלמועדואתמשמרתבנייישראל
סעוהעממחצרותויחנובמדברפ
לראשהפסגהויבנשבעקמזבחתו
לבנאפדולמטהבניאפרימנשיא
לוחתהאבנימלווחתהבריתאשרכ
לאמצאתילבתכבתולימואלהבת
בותאפרימוהמאלפימנשהולזב
ויאמראליואנייהוהאשרהוצא
לצודצידלהביאורבקהאמרהאל
הפסימאשרעליוויקחהוויעלכ
ולדימלכבבארצמצרימעדבאיאל
שאתאחיוולאקמואישמתחתיוש
```

ELS Map 9: Jerusalem to Bir El Abd

עברולכמאתנחלזרדונעבראתנחלזרד
ירשמוישבותחתמכאשרעשהלבניעשו
תתנליושתיתירקאעברהברגליכאשרע
אשרלכדנומערעראשרעלשפתנחלארנ
קחנומאתמשמימעירכלחבלארגבממלכ
חבהבאמתאישואתהארצהזאתירשנוע
להיכמנתנלכמאתהארצהזאתלרשתהחל
אתידכההזקהאשרמיאלבשמימובארצא
והאלהיאבתיכמנתנלכמלאתסמועלה
וכיהוהאלהינובבכלקראנואליומיג
תיקולויגדלכמאתברייתואשרצוהאתכ
עבדתמאשרחלקיהוהאלהיכאתמלכלהע
שיתמהרעבעיניייהוהאלהיכלהכעיסו
חאתבריתאביכאשרנשבעלהמכישאלנ
הבאתאבתיכויבחרבזרעואחריוויוצ
בניואתראמתבגלעדלגדיואתגוןנבב
ברבאזניכמהיומולמדתמאתמושמדרתמ
מועלשלשימועלה בעי מלשנאיועשהחס
יכנימיכולמעניטבלעלהאדמהאשר
האשהגדלההזאתאמיספיאנחנולשמע
המשפטימאשרתלמדמועשוובאראשראנ
ששמעישראליהוהאלהינויהוהאחדוא
רממביתעבדימאתיהוהאלהיכתידאו
פרעהבמצרימויציאנויהוהממצרימב
מיהואלהיכלפניכוהכייתמהחרדמתחר
כמביתעבדימידפרעהמלכמצימויד
עקרועוקרהובבהמתכוהסיריהוהממכב
ניכלאתערצמפניהמכייהוהאלהיכבק
הארצאאשרנשבעיהוהלאבתיכמוזכרתא
ושערוהוגפנותאנהורמונארצזיתשמנ
כלכמנבמדברישראלאדעונאתיכלמע

Ark Code

Terms on ELS Map 9	Translation	Symbol	Skip	Start	End
בר אל אבד	Bir El Abd	●	-1969	Deuteronomy 8 V16 L25	Deuteronomy 2 V13 L35
ירושלם	Jerusalem	☐	-3	Deuteronomy 5 V9 L70	Deuteronomy 5 V9 L55

DESCRIPTIVE REPORT AND CALCULATIONS FOR ELS MAP FIGURE 9

The encoded course from Jerusalem to Bir El Abd displayed on ELS Map Figure 9 corresponds to a **course of 249.4°**. The course from Bir El Abd to Jerusalem on this plot is 69.4°. Trig is as follows: X = 8, Y = 3. Y/X = .375. Arctan = 20.6°, this from 90 = 69.4°. The reciprocal course is 249.4°.
Actual course from Temple Mount in Jerusalem to the Bir El Abd wells is 248.8° True, a difference of less than one degree (in fact, 0.6°) from what is encoded.

Map 4 – Bir El Abd

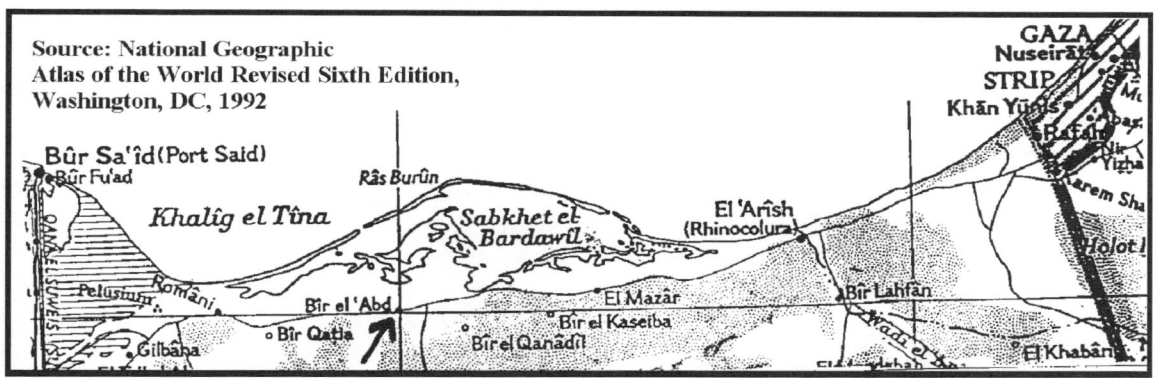

SITE	LATITUDE	LONGITUDE
Temple Mount	31° 46′ 39.7″ North	35° 14′ 04.4″ East
Bir El Abd	31° 05′ 00″ North	32° 59.4′ East

For ELS Map 9, *Jerusalem* is at its minimum skip in the Torah, while *Bir El Abd* is at its third shortest skip. The two ELS hits with Bir El Abd at shorter skips do not have Jerusalem encoded with them in CodeFinder's initial standard search window of 80 columns and 50 rows.

There is one last ELS map figure to consider, but it requires a bit more of an explanation than most. On ELS Map 10 where *Ark of the Covenant* (ארון ברית)

23

appears at skip +9,698, there is a *Jerusalem* (ירושלם) at skip +19,397 on the plot. Two letters left of the letter *bet* (ב) in ארון ברית, there is, as in ELS Map 1, a *tsadeh* (צ) again. The angle from the closest letter of *Jerusalem, mem* this time (מ), to this צ, corresponds to a course of 252.12° (only 0.22 degrees off the Java Applet Coordinate Calculator course of 251.9°). It would have been nice if the letter in between the צ in question and the ב in ארון ברית was a *kof* (ק) again, but it's an *alef* (א). At skip -1, we don't get a transliteration of *Zuqba*. We get one for *Zuaba* (צאב). This would seem to be a mismatch except for one small detail. Based upon an unclear map (Map 1), Zuaba was what I thought was the correct name for Zuqba when I made my presentation in Jerusalem. It wasn't until I arrived in Cairo and found the Qatia map (Map 3) that I altered my search from *Zuaba* to *Zuqba*.

It's fair to ask why any attention should be given to ELS Map 10 if an anchor spot on it is a transliteration for Zuaba. There are three reasons for doing so. First, there is a nearby place named Bir El **ZUABA**tiya (see Map 5). Bir means *well*. Almost every Egyptian site has El before it (some transliterations use Al). Nobody at the Northern Sinai Government office in El Arish, Egypt could tell me the meaning of either Zuqba or Zuaba. Nor were they familiar with either name. It is possible that Zuqba was someone's mistake earlier and that Zuaba is the real name.

Map 5 – The Pre-Expedition Map (expanded section)

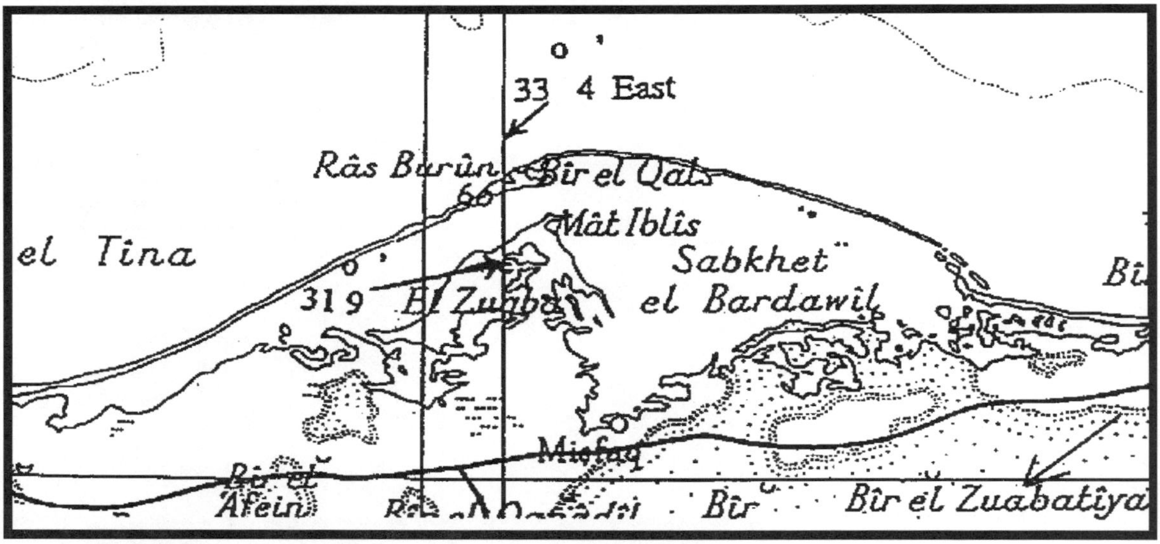

Second, on projecting Map 5 (from *Times Atlas of the World*) before a room of my students, half of them read *Zuaba* instead of *Zuqba*. A few saw *Zunba*, but only one saw it as Zuqba. For years I had worked with the photocopy above (the original color map was clearer).

ELS Map 10 – Zuaba, Jerusalem and the Ark of the Covenant

```
ינוויאמרואלפרעהלגורבארצבאנוכיאינמרעהל
ימוהיהכיתלכונלאתלכורייקמושאלהאשהמשכנתה
בהדוהקלתויספלחטאויכבדלבוהואועבדיווייחז
מדברסינאשרבינאילמובינסיניבחמשהעשרייומל
תכודמעכלאתאחרדבכורדבניכתתנליכנתעשהלשרדכל
מתוחקתעולומלוולזרעואחרייווזההההדבראשרתעשה
ימבשנהירדאהכלזכורדכאתפנייהאדנייהוהאלהייישר
כהוהנהעשואתהתהכאשרצוהייהוהכנעשווייברכאתממ
יאכללאיניחממנועודבקרואמנדראונדבהזבחהקרב
יראנההכהנוההנהאינבבהרתשערלבנוושפלהאיינה
אלהיכמעשההאשהצרצמאריימאשריישבתמבההלאתעשוווכ
ותשנייעשרנהמיהיההחלההההאחתוושמתאותתמשתיימע
תמלאהתהפקדובתובמאידברייהואהלאלמשהלאמראראכאת
ניעשהלעולתורתנוזרוידדברייהואהלאלמשהלאמרדברא
תבכולפנייולאמדלמההזהאצאנומממצרדיימואיאמדמשה
עמייהוהויייבההקהלההעדהעלמשהועלאהרנווייפנוא
יוויאמרמלאכייהוהלבלעמלכעמאנשיימואפסאתה
לכמועניתמאתנפשתיכמכלמלאכהכההלאתעשוווהקרבת
מכנרתקדמהורדהגבולהירדנהיוהירדנהיותואתיוייימ
ובאתמוירשתמאתהארצאשרייהוהאלהיאבתיכמנתנ
יתייתנייהוהאלייאתשנילוחתהאבניימכתביימבאצ
ראעליכאליהוהוהייהבכחטאנתוונתנלוולאלייעל
אהצעקההנערהמארשהוואייימושייעלהכיימצאאישנ
תלילהויוממולאתאמיינבחייכבבקרתאמרמייתנע
```

Terms on ELS Map 10	Translation	Symbol	Skip	Start	End
ארון ברית	Ark of Covenant	○	9698	Numbers 22 V35 L34	Deuteronomy 28 V67 L12
ירושלם	Jerusalem	□	19397	Genesis 47 V3 L60	Leviticus 18 V2 L35

						Deuteronomy 9 V10 L34	Deuteronomy 9 V10 L32
צאב	Zuaba		☐	-1			

שני לוחת האבנים כתבים באצ(בע אלהים) skip=+1

* The words running into Zuaba read: *Two stone tablets written* (*with the finger of God*). This describes what is in the Ark of the Covenant.

DESCRIPTIVE REPORT AND CALCULATIONS FOR ELS MAP 10

The ELS reference is 9698 characters between rows. There are 3 displayed terms in the matrix. The matrix starts at Genesis 47 V3 L60 and ends at Deuteronomy 28 V67 L12. The matrix spans 223089 characters of the surface text. The matrix has 24 rows, is 35 columns wide and contains a total of 840 characters.

COURSE CALCULATION: X = 31 COLUMNS Y = 10 ROWS; TANGENT VALUE Y/X = 0.32258064516129; ARCTAN = 17.88 DEGREES. SUBTRACT 17.88 DEGREES FROM 90 DEGREES TO GET COURSE FROM ZUABA'S FIRST LETTER (צ) TO JERUSALEM'S CLOSEST LETTER (ם). THIS EQUALS 72.12 DEGREES. THE RECIPROCAL **COURSE FROM JERUSALEM TO ZUABA WOULD BE 252.12 DEGREES.**

We are dealing with an investigation into the supernatural here, or into some other yet to be explained scientific phenomenon like quantum tunneling (as explained by Arthur C. Clarke and Stephen Baxter in a science fiction novel named *The Light of Other Days*). As such, however unlikely, there may be deliberate encoding of the name that I wanted to see; or there may be deliberate encoding of both names, because at some time both names were used on maps of the area.

Finally, it's not just true that a cursive "Q" on the chart can easily be misread as an "A" when the bottom of the "Q" corresponds to undulating salt marsh shoreline (as it does on Maps 1 and 5). But it is also true that a hand printed lower case "q" can resemble "a." Further, the "Q" on a typewriter is directly above the "A." Thus a single typo mistake could easily be copied from chart to chart. This would mean again that the true name could be Zuaba, not Zuqba.

I want to be perfectly clear about which course is probably the right one to take from the Temple Mount in Jerusalem to the Ark site. We have seen 251.565° pop up on six ELS map figures. This is the course we should first investigate. If we ask how far a course of 251.565° is from the Java course of 251.9° over the distance of, say 115 nautical miles, it's about 1,037 yards, but again, the Java calculator only provided a crude course estimate based on a perfectly spherical Earth.

Before discussing the history of the Ark, alternate beliefs about its location (or destruction) and the expedition that led to discovery of the above ELS maps and other Codes topics, let's compare some of the maps seen so far:

Comparison of Eight ELS Maps

ELS Map	Axis Term	ELS, ELS Axis Term Rank (#1 = SHORTEST)	TARGET TERM FOR JERUSALEM ירושלם	X COLUMNS/ Y ROWS = RATIO	Course From Jerusalem
1	ארון ברית	Skip –306, #1	צקב (Zuqba)	22/7 = 3.14	252.35 ° T
2	ירושלם	Skip –30, #3	צקב (Zuqba)	3/1 = 3.0	251.565° T
3	מקום ארון	Skip 2,628, #2	מקום ארון (Position of Ark)	18/6 = 3.0	251.565° T
4	מקום הארן	Skip 3,373, #1	מקום הארן (Position of the Ark) [measured from the 1st letter of מירושלם]	27/9 = 3.0	251.565° T
5	עגרת שלימה	Skip 37,187, #1	עגרת שלימה (Ugret Selima)	3/1 = 3.0	251.565° T
7	קתב אל כלש	Skip –10,560, #1	קתב אל כלש (Katib El Qals)	3/1 = 3.0	251.565° T
8	כתב אל כלש	Skip 18,833, #4	קתב אל כלש (Katib El Qals)	22/8 = 2.75	250.017 ° T
10	ארון ברית	Skip 9,698, #4	צאב (Zuaba)	31/10 = 3.1	252.12 ° T
MAP	AXIS TERM	ELS, ELS AXIS TERM RANK (#1 = SHORTEST)	TARGET TERM FOR (TEMPLE) מקדש	X COLUMNS/ Y ROWS = RATIO	Course From Temple
1	ארון ברית	Skip –306, #1	ארון ברית (Ark of Covenant)	12/4 = 3.0	251.565° T

The Average X/Y ratio = (3.14+3+3+3+3+3+2.75+3.1+3)/9= 2.998888
The average course = 252.35 + 251.565 + 251.565 + 251.565 + 251.565 + 251.565 +250.17 + 252.12 + 251.565 = 251.55888. This rounds off to 251.56° True

MAP	ALTERNATE AXIS TERM	ELS, ELS AXIS TERM RANK (#1 = SHORTEST)	TARGET TERM FOR FROM JERUSALEM מירושלם	X COLUMNS/ Y ROWS = RATIO	Course From "From Jerusalem"
4	מירושלם (From Jerusalem)	843, #15	זהב (Gold)	3/1 = 3.0	251.565° T

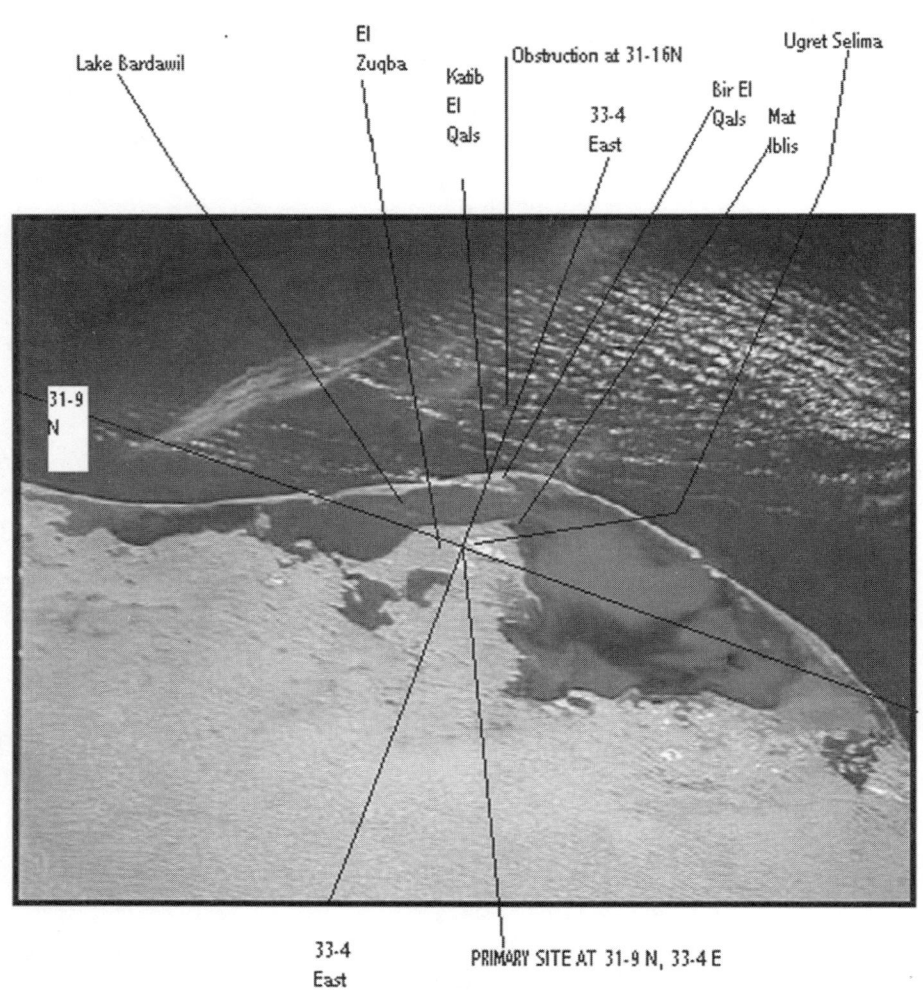

Lake Bardawil

El
Zuqba

Katib
El
Qals

Obstruction at 31-16N

Ugret Selima

Bir El
Qals

33-4
East

Mat
Iblis

31-9
N

33-4
East

PRIMARY SITE AT 31-9 N, 33-4 E

CHAPTER 2

ARK HISTORY: CONSTRUCTION TO LOSS WITH THE FIRST TEMPLE

Before covering my own expedition, it would be wise to review some of the other ideas or even claims about what happened to the Ark and where (if not destroyed) it might be today. This chapter will focus on the Ark's construction, known travels, and disappearance from Jerusalem at the time of the prophet Jeremiah.

In Exodus 25:10-16 God gave Moses instructions to build the Ark as follows:

They shall make an Ark of acacia wood, two and a half cubits its length; a cubit and a half its width; and a cubit and a half its height. You shall cover it with pure gold, from within and from without shall you cover it, and you shall make on it a crown all around. You shall cast for it four rings of gold and place them on its four corners, two rings on its side and two rings on its second side. You shall make staves of acacia wood and cover them with gold; and insert the staves in the rings on the sides of the Ark, with which to carry the Ark. The staves shall remain in the rings of the Ark; they may not be removed from it. You shall place in the Ark the Testimonial-tablets that I shall give you.

The Ark was to have a cover of pure gold, with two gold cherubim facing each other (Exodus 25:17-21). The Torah then assigns radio-like qualities to the Ark when God declares to Moses:

It is there that I will meet with you, and I shall speak with you from atop the Cover, from between the two cherubim that are on the Ark of the Testimonial tablets, everything that I shall command you to the Children of Israel.

Bezalel carried out the above instructions and built the Ark to God's specifications (Exodus 37:1-9).

Exactly how old is the Ark? The answer given depends on when one dates the Exodus. Dates given on the Internet seem to range between 1201 and 1460 BCE. When the Jerusalem Post covered my own foray into Israel and Egypt, the article discussing my presentation gave a date for the Torah's delivery to Moses as having occurred 3,311 years prior to the holiday of Shavuot in May of 1999. That translates to the year 1312 BCE for the Exodus and Ark construction. Some attempt to tie the 9th plague of darkness with a total eclipse of the sun in parts of Egypt that occurred on March 27, 1335 BCE. Others attempt to link that plague with an eruption on Thira. The Bible speaks of a thick darkness that could be felt (Exodus 10:21-22). This may well have been volcanic ash blown to Egypt by the winds, but most scientists place the eruption centuries earlier (between 1650 and 1625 BCE).

With respect to an earlier date for the Exodus, 1st Kings 6:1 indicates that the exodus preceded the time when Solomon began to build the Temple by 480 years. If it took thirteen years to build the Temple and the Temple was finished in 950 BCE, then construction began in 963 BCE and the 480 years added to this figure yields a date of 1443 BCE. Dr. Randall Price in his book, *In Search of Temple Treasures,* placed the Ark's construction at about 1446 BCE, a date that would be correct if the First Temple was completed in 953 BCE. Based on Scripture, the time frame of the 1440s BCE would seem to make the most sense, but it is obvious that there is no unanimous opinion with respect to the Exodus or Ark construction date.

After the death of Moses we read in Joshua 3:12-17 that when the Ark crossed the Jordan River, the river divided in miraculous fashion. In Joshua 6:4-20 it is stated that in addition to shouting and blowing trumpets before the walls of Jericho, the Ark was also paraded before the city before its wall fell.

Delving Into Ark History

The Tent of Meeting, which contained the Ark, was set up at Shiloh (Joshua 18:1) where it remained for 369 to 389 years after having been at Gilgal except for a brief period at Shechem. According to the Soncino Commentary for Judges 20:26-27, when the Bible states that the Ark was in Beth-el, this does not mean the city by that name, but literally *the house of God* which was in fact in Shiloh (Soncino for Joshua and Judges, 309).

Samuel, as a boy, slept in the "temple" (buildings around the Tabernacle according to Kimchi, or as an attendant to the Ark) where the Ark was kept. There the Lord told him of a curse for Eli, a priest who had sinned.

The Ark was captured by the Philistines (1st Samuel 4:11) when Israel lost 30,000 men in battle. Eli had judged Israel for 40 years as a priest. As soon as Eli heard of the loss of the Ark, he fell off his seat backward, broke his neck, and died (1st Samuel 4:18). The Philistines took the Ark from Eben-ezer to Ashdod (what is today a modern port city of Israel). There they set it before an idol of Dagon, their god. The next morning Dagon had fallen on his face. They set Dagon back up, but the following morning he had fallen again breaking off his head and hands. With that the Philistines gave up belief in Dagon (1st Samuel 5:1-5).

The Philistines continued to drag the Ark around for seven months, but it brought plagues wherever they went giving them boils (1st Samuel 5:6) that might have been caused by bubonic plague (Soncino 1st Samuel, p. 28). They carried it to Gath where this happened again, then to Ekron with the same results. On advice of their priests, the Philistines made golden images of boils and mice (which spread bubonic plague) as an offering to the God of Israel. They put the Ark and the jewels on a cart with two calves to pull it. Then the Philistines waited to see if the animals would take the Ark back to its home in Beth-shemish, a priestly city on the borders of the territory of Judah (probably the nearest Israelite town to Ekron). Sure enough, the animals took it straight there convincing the Philistines that they had sinned, and bringing great joy to the inhabitants of Beth-shemish. However, when the men of Beth-shemish looked inside the Ark, 50,070 of them were slain (1st Samuel 6:19). The inhabitants then requested people from Kirath-jearim to take it away (1st Samuel 6:21). These people brought it to the house of Abinadab where they sanctified his son Eleazar to keep the Ark (1st Samuel 7:1). It stayed in his home for 20 years.

King Saul did nothing with the Ark during his reign. Later, King David moved it without following the Biblical procedures of carrying it by Levites set forth in Exodus 25:14-15, Numbers 3:30-31, 4:15 and 7:9. Oxen had been pulling it on a cart, they stumbled, and Uzziah was killed when he touched the Ark while trying to steady it (2nd Samuel 6:6-7; 1st Chronicles 13:5-10). David then took the Ark to the home of Obed-edom the Gittite, a Levite from the family of Korah (later one of the doorkeepers of the Ark). The Ark stayed there for three months and Obed-edom was blessed (2nd Samuel 6:10-12; 1st Chronicles 3:13-14). These events occurred around 1,000 BCE.

David next transferred the Ark to Jerusalem, leading the procession while wearing a priestly ephod (2 Sam. 6:14). The Ark was then kept in the city of David in Jerusalem according to 2nd Samuel 6:12, but moved to the Tabernacle in Gibeon, the modern el-Jib six miles northwest of Jerusalem (1st Kings 3:4).

David wasn't permitted to build the first Temple to house the Ark, but he was allowed to make preparations for it. When he later fled Jerusalem during Absalom's rebellion, he took the Ark with him, but then commanded the high priest, Zadok, to return it to the Holy City.

Solomon brought an end to the high places in Gibeon; and after a dream, he offered sacrifices before the Ark in Jerusalem (1st Kings 3:15). About ten years later, around 950 BCE, he placed the Ark in the Temple that he had built.

Around 926 or 925 CE the fate of the Ark begins to come into question. In 1st Kings 14:25-26 we read:

> *And it came to pass in the fifth year of King Rehoboam, that Shishak king of Egypt came up against Jerusalem; and he took away the treasures of the house of the Lord, and the treasures of the king's house;* **he even took away all***; and he took away all the shields of gold which Solomon had made.*

Another Ark hunter, Michael Sanders, speculates that Shishak took the Ark and placed it in an Egyptian ruin that has been under Palestinian Authority control in the town of Dhahiriya. He points to pictures on the walls there that look like the Ark, but the forms displayed seem more like river craft, and the motif of the Ark is somewhat Egyptian anyway. Sanders has explored the site and found nothing other than questionable pictures to back his assertion, though he hopes to have more luck there when the political situation calms down.

Does 1st Kings 14:25-26 really point to when the Ark was taken into Egypt? The Ark is not specifically mentioned, but the text does state that **he even took away all.** The first problem here with the word ***all*** is that it directly follows the treasures of the house of the king, but it does not directly follow the treasures of the house of the Lord (i.e., the Temple). Dr. Randall Price (79-80) argues that Shishak's own record indicates that he captured 156 cities, but does not list Jerusalem among them. He then concludes that the text in question only means that he extracted tribute from the city, but he never entered the Holy of Holies where the Ark was kept. The section in question does mention shields of gold, and it is likely that what was taken were treasures of that nature or spoils of wars taken from defeated foes.

If we only had 1st Kings 14:25-26 to go on, we might argue that Shishak took the Ark and placed it in Dhahiriya, in the Valley of Kings, or at the site indicated by my own research. The problem with this line of logic is that it not only runs into the problems cited in the previous paragraph above, but that the location of the Ark is given again in the Bible. In 2nd Chronicles 35:1-3 we read:

> And ***Josiah*** *kept a passover unto the* Lord *in Jerusalem; and they killed the passover lamb on the fourteenth day of the first month. And he set the priest in their charges, and encouraged them to the service of the house of the* Lord. *And he **said** unto the Levite that taught all Israel, that were unto the* Lord: ***Put the holy ark in the house which Solomon the son of David king of Israel did build***; *there shall no more be a burden upon your shoulders.*

The Soncino Commentary here (p. 334-335) states of *Put the holy ark*, etc., that, "It must have been removed from its place in the Holy of Holies during the period of apostasy in one of the preceding reigns, and King Josiah now ordered it to be restored. A Rabbinical explanation is that he commanded it to be hidden in a secret place so that it would escape capture by an invading army."

The Soncino also provides a date for Josiah: 31 years of reigning in Judah (starting at age eight under guidance of priests and elders – see 2nd Kings 22:1), commencing in 637 BCE, nearly 300 years after Shishak's invasion. Price places these events at about 622 BCE. Therefore it would appear that: **if the Ark went to Egypt, it must have been in the time of the prophet Jeremiah and the invasion by Nebuchadnezzar.**

After Josiah had repaired the Temple, King Neco of Egypt went up to fight against King Carchemish of Assyria whose power was weakened by a war with Babylon. The Egyptian king wanted to recapture Syria. Josiah opposed the

Egyptian, despite an Egyptian plea to avoid hostilities. They fought at Megiddo. In the battle Josiah suffered a fatal wound. He was buried in Jerusalem with Jeremiah there to mourn his death (2nd Chronicles 35:24).

Josiah's son, Joahaz, assumed rule at age 23, but only ruled three months before being deposed by the king of Egypt. Neco set another of Josiah's sons, Eliakim, as king of Judah and Jerusalem – changing the new king's name to Jehoiakim. The Egyptian then took Joahaz to Egypt. Jehoiakim did evil in the eyes of the Lord. The death of Josiah, the assault on Jerusalem by an Egyptian king, and the rise of an evil king in Judah would all have served as reasons for Jeremiah or others to hide the Ark again.

The Lord repaid Jehoiakim's evil conduct with an invasion by Nebuchadnezzar, king of Babylon. Of Jehoiakim's fate in 2nd Chronicles 36:6-7 we read:

Against him came up Nebuchadnezzar king of Babylon, and bound him in fetters, to carry him to Babylon. Nebuchadnezzar also carried off the vessels of the house of the LORD to Babylon, and put them in his Temple at Babylon.

Nebuchadnezzar set up the son of Jehoiakim to rule Judah and Jerusalem. This king ruled only three months ten days. After doing evil he was, along with goodly vessels of the house of the Lord, brought by Nebuchadnezzar to Babylon. Nebuchadnezzar next set up Zedekiah, brother of Jehoiachin, as king over Judah and Jerusalem. Zedekiah ruled for eleven years, and again is judged as evil by the Bible. "He humbled not himself before Jeremiah the prophet speaking from the mouth of the Lord." (2nd Chronicles 36:12). Zedekiah brought the ultimate disaster to his country by failing to heed Jeremiah, refusing to honor God, and even choosing to pollute the Temple with abominations (idols). The result is set forth in 2nd Chronicles 36:18-21:

And all the vessels of the house of God, great and small, and the treasures of the house of the LORD, and the treasures of the king, and of his princes; all these he brought to Babylon. And they burnt the house of God, and broke down the wall of Jerusalem, and burnt all palaces thereof with fire, and destroyed all the goodly vessels thereof. And them that had escaped from the sword carried he away to Babylon; and they were servants to him and his sons until the reign of the kingdom of Persia to fulfill the word of the LORD by the mouth of Jeremiah...

Thus, after several attacks on Jerusalem with treasures of the Temple being taken by or offered to foreign kings, the First Temple was destroyed in 586 BCE. **There is no mention of the Ark being put into or seen in the Second Temple.**

The Second Temple was constructed with permission of King Cyrus of Persia. It was completed in 516 BCE; later it was rebuilt in splendid fashion by King Herod the Great; and finally it was destroyed by Titus and the Roman legion in 70 CE.

The Arch of Titus in Rome recalls the destruction of that Temple and portrays treasure taken from it, but does not display the Ark as one of those treasures. **This fact would seem to cast doubt on any theories that the Ark is in the Vatican treasuries.** There simply is no evidence that the Ark was available for capture when the Romans destroyed Jerusalem and its Second Temple.

Neither Nebuchadnezzar nor Titus were likely to have remained silent about the capture of the Ark had it come into their possession. Nor would the Bible be likely to remain silent about its capture, if such an event were known. Therefore, the only fates that would seem to make sense would be based around the Ark being hidden or removed by priests or Jeremiah. **This must have occurred sometime between its last mention in conjunction with Josiah in about 622 BCE and the destruction of the Temple in 586 BCE, a period of about 36 years.** When did Jeremiah preach? The Soncino places his prophetic career as occurring between the 13th year of Josiah's reign (625 BCE) and the fall of the First Temple in 586 BCE. We must assume that the man who cared the most about the Ark would also be the one to oversee its fate. Jeremiah was that man. Knowing that the Temple would be destroyed, his only options would be to (1) hide it beneath the Temple (as rabbinical tradition holds) or (2) remove the Ark from the Temple so that it would not suffer the same fate as all other Temple treasure. Whereas the Babylonians would have free reign of the Temple ruins, the later option would seem to make the most sense.

Now that we have a clearer picture of when the Ark disappeared, and who was responsible for its safeguard, let's turn to what is written in the Book of Jeremiah itself. Exactly what happened to Jeremiah when Jerusalem fell in 586 BCE?

Nebuchadnezzar slew the sons of Zedekiah before his eyes, and then put out Zedekiah's eyes before taking him in fetters to Babylon (Jeremiah 39:6-7). The remnant of Judea not taken into captivity came to Jeremiah and asked him to pray to the Lord to tell them where they should go (Jeremiah 42:1-3). Jeremiah did not give them an answer for ten days (Jeremiah 42:7). This may be because the Lord was not inclined to deliver a speedy answer. But it may also be because the communication device, (i.e. the Ark) that Jeremiah needed to pray before, had already been whisked away to a safe distance. The location could have been one that would take up to five days each way to reach and return from. This is not likely to fit the description of any place near or under Jerusalem that might be accessible by tunnel.

Jeremiah's answer to his countrymen about where to go was not what they wanted to hear:

> *...Thus saith the LORD of hosts, the God of Israel: If you wholly set your faces to enter into Egypt, and go to sojourn there; then it shall come to pass, that the sword, which ye fear, shall overtake you there in the land of Egypt, and the famine, where ye were afraid, shall follow hard after you there in Egypt; and there ye shall die. (Jeremiah 42:15-16)*

Azariah the son of Hoshaiah, Johanan the son of Kareah, and all the proud men accused Jeremiah of speaking falsely about the Egyptian prohibition (Jeremiah 42:2).

> ***But Johanan the son of Kareah, and all the captains of the forces, took*** *all the remnants of Judah, that were returned from the all the nations whither they had been driven to sojourn in the land of Judah; the men, and the women, and the king's daughters, and every person that Nebuzaradan the captain of the guard had left with Gedaliah the son of Ahikam, the son of Shaphan, and **Jeremiah the prophet**, and Barach the son of Neriah; and they came **into the land of Egypt;** for they hearkened not to the voice of the L*ORD*; and they came even **unto Tahpanhes**. (Jeremiah 43:5-7)*

Despite his warnings to kings and countrymen, Jeremiah could not turn his back on his wayward people. He hoped to reach them, even in Egypt, and convince them to turn back. But if he were to succeed, he would need a miracle. It would make sense to have the tool required for that miracle (the Ark) to be kept relatively close (but not close enough for wayward Jews to get a hold of). That way if his countrymen repented, they could return with the full protection of God as God had promised:

> *Be not afraid of the king of Babylon, of whom you are afraid; be not afraid of him, saith the L*ORD*; for I am with you to save you, and to deliver you from his hand. And I will grant you compassion, that he may have compassion on you, and cause you to return to your own land. (Jeremiah 42:11-12)*

Where did Jeremiah go to in Egypt? We saw mention above of Tahpanhes in Jeremiah 43:7, but in Jeremiah 44:1 we read the following:

> *The word of that came to Jeremiah concerning all the Jews that dwelt in the land of Egypt, that dwelt at **Migdol**, and at Tahpanes, and at Noph, and in the country of Pathros....*

So there was a Jewish community at **Migdol**. Now with respect to this name, we must be cautious. Migdol in Hebrew (מגדל) means tower. The meaning is similar in Arabic, though it could also mean fort. There were many of these forts/towers in Egypt, usually distinguished by the name of the pharaoh who constructed it or by some local circumstance. However, the area shown in this book to be the primary suspect Ark site, when the Torah Codes are applied to the search, is in the area of Baal Zephon. A chapter will be devoted to Baal Zephon later in this work, however, in Numbers 33:7 we read the following of the Exodus route:

> *They journeyed from Etham and turned back before Pi-hahiroth, which is before **Baal - Zephon**, and they encamped before **Migdol**.*

Therefore, Jeremiah traveled to Egypt and spoke to the Jewish community of Migdol, which may have been close to the suspect Ark site in this book. If he wanted to stay in touch with the Lord, even **without** the Codes, we now have reason to suspect that the Ark was taken to this area in Northern Sinai.

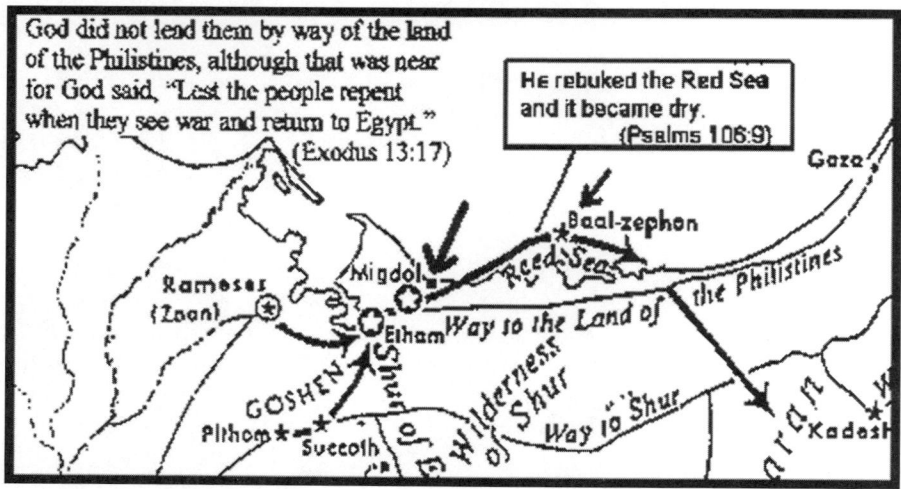

MAP 6: with Emphasis on Migdol and Baal Zephon

The above extract from the MacMillan Bible Atlas shows a popular suspect site for Migdol. British Admiralty Chart 56100 shows several ruins and one fort in the area today. All these lie between 31 degrees 1 minute and 31 degrees 4 minutes North; 32 degrees 30.5 minutes and 30 degrees 40 minutes East, ranging from about 21 to 29 nautical miles (24 to 33 statute miles) from the primary Ark site in this book. An Arabian camel go travel up to 100 miles in a day, so these distances would certainly be within easy reach of Jeremiah if he preached in such a Migdol and wanted to pray before the Ark. It lends plausibility to the idea that the Ark was taken to the site indicated by my Codes research.

How did the life of Jeremiah end? There seems to be unanimous belief that he died in Egypt, with some speculation in Funk and Wagnall's New Encyclopedia (unproven) that he may have been murdered by Jewish zealots. What is revealed in the Codes? The site of Jeremiah's death is quite clearly given there as the site in Egypt where the pillar of cloud and fire blocked the Egyptian army, and where Moses split the sea. This is precisely the area that the Codes reveals the Ark to be (see Figure 3 below).

Figure 3: Jeremiah's Death Site – Where Moses Split the Sea

Terms	Translation	Symbol	Skip	Start	End
ירמיה ימת	Jeremiah will die	◯	401	Exodus 13 V15 L43	Exodus 15 V13 L17
ויהרג	And he slew	▢	1	Exodus 13 V15 L21	Exodus 13 V15 L25
בארץ מצרים	In the land of Egypt	◡	1	Exodus 13 V15 L36	Exodus 13 V15 L44
בעמוד ענן לנחתם הדרכ ולילה בעמוד אש	In a pillar of cloud to lead them on the way And at night in a pillar of fire to give light to them	⌒	1	Exodus 13 V21 L19	Exodus 13 V21 L47
כל רכב מצרים	All the chariots In Egypt	⌒	1	Exodus 14 V7 L19	Exodus 14 V7 L28
בין מחנה מצרים ובין מחנה ישראל ויהי הענן	Between the camp of the Egyptians and between the camp of the Israelites and it was a cloud	⌂	1	Exodus 14 V20 L5	Exodus 14 V20 L37
ויט משה את ידו על הים	And Moses stretched out his hand over the sea	‿	1	Exodus 14 V27 L1	Exodus 14 V27 L16
לג-ד	33-4	⊔	-6	Exodus 15 V13 L20	Exodus 15 V13 L8

The ELS reference is 401 letters between rows. There are 12 displayed terms in the matrix. It starts at Exod. 13:15 Letter 16 and ends at Exod. 15:13 Letter 31. Figure 3 spans 2849 characters of the surface text. It has 8 rows, is 42 columns wide and contains a total of 336 characters.

Whereas all the evidence points to Jeremiah's death in Egypt, the first *a priori* terms to search for here in this matrix based on the all-important lowest ELS of the axis term (*Jeremiah will die*) would be terms like *In Egypt* or *In the Land of Egypt*. Both terms in the open text cross and share letters with the axis term. Is there any reference to a murder in the matrix? Possibly, as the term *and he slew* is there on the top line, though the open text refers to the Egyptians that were slain:

In Chapter One the geographic evidence, for Lake Bardawil as the site of the

37

sea being split, was discussed. If that was the body of water split, then El Zuqba was probably the peninsula where the pillar of cloud and pillar of fire temporarily blocked the path of the Egyptian army, dividing it from the Israelites. These pillars are mentioned not just once in crossing the axis term here. They are there twice – once with the phrase *In a pillar of cloud to lead them on the way and at night in a pillar of fire to give light to them* (Exodus 13:21) and a second time with the phrase *Between the camp of the Egyptians and between the camp of the Israelites and it was a cloud* (Exodus 14:20). The splitting of the sea is indicated with the crossing phrase *And Moses stretched out his hand over the sea* from Exodus 14:27.

The next chapter will examine why I believe that other sites often mentioned in conjunction with the Ark can probably be ruled out.

Chapter 3

ALTERNATE ARK SITE THEORIES

Was the Ark Destroyed?

Whenever I get a conversation going about my Codes research, there's almost always someone who comes up with an alternate theory. At times it seems like there are as many opinions about the Ark's disposition as there are religious sects on the planet. One such alternate idea is based around the belief that the Ark was destroyed.

It is certainly true that Jerusalem was attacked on many occasions, but as Josiah ordered the Ark to be put back in the Temple, we can be nearly certain that it existed during his reign, and was not melted down during an assault that preceded his rule. As was true in Chapter 2, the man at the center of the Ark controversy is Jeremiah. The crucial verse in question is Jeremiah 3:16:

And it shall come to pass, when ye are multiplied and increased in the land, in those days, saith the Lord, they shall say no more: The ark of the covenant of the Lord; neither shall it come to mind; neither shall they make mention of it; neither shall they miss it; neither shall it be made any more.

At first glance, Jeremiah's words would seem to cast doubt on any attempt to recover the Ark. But a closer look shows that he could not be describing any time that would be *between* his age and our own. For clearly, the Ark does come to mind among religious Jews and Christians and clearly both religions would love to get their hands on it. No mention of it? Just tell that to all the Indiana Jones fans! The Ark is obviously a source of great fascination and mystery for millions of people at the start of the 21st century. Whereas Jeremiah is considered a true prophet by billions of people on Earth, we must look for deeper meaning to his words. The only alternative is to throw his book out of the Bible. For starters, we need to read the next two verses of Jeremiah (Jeremiah 3:17-18):

At that time they shall call Jerusalem The throne of the Lord; and all the nations shall be gathered unto it, to the name of the Lord, to Jerusalem; neither shall they walk any more after the stubbornness of their evil heart. In those days the house of Judah shall walk with the house of Israel, and they shall come together out of the land of the north that I have given for an inheritance unto your fathers.

Jeremiah was obviously describing a time that has not yet arrived, even as I sit at my computer today. In fact, he seems to be describing the Messianic Age. For starters, Jerusalem is to be *The throne of the LORD.* As of today, it is still at the very heart of the Arab-Israeli conflict, the scene of nearly constant terrorist attacks, a place where one can pay for a slice of kosher pizza on Ben Yehuda Street with his or her life.

So what can Jeremiah mean about not missing the Ark? He must be referring to a time when the Ark doesn't have to travel any more, when its purpose has been fulfilled. That purpose, I believe, is to help restore the Temple. But once it is restored, Jerusalem itself becomes *The throne of the LORD,* and the Ark is unimportant. In that day all mankind will know God, and quite unlike today or any other period in the history of mankind, *neither shall they walk any more after the stubbornness of their evil heart.* The Ark may well be unimportant in that new era, but until we reach such a time, the Ark remains of utmost importance. In fact, I believe that it is the essential key that will usher in the long-awaited Messianic Age.

While I feel certain that Jeremiah knew how central the Ark was to God's ultimate plan, and while I am also certain that he hid it far from the prying hands of Temple Mount trespassers that would scavenge the site throughout the many dark centuries to come, it is incumbent on me to at least briefly examine other theories about who might have taken the Ark.

Did the Romans Take the Ark?

It is obvious that Rome must be discussed. In the year 70 CE a Roman general by the name of Titus destroyed the Second Temple. The date was the 9th of Av on the lunar Jewish calendar (August 2 of the year 70 if my CodeFinder calendar is correct). It was the same day on the Jewish calendar as the destruction of the First Temple. Jews still fast today for about 25 hours each 9th of Av in mourning for the loss of both Temples.

The odd thing is that Israel could have rebuilt the Temple in 1967. But on Saturday June 17, 1967, shortly after the end of the Six-Day War, Defense Minister Moshe Dayan elected to defile the Jewish Sabbath and his faith. He entered the Al-Aksa Mosque, and as a good will gesture, offered five leaders of the Supreme Muslim Council (the Waqf) – the focal point of all Jewish hopes – the Temple Mount. The rabbinical community didn't significantly oppose this treasonous act because they didn't want the Temple rebuilt before the Messiah appeared. In fact, most rabbis expect that the Messiah will restore the Temple. Indeed, this feat will help establish his identity. By contrast, fundamentalist Christians tend to believe that Jews will first restore the Temple, possibly with the help of an Antichrist, then

Jesus will return. Who's right? Fundamentalist Christians and Orthodox Jews both feel we're in *the last days*. If they are right, the facts will speak for themselves when the events play out.

How do we know that Titus didn't take the Ark back to Rome? To view the answer, take a trip to Rome. Right next to the Coliseum is the Arch of Titus. On it the Romans proudly display treasure taken from the Temple. Nowhere on the Arch is the Ark of the Covenant displayed. Nor, as the Ark wasn't even in the Second Temple, should the Romans have found it there. Indeed, the Ark was missing for at least 656 years before they arrived. Is the Ark under the Vatican? If it is, and we'll look at that possibility in a bit, it didn't get there by the hand of Titus.

Is Vendyl Jones on the Right Track with the Copper Scrolls?

At about the time Titus was demolishing the Second Temple, some unknown Jewish scribe was supposedly producing the Copper Scroll which allegedly lists hiding places of some Temple treasures and the Temple taxation money. The scroll, labeled 3Q15, was found along with other manuscripts that were written on papyrus or leather in 1952 on an expedition sponsored by the Jordanian Department of Antiquities. It was so badly oxidized that it had to be cut open at the Manchester College of Technology in 1956 to avoid crumbling that would have occurred if it was unrolled. The first translation was published by John Allegro in 1960.

Vendyl Jones is a former Baptist minister who became disillusioned with the New Testament. He served in the Israeli Army. He also founded the B'nai Noach (Sons of Noah) movement which is (under Rabbinical sponsorship) an organization that seeks to bring the nations of the world to an understanding of Torah as it relates to the grand design that God has for Jews and Gentiles. Jones, with encouragement of several rabbis, has been attempting to use information from the Copper Scroll to search for the Ark. But what is listed on the Scroll? Basically, it's a list of locations for gold and silver treasure from Jerusalem and from the *Second* Temple, the one that did *not* hold the Ark. Most of the sites mentioned are unknown today. There are spelling mistakes and there is corrosion that makes it difficult to read in its entirety. There is also much speculation that the text is based on fable, but Jones has shown that there is reason to believe it is not. He has found items that he believes were from the Temple. No gold of course, but in April of 1988, he found a small juglet of thick oil. According to the Pharmaceutical Department of Hebrew University, this substance was probably Holy Anointing Oil (Shemen Mischak, the oil that was used as a sweet fragrance on the sacrifices and as the Holy Oil for anointing the priests and kings of ancient Israel). It was the first find of an item mentioned in the Copper Scroll.

In a 1992 excavation, his efforts resulted in the recovery of a reddish snuff-looking material. It was analyzed by Dr. Marvin Antelman, then a consultant to the Weitzmann Institute; and subsequently, the pollens in the material were identified by Dr. Terry Hutter, a paleobotanist. They identified the material as a compound of nine specific spices in a highly refined state. Two additional inorganic ingredients, Karsina Lye and Sodom Salt, were found close by in the same cave, apparently ready to be mixed with the spices, to comprise the ingredients of the Holy Incense, the *Qetoret*, listed in the Torah and the Talmud. This was the same compound burned on the Altar of Incense in the Holy Temple. A total of 900 pounds of the Incense was eventually found. It seems likely that even if the oil and incense were from the Temple, we would be dealing with artifacts produced during the time of the Second, non-Ark possessing Temple. However, according to a Vendyl Jones article by Gerald Robins carried in the Jewish Herald Voice Houston newspaper in 2000, the Scroll is said to contain the following text:

> *In the desolations of the Valley of Achor, under the hill that must be climbed, hidden under the east side, forty stones deep, is a silver chest, and with it, the vestments of the High Priest, all the gold and silver with the Great Tabernacle (the Mishkan) and all its Treasures.*

Certainly the High Priest of the Second Temple had vestments. Treasures are also to be expected. What is important here is reference to the Great Tabernacle (the *Mishkan*) and all its Treasures. This reference is not repeated in other translations of this document at other Internet sites. What is listed on multiple Internet sites is only the following translation:

Column I
> *In the ruin of Horebbah which is in the valley of Achor, under the steps heading eastward about forty feet: lies a chest of silver that weighs seventeen talents (yard stick).KEN* (Note: KEN are mysterious Greek letters in the original text).

S*acred vestments* and *oil* are mentioned elsewhere on the scroll, but the above text based on The Wise translation of the Copper Scroll from *The Dead Sea Scrolls, a new translation* (Wise, Abegg & Cook. HarperCollins, 1996) and the Florentino Garcia Martinez translation from *The Dead Sea Scrolls Translated* (Brill/Eerdmans, 1996) has no mention of the tabernacle at all! In fact, in scanning the Internet, I am unable to find any site other than those backing or describing Vendyl Jones that mention anything about the Ark or the Tabernacle in conjunction with text found on the Scroll. This, from the viewpoint of Torah Codes research, is of fundamental importance, because the way some of us use the Codes would strongly suggest that if we find the Tabernacle, we should find the Ark still with it. In the Babylonian Talmud (Tractate Yoma 72a) it states that although the Tabernacle and its contents (that would include the Tent of Meeting) were hidden away, they will one day be found again. What better place to keep the Ark when away from the Temple than in the same Tent of Meeting used to house the Ark while Moses was roaming around the Sinai?

We will examine the link between the Ark and the Tent of Meeting as seen in the Torah Codes briefly. But before doing so, I have often been asked to look into claims by Venyl Jones and his supporters (hereafter referred as the VJRI for Vendyl Jones Research Institute) that the Copper Scroll deals with objects hidden in the *First* Temple. The Scroll itself has, once again, no reference to the Ark. So what are they talking about?

The VJRI bases its argument on a text known as *Emek HaMelek* (Valley of the King). It is allegedly the complete text of a missing Mishnaic text called *Massakhet Keilim*. It describes various vessels that were hidden away by Jeremiah the Prophet. And here, as the story was carried in the *Jewish Herald Voice Houston* newspaper, the problems begin. Its writer, Gerald Robins, wrote his story based on an interview with Jones. It states that the First Temple treasures were hidden in the Jewish year 3331 (429 BCE), seven years before the destruction of the First Temple in Jerusalem in 422 BCE. The problem here is that the First Temple was destroyed in 586 BCE. Seven years before that would place Jeremiah's actions as having taken place in 593 BCE. The difference from the Jones account is a not so trivial 171 years!

The author of *Emek HaMelek* (a book published in Amsterdam, Holland in 1648 CE) was Rabbi Naftali (ben Elchanan) Hertz. The text refers to five holy men who were assigned the task of hiding the items in question. They were Shimor HaLevi, Chizkiah, Tzidkiyahu, **Haggai the Prophet and Zechariah the Prophet**. Now we must ask, "when did Haggai and Zechariah live?" The *Soncino Books of the Bible* point to Haggai 1:1 and Zechariah 1:1 in yielding a date of 520 BCE and state that Zechariah began his career exactly two months after Haggai – both in the second year of Darius (the First*)*. *Funk and Wagnalls* dates Darius I from 558? to 486 BCE. *The Chronicle Encyclopedia of History* lists 522 BCE as the year that Darius came to power. Now if we assume that the Ark was hidden in 593 BCE, then from that date to the time both Haggai and Zechariah began their careers as prophets would be 73 years. That is, the Ark was hidden 73 years (593 – 520) before these men were old enough to make their mark in the world. With a discrepancy this large, we can safely say that these men were probably not with Jeremiah when he hid the Ark. *Emek HaMelek* does mention a copper *plate*. It was alleged to record the location of treasures from the First Temple, but since the Copper *Scroll* does not mention the Ark, it can not be the item that vanished 2,241 years before Rabbi Hertz's book. It is true that copper is an unusual way to pass on records, but all we may have witness to here is that the method was used more than once. Further, the Copper Scroll contains Greek letters. Since Israel was not conquered by Alexander the Great until 332 BCE, there would be no reason for anyone associated with the First Temple, destroyed 254 years earlier, to be using Greek. In summary, the dates just don't fit for the Copper Scroll to be a First Temple artifact; and the bottom line is: the Copper Scroll does not mention the Ark.

Now let's return to what the Torah Codes have to state about the Ark's current location in conjunction with the Tent of Meeting. A leading Torah Codes researcher named Dr. Leib Schwartzman employs a dialogue mode of search. Here one types in a question to search for at an equidistant letter spacing (ELS), then looks in the crossprint for the answer. The all-important lowest ELS for the question, *Where is the Ark?* (איפה הארן), is at skip 2,101. Figure 4 pairs the question in a 135-letter matrix with *Tent of Meeting* (אהל מועד) three times and with *fortress* (מצד).

Figure 4
Where is the Ark at Skip +2,101

(Minimum Axis Term ELS)

איפה הארן = Where is the Ark?
   Start: Leviticus 6:23 Let 21
   End: Leviticus 14:43 Letter 31
אהל מועד = Tent of Meeting (three time on the matrix. These words are found in Leviticus 6:23, 9:5, and 15:29.
   מצד = Fortress

Figure 5 – Find the Ark at Skip -104

(Minimum Axis Term ELS)

מצא הארן = Find the Ark
   Start: Leviticus 9 V15 L35
   End: Leviticus 9 V3 L45
אהל מועד = Tent of Meeting (Leviticus 9:5)

Figure 6 – Find Ark at Skip 75

(Minimum Axis Term ELS)

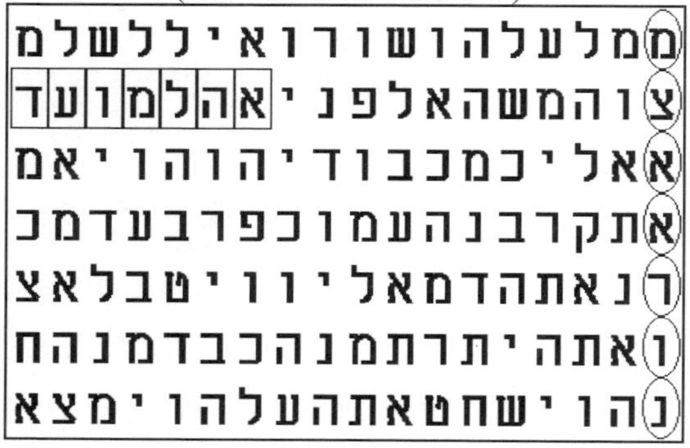

מצא ארון = Find Ark
   Start: Leviticus 9 V3 L53
   End: Leviticus 9 V11 L28
אהל מועד = Tent of Meeting (Leviticus 9:5)

It is especially significant that the first letter of the axis term ELS question (*Where is the Ark?*) is also the first letter of *Tent of Meeting* in the open-text.

A somewhat similar match shows up when we alter the axis term from the question *Where is the Ark?* to the command *Find the Ark* on Figure 5, or to *Find Ark* (not as good grammatically as *Find the Ark*) on Figure 6. All these plots have the axis term at its minimum ELS. This is critical here because Tent of Meeting is a high frequency term. How likely is it to get *Tent of Meeting* intersecting or so close to these three axis terms? A spreadsheet (methodology explained in Appendix A) indicates that for Figure 4, it was one chance in 40.8, for Figure 5 it was one chance in 29.8, and for Figure 6 it was one chance in 18.4. Taken apart, these figures are not significant, but when combined the chance that the minimum ELS for each axis terms would come so close to Tent of Meeting was only one chance in 22,430. That is significant.

The redundant matrices below are significant, because they may simplify what we are looking for when we get to the prime Ark site for my research. Find the Tent of Meeting and the entire Tabernacle and you'll find the Ark. It is probably hidden below the sand dunes of El Zuqba, but at least it adds to the size of the area dug that may result in a first indication that we are on the right track.

Are the Rabbis right, is the Ark in Jerusalem?

Whenever I broach the topic of the Ark's location with Orthodox rabbis, I get an almost immediate response that the Ark is still under Jerusalem, waiting to be recovered from a vault location under the Dome of the Rock Mosque on the Temple Mount. Some of these rabbis have informed me that they were told by another rabbi that it has even been found there. So why, they want to know, am I wasting my time researching a site in Egypt? I could focus on the Talmudic opinion that there were two Arks, and each contained one set of Tablets (*Berakhot* 8b). With this line of reason it's possible to argue that one Ark was taken to Egypt by Jeremiah while the other remained behind in Jerusalem.

The problem with the above line of reason is that nowhere in Scripture do we clearly read of two arks. Given that the Ark is referred to about 203 times in the Tenach (Old Testament), we should read about dual appearances if we are really dealing with two Arks. However, the issue may be somewhat clouded by the many terms used to refer to the Ark (or Arks). Unlike my own experiment that looked primarily for encodings just in conjunction with the term Ark of the Covenant (ארון ברית) as it appears six times in Torah, there are many terms that we all assume refer to the same Ark, but which may in fact refer to different Arks. They include the following additional Hebrew terms:

The Ark	Ark of Testimony /Witness	Ark of the Covenant	Ark of the Lord	Ark of the God of Israel
הארן	ארון העדות	הארון הברית	ארון האלוהם	ארון אלהי ישראל
	ארון העדת	הארן הברית	ארון אלוהם	
	ארן העדת			

Where do the stories of rabbis spotting the Ark come from? In 1983, Rabbi Yehuda Getz – the former Rabbi of the Western Wall – was tunneling through the Western Wall of Temple Mount. He was attempting to reach the foundation of the Second Temple. Randall Price writes that it was then that Rabbi Getz and Chief Rabbi Shlomo Goren allegedly claim to have seen the Ark of the Covenant according to statements they later made to the press. Moslem guards on the Temple Mount, who heard the underground activity, interrupted their exploration of the site. When the Arabs arrived a fight ensued. To defuse the volatile situation, the Israeli Government sealed up the wall with six feet of reinforced concrete.

Price (pgs 181-182) names Rabbi Matiyahu Dan HaCohen, founder of Ateret Cohanim Yeshiva, as a source of Ark-siting stories. But on further examination, what he cites is mere hearsay, as the story is only handed down via Dr. David Lewis, noted author and founder of Christians United for Israel. It was Lewis who allegedly recorded Rabbi HaCohen's statement as follows:

HaCohen told of how they were excavating along the lower level of the Western Wall of the Temple mountain . . . At the end of the tunnel, Rabbi HaCohen said, "I saw the golden ark that once stood in the Holy Place of the Temple of the Almighty." It was covered with old, dried animal skins of some kind. However, one gold, gleaming end of the ark was visible. He could see the loops or rounds of gold through which the poles of acacia wood could be thrust so that the ark could be properly carried by four dedicated Levites. HaCohen and his friends rushed out to the home of Chief Rabbi Shlomo Goren. They awakened the rabbi and excitedly told him that they had discovered the holy ark of the covenant! Goren said, "We are ready for this event. We have already prepared the poles of acacia wood and have Levites

who can be standing by in the morning to carry out the ark in triumph."
(David Allen Lewis, Prophecy 2000, p.176)

The above story sounds great, but it is a absolutely denied by Rabbi HaCohen who also denies that he ever told such a story. When Randall Price asked Rabbi Goren about the story in an interview conducted in Goren's Tel Aviv office on January 24, 1994, Goren was emphatic:

They are all liars! They are just telling you stories! How can anyone say they saw the Ark? The Ark is hundreds of meters down ... If [anyone] would see the Ark he wouldn't remain alive even for one minute! (Price, 182).

How close were the rabbis to the Ark? In the same interview with Price, Goren declared:

I imagined that [I was there] when I had dug in about 50 yards in a straight line from the place where the chamber of the Ark was. But it was still very deep-maybe 100 meters. If [Charles] Warren dug over 100 meters and he didn't get to the end [bedrock], what can one say about the Temple, its foundation, and the chambers beneath it! I believe that the Ark is somewhere beneath the Temple and the problem [now] is one of digging down a hundred meters.

There is another rabbi-related Ark siting story floating around, that of Rabbi Yehuda Getz (who was the Chief Rabbi of the Western Wall and Holy Places in Israel). Allegedly, Rabbi Getz feared entering the chamber to gaze at the Ark. Instead, he used a mirror to look around a corner of the tunnel, and thus saw the reflected image of the Ark.

When Price questioned Getz about these stories (Price, 183), he was given the following response during an interview on January 25th, 1994):

No... no... that is not what I said. These are all stories.... I am not responsible for someone else's remarks. It is important to know the truth, since millions of Christians and people who love Israel read such material.

So, for the reasons cited above, and others laid out by Price in his book (*In Search of Temple Treasures*), we can probably put these stories to rest. Ah, you ask, but what does the Code say about these matters?

To find out, I searched for Shlomo Goren, the rabbi at the center of most of the controversy. On Figure 7, his name appeared at its third minimal ELS (on a rounded torus matrix) encoded with the *Ark of the Covenant*. It requires a row split of 2 to see the Ark with his name. What does directly intersect his name is significant, though there may be two ways to interpret it: the phrase *And no man knows his (its) burial place unto this day!* This phrase not only shares a letter with the rabbi's first name (Shlomo), but it also touches seven letters of *Ark of the Covenant.*

Since the burial phrase intersects *Shlomo Goren*, it could mean that no man knows where the Ark is located until Shlomo Goren, but he now knows. Or it could mean that he is one of many who still do not know. His partner, Rabbi Getz, passed away in 1995. Both rabbis are highly regarded. One would hope that they are honest men. If they have indeed honored the Torah's teaching, *You shall not deny falsely, and you shall not lie to one another* (Leviticus 19:11), then there is only one way to interpret the matrix below. Rabbi Goren may believe that the Ark is under Temple Mount, but he does not know its actual whereabouts to this day.

Figure 7 – Rabbi Shlomo Goren and the Ark of the Covenant

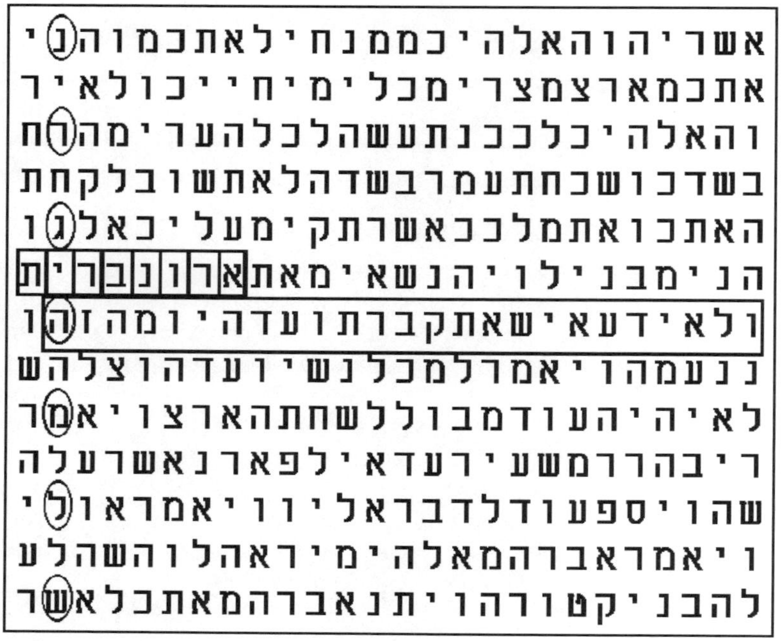

Terms	Translation	Symbol	Skip	Start	End
שלמה גרן	Shlomo Goren	◯	−11114	Genesis 25 V5 L15	Deuteronomy 12 V10 L48
ארון ברית	Ark of Covenant	▢	1	Deuteronomy 31 V9 L 47	Deuteronomy 31 V9 L54
ולא ידע איש את קברתו עד היום הזה	And no man knows his (its) burial place until this day.	▭	1	Deuteronomy 34 V6 L30	Deuteronomy 34 V6 L54

For Figure 7 the ELS reference is 5557 characters between rows. There are 4 displayed terms in the matrix. The matrix starts at Deuteronomy Ch 12 V 10 Letter 24 and ends at Genesis Ch 25 V 5 Letter 16. The matrix spans 66710 characters of the surface text. The matrix has 13 rows, is 26 columns wide and contains a total of 338 characters.

Is the Ark on Mount Nebo in Jordan?

The idea that Jeremiah took the Ark and went to Mount Nebo in Jordan is attributed to the Apocryphal book of Second Maccabees:

> *And it was contained in the writing, that **the prophet**, being warned of God, commanded that the tabernacle and the ark should follow with him, when he **went forth into the mountain where Moses went up and beheld the heritage of God. And Jeremiah came and found a chamber in the rock, and there he brought in the tabernacle, and the ark**, and the altar of incense; and he made fast the door. And **some of those that followed with him came there that they might mark the way, and could not find it.** But when Jeremiah perceived it, he blamed them, saying, Yea **and the place shall be unknown until God gather the people again together**, and mercy come: and **then** shall the Lord disclose these things, and the glory of the **Lord shall be seen, and the cloud.** (2 Maccabees 2:4-7).*

The above text was written in Greek sometime between 161 BCE and 125 BCE. It again indicates that Jeremiah, our prime suspect, took the Ark. As was seen with Figures 4, 5, and 6, he took it with the Tabernacle (that includes the Tent of Meeting). But that's as far as the text goes at first in backing my theory, and it's where I have to go to work in addressing the Nebo site.

The main problem is that the text states that Jeremiah **went forth into the mountain where Moses went up and beheld the heritage of God.** This statement is correlated with Deuteronomy 32:49-50, which is where God tells Moses the following:

> *Ascend to this mount of Abarim, Mount Nebo, which is in the land of Moab, which is before Jericho, and see the Land of Canaan that I give to the Children of Israel as an inheritance, and die on the mountain...*

The above would seem to argue strongly for a Mount Nebo site, but look again at Second Maccabees. It does not state that the Ark was in fact buried there. Indeed, it does state *some of those that followed with him came there that they might mark the way, and could not find it.* This appears to be deliberate on the part of Jeremiah. He was so certain that they would not find it there that he declares, *"**the place shall be unknown until God gather the people again together**, and mercy come: and **then** shall the Lord disclose these things, and the glory of the **Lord shall be seen, and the cloud."** The Ark was thus absent from the Second Temple, and remains missing to this very day.

There is a general consensus that the apocryphal book was referring to Mount Nebo. Setting aside the question of how its Greek writer knew about the details of this incident that occurred at least 425 years earlier, the fact is that the text does not specifically name Mount Nebo. Rather, it simply states that Jeremiah ***went forth into the mountain where Moses went up and beheld the heritage of God.***

While, despite Palestinian protests, it is true that Israel is the heritage of the Jews, Deuteronomy 33:4 states *The Torah that Moses commanded us is the heritage of the Congregation of Jacob*. This, the Koran does not dispute. And this heritage was received on another mountain – in Egypt, Mount Sinai. In 1979, and again in 1987, I enjoyed climbing the Jebel Musa 7,497-foot peak at 28° 31' North, 33° 57'East generally believed to be Mount Sinai. But the actual peak is still a matter of great controversy. According to a chart in Bowditch's American Practical Navigator, unobstructed views from the top of Jebel Musa can extend up to 113 statute miles on a clear day (common in that part of the desert). For the adjoining Jebel Katherina peak at 8,651 feet, the unobstructed view is about 122 statute miles. By air, Eilat in Israel is about 104 statute miles from these two peaks. Thus Moses might have actually received the Torah as an inheritance and spotted his people's other inheritance, Israel, for the first time at Sinai.

Mount Nebo rises nearly 4,000 feet above the lowest point on Earth, the Dead Sea below, but is 2,643 feet above sea level. At that altitude, an unobstructed horizon would be about 68 statute miles away. Deuteronomy 34:1-3 describes how much of Israel may be seen from there.

Did Jeremiah leave the Ark on Mount Nebo? If he did, his contemporaries who followed him there couldn't find it at that location according to Second Maccabees. However his visit to this area before leaving for Egypt may suggest that he was deliberately reversing the pathway of the Exodus. If this were the case, it would be easy to see why this plan places him back in Egypt at Migdol, an area passed on the early stages of leaving Pharaoh's rule some seven centuries earlier.

Mount Nebo has been searched for the Ark in modern times. An American named Tom Crotser announced the discovery of the Ark under Mount Pisgah, the highest peak in the Mount Nebo range in Jordan on October 31, 1981. This is the same peak Michael Drosnin claims (*The Bible Code*, p. 66) that Libyan terrorists will attempt to use to launch an atomic artillery attack on Jerusalem (discussed later in this book).

What Crotser and his associates allege to have found on Nebo was a 600-foot tunnel with a room at the end measuring 10 feet by 12 feet. There he said he saw an object covered with a blue cloth with another wrapped object to its side. He goes on to say he removed the cover and took pictures of a golden-hued metal box that measured 62 inches long, 37 inches wide and 37 inches deep. Although there is dispute about the size of a cubit, these proportions at least match the Ark's description as being two and a half cubits long by one and a half wide by one and a half deep.

Pictures were taken by Crotser. The Biblical Archeological Society asked renowned archeologist Seigfried Horn to investigate. His conclusions were published on page 69 in the May/June 1983 issue of *Biblical Archeology Review*. There he revealed that only one slide was clear, and that object was a modern fabrication that "appeared to bear the markings of a machine-tooled design." He also is mentioned on page 20 of *Ark of the Covenant* by Jonathan Gray. In that text the description given by Horn is of a "nail with a modern style of head" protruding from the upper right hand corner of the box, with decorative strips obviously machine produced, i.e. not the genuine article." Further, the initial description of the object by Crotser's associate, Tim Bollinger, as given to the *Dallas Morning News*, was that its size was five feet long (60 inches), four feet high (48 inches) and four feet wide (48 inches again). Those measurements do *not* match the proportions outlined in Exodus 25:10 and 37:1.

Crotser had also described a cave entrance that was covered by a tin sheet, with the last 300 feet of tunnel lined on its sides with ancient tombs that resembled catacombs. Randall Price (*In Search of Temple Treasures*, p. 128) identifies this site with the burial cave for the monks of the Church of the Franciscan Fathers of Terra Santa. Crotser thinks the monks are deliberately hiding the Ark. When pressed on the issue, Crotser told Dr. Shorrosh in an interview for *The Wichita Eagle-Beacon* that, "the mercy seat had probably been taken by Jeremiah to Ireland along with King Zedekiah's daughter when Jerusalem was destroyed."

The bizarre Irish claim is plainly refuted by the Bible's account of Jeremiah journeying to Egypt. Indeed, Ireland was nowhere on Jeremiah's 'radar screen', as it isn't even mentioned once in the entire Bible (even if we include the New Testament). Nor does Ireland even appear to be on anyone else's radar screen then, as it wasn't even cited in any literature until around 500 BCE when the Celts came on scene. Funks and Wagnalls New Encyclopedia indicates that Ireland was mentioned under the name of Ierne in a Greek poem in the 5th Century BCE, but that little was known of its inhabitants until the 4th century CE. So why would Jeremiah – with his great desire to serve God and the Jewish people – run to such a place where there was a Jewish population of zero?

For the record, the *mercy seat* is generally rendered as *the cover* of the Ark in Jewish translations. The last thing that I can imagine Jeremiah doing would be to remove the Ark's cover and abscond with it while leaving the Ark behind. Such behavior might be expected of a thief who could not lift the entire heavy golden Ark himself. Nowhere, however, does Jeremiah appear to be a man of such character. In short, this idea is truly way out of line.

Crotser promised to release photographs to a London banker, David Rothschild, who he thinks is the direct descendant of Jesus (Price, 129). Rothschild declined to take delivery of the pictures. Price quotes Adnan Hadidi, director of the Jordanian Department of Antiquities as saying, "The whole story, as far as we are concerned, is nonsense. This is an irresponsible group." What was the motive here? As the group's stories of the Ark's size are not consistent, it seems likely the true motive was to gain access to funds they thought might be derived from David Rothschild (i.e., a scam that Rothschild didn't fall for).

Is the Ark Hidden Under the Site of Calvary?

To an Orthodox Jew, Ron Wyatt's claim that the Ark was put under Calvary – site of the crucifixion of the Nazarene – is one that seems hard to swallow. His claim is that this was done as an offering of final blood atonement. While the Torah does place value on the blood offered during animal sacrifices, nowhere does it request human blood sacrifice. When Abraham was ready to offer Isaac's blood, a ram was provided at the crucial time. The Torah (Leviticus 18:21) decries those who offer their own children to the false god Molech.

Here again, I will refer briefly to Randall Price's book, *In Search of Temple Treasures*. He notes Wyatt's claim to have photographed the Ark with a 35 mm camera, a Polaroid camera, and video (all of which produced pictures that were whited out) on January 6, 1982. Wyatt claims that he also saw the Ark himself through a colonoscope which was inserted through a hole drilled through the Ark's case.

Price writes with a decidedly Christian viewpoint, however, he views the claims by Wyatt the way I do. Putting aside the issue of why God would want the Ark placed in an area that was a cemetery since the time of the First Temple (i.e., an area that would defile the Ark), the reality is that Wyatt's life-long claims read like the script of the movie *Forest Gump*. Wyatt boasted that he has found (1) Noah's Ark, (2) the chariots of Pharoah under the Red Sea, (3) the 12 altars built by Moses, and (4) Abraham's family tomb in Hebron, but not under the 2,000-year old site revered by Jews and Muslims alike. He made other amazing claims, but Price then goes on (Ibid, p. 155-156) to show that on his literature Wyatt listed degrees that he was never issued. Further, Price quotes Dr. Jim Fleming – founder and former director of the Jerusalem Center for Biblical Studies and an editorial advisor for *Biblical Archeology Review* – as stating that he observed Wyatt planting false evidence at archeological sites. Wyatt passed away in 1999. Whereas he did so without ever proving his claims about the Ark, we can probably safely put his claim in the same category as Tom Crotser's claim to have seen the Ark in Jordan.

What about the Knights Templar and Vatican stories?

There are many stories on the Internet about the Knights Templar finding the Ark. I had intended to spend a good bit of time investigating these claims and assertions that I had heard about them transferring or losing the Ark to the Vatican. However, at http://www.templarhistory.com, I found an article by Patrick Byrne, author of *Templar Gold* that appeared to indicate just the opposite of what Mr. Byrne was attempting to espouse, the idea that the Ark was retrieved by the Knights Templar.

Before discussing the crucial statement, let's review just a very brief aspect of the Templars. Their full name is *the Poor Knights of Christ and the Temple of Solomon.* The organization was founded during the early Crusades in the 12th century. Their short name, the *Templars*, was derived from the fact that in 1104 CE while under the leadership of Hughes, Count of Champagne, they were given part of the former Temple of Solomon in Jerusalem as their headquarters. While living in what now constitutes the Al Aqsa Mosque, the Templars are believed to have spent ten years digging under the Temple Mount.

Mr. Byrne asserts that Captain Wilson, Lieutenant Warren and a team of Royal Engineers uncovered evidence to back the idea of Templar digging. In 1867, they re-excavated the area and uncovered tunnels extending vertically from the Al Aqsa mosque, down to about 25 meters before fanning out under the Dome of the Rock Mosque. Supposedly, Crusader artifacts are found in these tunnels.

The Templars of old were – after a long and torturous relationship with the Vatican – eventually slaughtered and/or disbanded, but passed their torch to the Masons of today. Mr. Bryrne states that, "The earliest written copies of Masonic ritual state unequivocally that the ancient Masons found the Ark of the Covenant hidden in a cave under the site of King Solomon's temple." Then he quotes Templars as have having issued the following statement:

*"In pursuance of your orders, we repaired to the secret vault, and let down one of the companions as before. **The sun at this time was at its meridian height, the rays of which enabled him to discover a small box**, or chest, standing on a pedestal, curiously wrought, and overlaid with gold: **he gave the signal of ascending, and was immediately drawn out.** We have brought the ark up, for the examination of the grand council."*

The Ark is not a small box. Nor would it be easy to immediately draw it out from 25 meters, as it contains a large amount of very heavy gold. These facts, however, are of slight importance here. What is important is the significance being placed on the sun's altitude, which was at meridian height.

If the Ark was located in Syene, Egypt, then the story might make sense. For in Syene, as Eratosthenes was aware when he first measured the circumference of the Earth, the sun is directly overhead at local apparent noon on the summer solstice. Rays from the sun there do indeed go straight down a vertical shaft and they would certainly shine powerfully off the surface of a golden Ark. However, the Temple Mount is not this far south. Indeed, the Temple Mount is at 31 degrees 46 minutes 39.72 seconds North. The vertical rays of the sun never go north of the Tropic of Cancer that is located at 23 degrees 27 minutes North. As a result, the sun never gets higher than 81 degrees 40 minutes 20.28 seconds above the horizon at the Temple Mount. This is 8 degrees 19 minutes 39.72 seconds short of being directly overhead. On the winter solstice the sun's maximum height at the same location is only 34 degrees 56 minutes 20.28 seconds above the horizon.

Now, let's assume that the sun was at this maximum summer angular altitude at precisely the moment that the Knights were looking down a 25-meter hole. If the hole were one meter wide (big enough for a man to fit through) then the direct sunlight would only penetrate about 6.85 meters, which is nowhere near the 25-meter depth found by the Royal Engineers. If it were two meters wide, then the sun might penetrate to about 13.7 meters, still short of the floor of any room at 25 meters that might hold the Ark. For a sliver of the sun to reach the bottom, the hole would have to be about 3.647 meters wide (11.965 feet). And of course, this huge hole would have to be dug precisely in the right spot. Yet even today the rabbis argue about the precise location of the Holy of Holies and Temple on the surface of the Temple Mount.

Now, it is true that the Royal Engineers supposedly uncovered not just one tunnel, but tunnels (exact amount unspecified). This would seem to argue for holes that are smaller in size, i.e., not wide enough for the sun to penetrate 25 meters. Therefore, as the Temple Mount was not destroyed by these tunnels (which multiple huge holes would in fact do), we can conclude that any tale of the sun's rays shining off a golden Ark down 25 meters is likely to be a hoax. If this is so, there is no reason to go further in the study of the Templars to explore where (including to the Vatican) that the Ark might have gone as a result of such tunneling activity.

J.R. Church published, *THE ARK OF THE COVENANT – WE HAVE FOUND IT,* Prophecy Publications, 1993, pp. 13-15. In it, he says the Ark is underground at the Vatican. From the 7th century, there is a record that allegedly shows Pope Vitalian (CE 657) had the Ark and the two stone tablets. Church met a Benedictine monk who claimed to have seen it in the vaults of the Vatican, thirty miles east of Rome. The story goes that four stories down was the Ark, golden articles and old drapes from the tabernacle. But with no evidence that the Ark was in the Temple when Rome conquered Israel, and with the Knights Templar excavations discredited, there is no means apparent for the Vatican to have acquired the Ark. If they have it, why not produce it?

We have seen claims that the Ark was seen in Jerusalem under the Temple Mount, at Mount Nebo, in a cave under Calvary, and in Rome. One Ark can't be in all those places at the same time. The world is full of liars and incompetents. Nowhere is this more apparent than with respect to Ark sitings. Before returning to my hunt, let's examine one last claim that the ark is in Ethiopia.

Is the Ark hidden in Ethiopia?

One of the most publicized ideas about the Ark being removed from Israel relates the belief that it is now intact and well in Ethiopia. This belief was given some credence by Graham Hancock in his book entitled, *THE SIGN AND THE SEAL*. In it, Hancock claims to have traveled to Lalibela – a town in the region of Axum, Ethiopia – where he interviewed the priest who claimed to be the guardian of the Ark.

Hancock wanted to know if the Ark was stolen by Prince Menelik, a son of King Solomon that was supposedly born to the Queen of Sheba when she returned to Ethiopia. The monk then allegedly provided the following story:

When he had reached the age of twenty, Menelik himself travelled from Ethiopia to Israel and arrived at his father's court. There he was instantly recognized and accorded great honour. After a year had passed, however, the elders of the land became jealous of him. They complained that Solomon showed him too much favour and they insisted that he must go back to Ethiopia. This the king accepted on the condition that the first-born sons of all the elders should also be sent to accompany him. Amongst these latter was Azarius, son of Zadok the High Priest of Israel, and it was Azarius, not Menelik, who stole the Ark of the Covenant from its place in the Holy of Holies in the Temple. Indeed the group of young men did not reveal the theft to Menelik until they were far away from Jerusalem. When at last they told him what they had done, he understood that they could not have succeeded in so bold a venture unless God had willed it. Therefore, he agreed that the Ark should remain with them. And it was thus that it was brought to Ethiopia, to this sacred city... and here it has remained ever since.

Hancock wanted to know if the Ark was ever shown in public. He states that the priest responded as follows:

In the very distant past the relic had been brought out during all the most important church festivals. More recently its use in religious processions had been limited to just one occasion a year. That occasion was the ceremony known as Timkat that took place every January.

During the Timkat ceremony, Ark replicas (*Tabots*) are paraded. Even the miniature boxes are draped in colorful embroidered silks with silver and gold brocades, shielded from the prying eyes of the pilgrims and tourists. When, in 1986, Hancock pressed the issue by offering to come back the following January to see the Ark itself paraded, he says he was told:

You must know that there is turmoil and civil war in the land... Our government is evil, the people oppose it, and the fighting comes closer every day. In such circumstances it is unlikely that the true Ark will be used again in the ceremonies. We cannot risk the possibility that any harm might come to something so precious ... Besides, even in time of peace you would not be able to see it. It is my responsibility to wrap it entirely in thick cloths before it is carried in the processions...

Hancock states the monk explained the wrapping in terms of protecting the laity from it, as "The Ark is powerful." Thus what we have is one (half blind) man from the chapel besides Saint Mary of Zion Church claiming to possess the Ark. When he brings out the relic to parade it before the people, it's hidden under thick cloths, so that what is seen is of little or no scientific value in terms of establishing the credence of the monk.

What has happened since Hancock's 1986 trip? Well, from January 12-29, 2003 there was an Ethiopian Expedition conducted by Chuck Missler. In evaluating what Mr. Missler learned, it is important to focus on issues related to consistency in stories between his account and that previously related by Hancock. This is especially true with respect to the account of *how* the Ark got to Ethiopia. We saw above that the monk at St. Mary of Zion Church claimed that the Ark was stolen during the reign of King Solomon, who ruled from about 965 BCE to 931 BCE. But after Missler came back from the Church site, he published the following report:

> *Based on our understanding of 2 Chronicles 35, it appears that the Levites had removed the Ark of the Covenant from Jerusalem to protect it from the ravages of Manasseh and sought protection under Pharaoh Necho. (Pharaoh Necho, incidentally, was an Ethiopian, descended from XXV Dynasty, known as the Ethiopian Dynasty). This relic, along with its Levitical retinue, apparently remained ensconced at Elephantine Island in Egypt for two centuries before it was moved south to Tana Qirqos Island on Lake Tana in Ethiopia, where it remained for eight centuries before moving to Axum, where it has been secured in a highly protected bunker-like building to this day.*

Manasseh ruled Israel from 687-643 BCE. **The difference between the end of Solomon's rule and the beginning of Manasseh's is a not so trivial 244 years. As for 2 Chronicles Chapter 35 (Verse 3), that is where Josiah instructed the Levites to put the Ark back in the house which Solomon built!** If the Levites still had the Ark during Josiah's reign, it follows that neither Azarius, nor Menelik had the Ark in their possession. What they might have had is a replica (i.e., a simple souvenir) of the Temple in Jerusalem and its Ark. Souvenirs are still a big business in Jerusalem to this day. I myself have two models of the Second Temple (one is a Chanukah menorah, the other is a charity box). Is there any evidence supporting a tradition of such souvenirs being in use in Axum, Ethiopia today? There certainly is. Missler describes the January ceremony in Ethiopia as follows:

> *The actual Ark does not leave its secluded vaults, nor does the Guardian leave its side. Ceremonial replicas and other elements are used in the celebration.*

Even the Ark replicas are guarded, though I found reference on the internet that indicated Graham Hancock was shown samples in the British Museum. Supposedly they were not in the shape of an oblong chest, like the Ark of the Covenant. Rather, the samples there were simply wooden slabs with writing on them. At first this caused him to doubt the whole story, but later he took the view that they were replicas of the Tablets of the Law which were put in the Ark.

There is evidence that copies of the Ark were made. One of these may have found its way first to Elephantine Island, which lies in the middle of the Nile, near Aswan, Egypt. A Jewish colony there built a copy of the First Temple during Manasseh's reign. It was destroyed around 410 BCE, but an Ark copy might have found its way to Ethiopia. Why wouldn't Jeremiah want the real Ark taken to Elephantine? No legitimate Jewish prophet could sanction what would appear to be the permanent moving of the Temple from Israel back to Egypt. As was shown in Chapter 2, God clearly opposed any movement of Jews there. And what is the evidence that copies of the Ark were made? As was shown before, Jeremiah 3:16 states, *"The Ark of the Covenant… neither shall they miss it; **neither shall it be made any more.**"* It is the final part of the verse in question that strongly implies copies had been made. If a copy were made during the reign of Solomon and then given to the Queen of Sheba as a *souvenir*, it would certainly have been made with real gold. It would be a priceless ancient artifact, easy to confuse with the real Ark. The difference would be that it would not contain the Tablets written with the finger of God. This, at best, may be what is to be found in the church at Axum, Ethiopia today. The real Ark remains to be found. In the next chapter, I'll begin to cover what has transpired and what needs to be accomplished to complete my own quest for the real Ark hidden away in Egypt.

High priest with Ark of the Covenant, menorah, altar of incense and table of showbread.

CHAPTER 4

MOTIVATION TO SET SAIL

On Wednesday April 21, 1999, I left my former teaching job in Lantana, Florida and began a sea voyage to the Middle East. It was somewhat unusual that I was the one invited aboard the *Splendor the Seas* as a guest lecturer on the Bible Code. I'm not Dr. Eliyahu Rips who helped discover the Code, though I was sailing to present my paper at the ITCS conference in Jerusalem. I wasn't a Ph.D. in math or even an Israeli fluent in Hebrew. But even though I was then somewhat of a novice at Codes research, I had apparently found enough interesting material to merit the speaking engagement for Royal Caribbean Cruise lines.

By the time I sailed, I knew there were those who loved me for what I was attempting, and those who feared me. The main concern of my opponents (mine too) was whether an Ark find would in some way impinge on our concept of free will. What if I really do find the Ark of the Covenant? Does this mean that the Code does pre-record all of history as Drosnin seemed to indicate? Can we change the future? Do we have the right to do so if we can?

If I succeed in finding the Ark, will it be because I was clever enough to break the Code and hit upon one of its main purposes, or is it because I'm programmed by the Master of the Universe? I pray the prior reason is correct, for if the latter is true, then am I or any of us anything more than the computer used to write my story? Don't get me wrong, I love my life and all the blessings bestowed upon me by the Creator, but cherish my individuality. I like to think of myself as a friend of God, ready to work very hard for a common purpose, not a *puppet on a string*.

I could have flown to Israel, delivered my paper on the Ark's location as indicated by the Codes, and then gotten back in time to save my job. I could have except for one small problem – a simple statement by the Codes that seems to foretell a plane crash in conjunction with the Ark site. If nothing else, it was a good excuse to put to sea with my wife Kathy (a Korean convert to Orthodox Judaism), and with my six-year old son David. It would be less than honest, however, if I didn't mention my love for the sea. I'm a U.S. Coast Guard officer, currently on recall to extended active duty (after seven years in a retired status). I also have ten years of prior service as a naval officer.

Originally I got into Bible Code research because of my military defense and disaster response planning experience. Drosnin claimed many past disasters had been foretold in the Bible Code. He predicted future disasters including an asteroid or comet threat for 2006 or 2012, and an atomic attack directed against Jerusalem by 2006 at latest. You don't need the Codes to know that there are people like Bin Laden who would love to nuke Israel. As for the more cosmic threat, I ran my own check to see if the famous Tunguska asteroid of June 30, 1908 (1 Tammuz, 5668 in Hebrew) in Siberia was in the Codes. Figure 8 shows the best plot that I could obtain for this asteroid that shattered at an altitude of 7.6 kilometers with an explosive force equal to a 15-40 megaton hydrogen bomb.

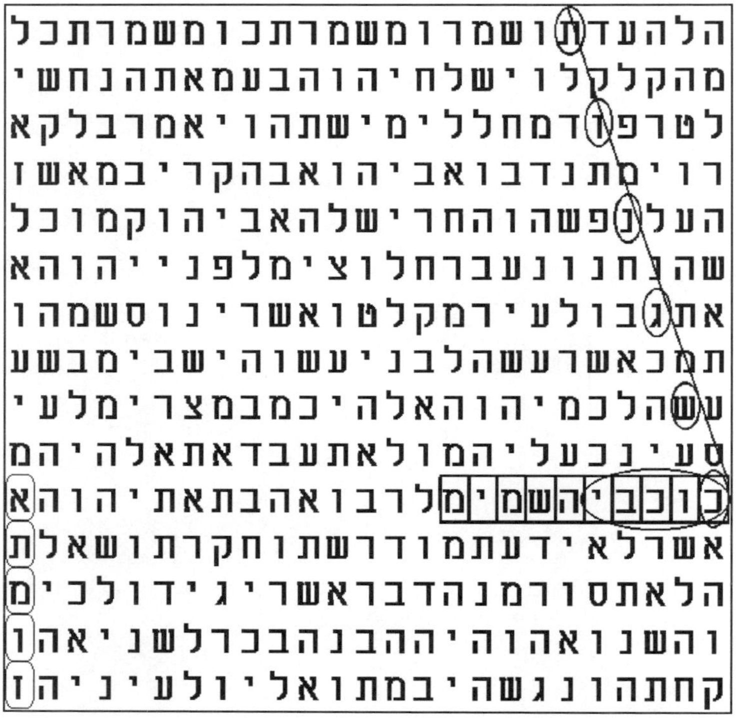

Figure 8
The Tunguska Asteroid

Terms	Translation	Symbol	Skip	Start	End
תונגשכ	Tunguska	◯	9951	Numbers 18 V2 L68	Deuteronomy 10 V22 L42
כוכבי	asteroid	⬭	1	Deuteronomy 10 V22 L42	Deuteronomy 10 V22 L46
כוכבי השמים	the stars of heaven	▢	1	Deuteronomy 10 V22 L42	Deuteronomy 10 V22 L51
א תמוז	1 Tammuz	◯	4976	Deuteronomy 11 V1 L12	Deuteronomy 25 V9 L21

For Figure 8 the ELS reference is 4976 characters between rows. There are 4 displayed terms in the matrix. The matrix starts at Numbers 18 V2 L63 and ends at Deuteronomy 25 V9 L21. The matrix spans 69689 characters of the surface text. The matrix has 15 rows, is 25 columns wide and contains a total of 375 characters.

On Figure 8, a transliteration for *Tunguska* intersects and shares a letter with the word for *asteroid*. The word for *asteroid* is also the first five letters of the open text phrase *stars of heaven*. The actual Hebrew calendar day and month of the incident are 15 columns left of the phrase *stars of heaven*. This plot may look good, but there are many ways to spell *Tunguska*, and there were words sought, but not on this plot like *Russia, Siberia*, and the year of the impact. When these factors are considered, the plot has about one chance in 97 to exist (see Appendix A for the math). It isn't really very significant. That's why I believe that to prove the Code is real, we must learn to make extraordinary predictions that aren't based on what's called *wiggle room*. We must consider not only what we see on a plot, but what was searched for and not found. It also means that we would be best to include the need for extraordinary corroborating physical evidence in our list of demands. For me, this equates to recovery of the Ark of the Covenant.

I first learned about the Code through a June 9, 1997 Time Magazine article about Drosnin's best seller, *The Bible Code*. Drosnin had found Rabin's assassination before the fact and had warned the Prime Minister personally only to be told that Rabin was not a mystic and that the Israeli leader didn't buy it. The rest is history.

The story of Rabin's assassination seemed impressive; but then again, the open text really spoke of a manslayer rather than an assassin; and an unfortunate reality in this world is that political leaders (especially in the volatile Middle East) *do* run the risk of assassination. Perhaps Drosnin's personal warning to Rabin was merely followed by an unfortunate coincidence. And Drosnin was wrong about a Third World War starting in 1996 (though, for reasons stated later, he may unwittingly have prevented it by warning Netanyahu about an assassination attempt in Amman). Further, although the method is used at times in Israel, I question his practice of often ignoring the fact that the first digit (letter) of a year is often missing on his plots. Something much more convincing would be needed to sway a justifiably skeptical scientific community.

Drosnin also claimed that Dr. Rips found the date of the first Iraqi Scud missile attack against Israel three weeks before the attack. I questioned Rips about this by e-mail. He denied the authorship of the Scud plot, but stated, "I have seen the table with *Fire on 3 Shevat* several days before it, in fact before January 15. I did not discover this table myself, but I know the person that did find it." Apparently Dr. Rips is more than reluctant to reveal the author of this prediction (probably Doron Witztum) because it is, he believes, against Jewish law to use the Torah to make such a prediction.

Wars, earthquakes, the Holocaust, comet impacts and Armageddon were all there according to Drosnin. I was the main plan writer for Maritime Defense Zone Pacific/Coast Guard Pacific Area for several years before beginning my research (and I am again today). I knew some Hebrew, was familiar enough with the scientific method, and wasn't too bad in math. How could I turn my back on potential intelligence like this? Here was an opportunity to save millions of lives.

So I bought the software and was "hooked."

I'm not a gullible man, and I don't believe that anyone (including my military superiors) should accept the validity of the Code without extraordinary, irrefutable, hard, physical evidence. An endorsement by a Ph.D. in math is nice, but you may be sure that for every positive endorsement out there, there will be those (like Professor Brendan McKay of Australian National University) with an opposite opinion. This is quite proper, for good science is only soundly founded upon the rock of skepticism.

Ten percent of Americans (I'm one of them) claim to have seen a UFO and more than half of the population believes in flying saucers. To science this is meaningless. Even my own experience on my 10th birthday is meaningless to me from a logical perspective. I only saw an unidentified flying object. To prove that this was more than just a strange light in the sky requires physical evidence – a captured spacecraft or an alien dead or alive. Nothing less is acceptable proof, only direct evidence (though I have been privy to some very strong evidence in that field of investigation). In science the burden of proof is always on those claiming the extraordinary. There are too many people all too ready to perpetrate a hoax for motives of fun, profit, or politically driven disinformation.

When I sailed, I hoped to find the Ark or provide the Egyptian government with evidence that it is buried in the area indicated by the Codes, by early August of 2000. Drosnin wrote that a prime purpose of the Codes was to avert a limited nuclear war on the 9th of Av in either 2000 or 2006. For 2000 this equated to August 9-10. Physical proof of Code reality was thus really required sufficiently before that time to allow military intelligence the opportunity to respond to the threat properly. However, the years shown on Drosnin's plots were not statistically significant, so it's likely that I'll continue my investigations until I'm certain that the Code is or is not real.

Why would God go to all the trouble to write such a Code? Who can fathom the will of the Almighty? Why do humans have kids? Children make life interesting and meaningful. If one impression has come through clearly, it is that the Creator of all life is a life form Himself – infinitely superior in intellect, but not all that different from us with respect to personality. So why embed a Code? Perhaps he did it to impress us with His power, His existence, and His love. The Lord worked hard for those six days to create us. Surely He wants to keep us from destroying His handiwork.

Beyond the above, the Code may be to God what DNA is to the life He has created. Indeed, as will be shown later in this book, there is a similarity between the structure of DNA and the word patterns shown on many plots produced or studied. People facilitate the reproduction of what may be the Divine genetic code every time they produce another copy of the Torah.

The problem with most interesting and possibly encoded items is that one could reasonably expect such encoding to occur only once unless they were really seen as important by the Code's author. Once does not a pattern make. So what was important to God, or at least, what was important enough to encode massively – perhaps more massively than anything else in the Torah and with a repetitive pattern that would prove undeniable?

I was always very fond of Steven Spielberg's films. His *Close Encounters of the Third Kind* came to mind the night I found the Ark's probable coordinates. But his *Raiders of the Lost Ark* first drove home the idea that God spoke to Moses from above the covering of the Ark, from between the wings of the cherubim. The Ark was kept in the very center of God's house – the First Temple. Such a find (if based exclusively upon the Code) would clearly prove the existence of God. This was something important enough to Him to list as the first of His Ten Commandments. Indeed, a find like this could open the way to a Third Temple (which might use, rather than destroy, today's Dome of the Rock Mosque) designed to facilitate worship of the Creator by all humanity. It might usher in the Messianic Age itself. Religious wars could well cease as religious leaders of all faiths came to the gradual realization that it was time to go back to kindergarten with respect to their comprehension of God and His Bible. So I turned on my ancient 40 MHZ computer in October, 1997, and typed in eight letters – *alef resh vav nun bet resh yud tav* which is read as *Aron Brit* – Ark of the Covenant. After about 30 minutes, the old slow poke computer spit out the number "1" and I knew that there was a hit.

The Ark could be found at an ELS, but did it really mean anything or would it be just a natural outcome of probability? I had asked the program to search at skips +2 to +1,000 and at skips -1 to -1,000 initially. Only the Torah was searched.

The computer started with each letter *alef* (א) in the Torah. It then searched for the eight letters of *Ark of the Covenant* (ארון ברית) at spacing of 2, 3, 4, 5 etc., out to 1,000 letters. There are 304,805 letters in the Torah. The letter *alef* accounts for 27,059 of them, so there were many places to start such a search for the remaining seven letters at an ELS.

The original program used in my search (Torah Codes 1.0) was primitive, slow, and extremely incapable by today's standards. It would not allow me to see the matrix on my screen that contained the encoded words sought, and it was necessary to actually print the section to look for related key words (positional in nature here). The program limited the printout to not more than 3,000 letters held in the memory per line of Torah text, so I restricted my search for the next few nights to an ELS skip range of +2 to +3,000 and –1 to –3,000. The "1" seen on the first night was the only hit known of for a long time until I bought a more powerful computer and CodeFinder software. The first night's hit was at an ELS of –306 letters. The other six encodings would not, with my initial slow computer and software, be found for over a year.

I am (in my own rebellious way) a religious man. Indeed, I consider myself to be a *modern* Orthodox Jew; but I've also taught science for 30 years, and in this investigation my "bible" is the scientific method (discussed in the next chapter). My purpose was to determine if the so-called "Torah Code" contains useful, empirically testable data, or whether the phenomenon is merely due to the chance pairing of letter combinations. Throughout my research, the sole measure of success has always been whether or not the Code would lead me to the Ark.

CHAPTER 5

TIME TO REALLY LEARN THE SCIENTIFIC METHOD

I was 50 years old when I first found the Ark encoded at an ELS skip of –306. A person tends to get somewhat set in their ways by such an age, and after teaching about the scientific method for so many years as a science teacher, I thought I really understood it. Harold Gans – U.S. government code breaker and Torah Codes guru – was quick to put me in my place.

"There were many *subtleties* that must be taken into account with such an experiment," he said. "How's your math?" he wanted to know. By math, he meant my background in statistics and probability. At the time that background went no further than an elementary probability course taken at Temple University in Philadelphia thirty years earlier. "You must write me telling me about everything that you found and everything that you looked for but did not find," he demanded. And so it was that I produced my first *Experimental Report on the Search for the Ark of the Covenant in the Torah Codes*. I was impressed by my own effort, but Harold wasn't overawed. He's a stickler for strict procedure with a passion for discriminating between finds that were *a priori* (searched for deliberately) versus those found after the fact and not originally sought out *(a posteriori)*. I quickly assumed his passion for this distinction, but found him a difficult man to convince initially. On the other hand, neither Harold nor anyone else working with less than ELS map figures has yet convinced me of the Code's reality with statistical evidence alone (though Dr. Haralick made great strides in this area).

I once read a particularly interesting fortune cookie. It read, *Words without deeds are just weeds.* I would add a second related thought. *When dealing with the bizarre, data without substantiating physical proof should not readily be accepted as truth.* That's why a Codes-based find of the physical Ark is so important.

An *a priori* find is one where the key word sought is specified ahead of time. Mr. Gans or others might have initially challenged whether or not some of my findings were *a priori* or not for the Figure 1 series. But when you see the same key words not only found over and over again on one plot after another, but even at the *a priori* angle, it is obvious that these are the position-related *a priori* key words sought. Where interesting data is found after the fact, it will be so labeled throughout this book. These *a posteriori* finds are not included in probability calculations. It was an *a posteriori* find that helped launch the Ark search project (the phrase *Egyptians were burying* that runs into *Ark of the Covenant* on Figure 1A), but this was a surprise on the first night of my search. There was no way that I could anticipate its presence, so it has no statistical significance at all.

It is often said that, "The queen of science is mathematics." In general, whatever is scientifically verifiable may be described in a mathematical way that is not subject to opinion. People have attempted to describe God mathematically, but (at least until the advent of Torah Codes) opinions have rendered the attempts futile. Jews proclaim the unity of the Godhead whenever they recite a prayer called the Shema: *Hear O Israel, the Lord our God, the Lord is One.* The Muslim concept of God is basically identical with the Jewish teaching. Ask any Christian how many gods he or she believes in, and the answer will be One again, but with a qualifier.

Much of Christianity holds the concept of the Trinity – they believe the One Godhead has three components: Father, Son, and Holy Spirit. Hindus will tell you that there are 330,000,000 gods. Without hard proof, all of these are opinions that fall outside of the realm of science.

The discussion of math brings us to the question of Drosnin's book, *The Bible Code.* Before proceeding, I want to thank Mr. Drosnin for his fascinating study. Many of his plots are extraordinary and they certainly caught my attention well enough to motivate the launching of my own project. Mr. Drosnin has performed a *mitzvah* (a good deed) even if he does believe that the *aliens* (discussed later) traveled back in time from the future to pre-record warnings about impending doom here on Earth.

The problem with Drosnin's book is that other than reprinting the WRR study, it contains no math. In all fairness, Mr. Drosnin is a journalist and not a mathematician. Dr. Rips told me that he did check the statistical significance of much of Drosnin's work, but we need to see evidence of the math to be certain that it is sound. If Drosnin's work was short on math, it should be noted that even the *"experts"* are far from an agreement about how to properly evaluate the significance of Codes plots. Lacking the solid evidence I seek – until this happens in my opinion – Codes experts are going to find it hard to convince others that they should be taken seriously.

Now while it is true that the Torah Code itself concerns religion, the moment that the WRR team published their paper in *Statistical Science* in 1994, science and its scientific method became the true owners of this field of study. This is a hard truth that even Dr. Rips is slow to comprehend. I say this because he has refused to accept my findings due to a rabbinical opinion that the Ark of the Covenant is still in Jerusalem. This rabbinical opinion is based upon a section in the Talmud that actually contains conflicting opinions. The opinions of rabbis are interesting, even important at times, but they are neither critical nor governing for a scientific study which must examine *all* possibilities (even Drosnin's *aliens* or human time travelers from the future).

What exactly is the Scientific Method? It is a way to investigate a phenomenon that is as basic to science as the Ten Commandments are to monotheistic religion. Briefly, the steps are as follows:

1. State and understand the problem.
2. Collect information.
3. Form a hypothesis (an educated guess that explains what is causing the phenomenon).
4. Do an experiment to test the hypothesis.
5. Record data from the experiment.
6. Check the results.
7. Repeat the experiment.
8. Form a conclusion.
9. Publish the results.
10. List new problems.

Whenever one of the above steps is missing, an investigator is likely to run into trouble getting his or her findings accepted by the scientific community. This is especially so where the conclusions are bizarre, as are the conclusions of any experiment supporting the existence of a computer code in the Bible. Drosnin claims this code is capable of revealing the future. He says it seems to lay out ahead of time, the fate of individuals that are at least newsworthy enough to make the New York Times. It might even lay out the fate of every human being to exist for all time. What could be more bizarre?

Let's return now to the ten steps as given above for the scientific method and briefly apply them to Code studies. The first step is to state or understand the problem. Drosnin correctly recognized that the Witztum, Rips and Rosenberg study (hereafter referred to as the WRR Study) made a bizarre claim that 66 sages were predicted in the Torah thousands of years before they lived. While the existence of Biblical predictions about key figures (kings, the Messiah, etc.) is generally accepted by most western religions, 66 sages, if really predicted, would indicate a much more detailed picture of the future than most would have accepted based upon general understanding of the Bible. Further, the very idea conjures up almost laughable questions. Does God like a laptop versus a standard PC, and which brand? How many gigabytes and how fast was the computer used? Is His computer still under warrantee and where, 3,314 years ago, could He turn to for service if the darn thing malfunctioned? In short, the WRR claim of a computer code in the Torah is bizarre enough. That it went unchallenged for three years seemed stranger still.

The second step of the scientific method is to collect information. Drosnin (as "a skeptic," he claims) went to see Dr. Rips for a few weeks. Rips showed him enough good plots to sway him, then taught him how to search for his own predictions. At this Michael Drosnin excelled. For me, the initial exploration phase involved looking for things like the Tunguska asteroid impact or the Roswell incident. So initially there was not a lot of difference between Drosnin's approach and my own.

Step Three involves forming a hypothesis. Drosnin did make some guesses about the future, but they weren't really formal hypotheses. When he told Prime

Minister Rabin that, "the only time your name comes up in the code, *assassin will assassinate* crosses it," it seems remarkable that he was proven correct until one realizes that many Middle Eastern leaders meet with such a fate. It's a dangerous neighborhood as Egyptian President Sadat, King Abdullah of Transjordan, and President Gemayel of Lebanon discovered (the Israelis also had a plot to assassinate Saddam Hussein, but it went amiss). In short, the probability of assassination is too high to make such a prediction an acid test of the Code's validity (unless the prediction comes with date and location). The moment an individual finds the need to hire bodyguards is the moment the assassination test becomes insufficient unless the prediction is linked with a specific date. Even then, it is important to ensure that a potential assassin does not learn of the prediction before acting.

Step Four of the Scientific Method involves performing an experiment. I'm not certain that, in the classical sense, Drosnin actually carried out a formal experiment. He does mention the concept of a *control* text, but his book did not document its use sufficiently (probably because it was written to appeal to the masses rather than to the harsh demands of pure science).

What exactly is a *control?* It is a comparison sample test that allows one to see whether or not results obtained in an experiment really are significant or even extraordinary. Suppose, for example, we are told that 50% of a population who take a new drug for treating the common cold state that they feel better the next day. Is the pill effective? One cannot tell the answer from the information just supplied. Perhaps 50% would feel better with no new drug given. If so, the drug probably had no effect at all. If only 10% felt better without taking anything the next day, the drug may well be effective, but if 80% would have felt better the next day without taking anything, then the drug may actually have slowed the recovery process. Beyond this, to fairly compare the *experimental* group that took the real medicine with a *control* group that took the fake medicine (placebo pills), one must demonstrate that there is no significant difference between the two groups other than the medicine taken. It would be unfair, for example, to compare a group of men taking the pill with a group of women not taking the pill. Age would have to be controlled. We might well want to look at diet, or at other medication taken, or at ethnicity, or any number of other variables that might distort our results and lead us to an inaccurate conclusion. There is a formal statistical test (chi-square) shown in the Appendix A at the end of this book that allows us to see if two groups are essentially the same or different. Use of it would have greatly enhanced Mr. Drosnin's work.

Step Five of the Scientific Method calls for recording the results or data. Although Drosnin's Bible Code books do contain footnotes, they are very incomplete (and at times incorrect). For example, where he cites the fact that *Clinton* and *President* touch in the Code, he could save fellow researchers time by stating that the skip for Clinton is 33,720 letters. By the way, what he missed in this plot was the entire Monica Lewinsky scandal (see Figure 9). Two letters right of the letter *tet* (ט) in Clinton is the word הזוב (*one who spills sperm*). The word that goes through the *tet* in his name is יטמא (*will be contaminated*). Monica (מניכ), at skip

67,442, appropriately enough, hugs Clinton from the bottom up, touching his name twice with her letters *mem* (**מ**) and *nun* (**נ**). What immediately follows the *mem* (**מ**) of her name is *eater* (**אוכל**). The next word (**גנה**), at skip −1, means *censure* and it has been said that impeachment is the highest form of censure. Finally, the entire verse that runs through Clinton's name discusses the need to clean clothing contaminated by sperm (like the blue dress). As Clinton appears at a skip (33,720) large enough to span four Torah books, this find might be evidence that the text in use today is the original. It also raises a lot of questions about the nature of time and free will.

Figure 9
Clinton Lewinsky Scandal

Terms	Translation	Symbol	Skip	Start	End
קלינטון	Clinton	○	33720	Genesis 24 V8 L25	Numbers 26 V24 L30
הזב	Sperm spiller	▭	1	Leviticus 15 V9 L20	Leviticus 15 V9 L22
יטמא	will be contaminated	◻	1	Leviticus 15 V9 L23	Leviticus 15 V9 L26
מנכ	Monica	⬭	67442	Leviticus 15 V9 L25	Genesis 24 V8 L22
אוכל	eater	⬭	1	Leviticus 15 V9 L26	Leviticus 15 V10 L3
גנה	censure	⊔	-1	Leviticus 15 V10 L6	Leviticus 15 V10 L4
נשיא	President	◻	1	Numbers 7 V2 L8	Numbers 7 V2 L13

For Figure 9 the ELS reference is 33720 characters between rows. There are 7 displayed terms in the matrix. The matrix starts at Genesis 24 V8 L21 and ends at Numbers 26 V25 L7. The matrix spans 202333 characters of the surface text. The matrix has 7 rows, is 13 columns wide and contains a total of 91 characters.

In this kind of research it is important that the following data should be supplied for the start and end of words: book, chapter, verse, word, letter and interval (skip). This is more than a common courtesy, it is essential for other scientists who are duty bound to repeat the experiment as part of the procedure required for validating any find.

Step Six of the scientific method requires us to check the results. I wrote over 50 drafts of my Experimental Report because two things were constantly happening: new findings, and mistakes caught. The more math used (even with a computer), the higher the probability of error. Many times I would e-mail Dr. Haralick and others a spreadsheet only to find that I later needed to transmit an *oops message.* I had found there was a glitch that had to be corrected, or that there was an error in my Hebrew that is limited to about 800 to 1,000 words. For months I was using the dictionary derived verb *coordinate* instead of the noun *coordinate.*

Step Seven of the Scientific Method calls for us to repeat the experiment. This is necessary because the results of any experiment may be a fluke. But when similar results are obtained over and over again, then we may be more confident of our findings. We have seen on six occasions (ELS Map Figures 1, 2, 3, 4, 5 and 7) the angle between *Jerusalem* or the *Temple* (in Jerusalem) to *Ark of the Covenant, Zuqba, Position (of) Ark, Position of THE Ark, Gold, Ugret Selima,* and the nearby fort *Katib El Qals* was 251.565° True. This redundancy between Jerusalem and Ark site names or related terms is far beyond what would be expected by chance alone.

Step Eight calls for forming a conclusion. There are obviously various levels of confidence that one may select from before reaching this step. Many times we do not have the luxury of time to be 100% certain. I may not agree with Michael Drosnin with respect to his scientific procedure (protocol), but I do thank him for alerting the world as to the dangers of an atomic attack against Jerusalem. Most (but not all) of his plots *are* significant. Frankly, he didn't have much time to alert us as to the dangers, though it would have been better if he could have had Dr. Rips clean up the presentation of his material somewhat. An effort to do so with respect to this threat will be presented later in this book. Indeed, I resigned my former job and set sail for the Middle East in an effort to personally thwart the dangers outlined in Mr. Drosnin's book.

Step Nine of the Scientific Method requires publication of results. It's essential for scientists to share results and to have the opportunity to criticize the findings of others. This is especially true with respect to claims that are bizarre, as is the case with the Bible Code. I am certain that there will be many efforts made to discredit my work. I welcome them so long as these attacks are scientific rather than religious in nature. Only those ideas that can withstand the most heated attacks and come through unweathered are or should be incorporated into the body of scientific knowledge. What if I have overlooked something and the Bible Code is bogus? If it can be so proven, terrific! We do have complete free will. If the Torah Codes are not conclusively proven, many people might make wrong life choices and others might make incorrect conclusions about the meaning of Bible text. If the Codes are false, it is very important to prove this and to prove it quickly. Should that be the sole outcome of my efforts, so be it. We don't need a modern replacement for fortune cookies, we need to evaluate data and make decisions on the basis of logic and reality.

My research is an effort to determine the nature of reality. There are two ways to approach it. There is the reality that people would like to believe exists, and then there is that reality that is. From a scientific perspective, only the second kind of reality is of interest. The purpose of science is, in fact, to clarify the nature of reality. All else is illusion.

The last step of the Scientific Method is to list new problems. It is somewhat premature to list all the new problems here at this time. We have not yet found the Ark and thus are yet to provide the ultimate validation of the Codes. I will, therefore briefly describe new problems inherent in the ultimate findings of my experiment if we *do* find the Ark and if we do *not* find it.

If we *do* find the Ark in the prescribed area, which is within one half nautical mile of 33 degrees 4 minutes East, and between 31 degrees 8 minutes 20 seconds and 31 degrees 16 minutes North, then the following problems are of concern:

(1) We must safeguard Egyptian sovereignty to ensure that the find does not trigger a war. No attempt should be made to move the Ark out of Egypt without the expressed consent of the Egyptian Government.

(2) We must solve the issue of where to house the Ark. While my primary recommendation would be that the religious leaders of Judaism, Islam, and Christianity should solve this issue, my belief is that it should be placed in the Dome of the Rock Mosque. Let God then make His Will known as to how that structure should be employed.

(3) We must emphasize that the Codes are easy to misuse and misinterpret without a firm knowledge of the mathematics involved as presented in my formal Experimental Report. Mr. Drosnin states that Hiroshima is encoded at a skip of 1,945. This equals the year that the atomic bomb was dropped on that city. It seems quite impressive, but there are several ways to spell the transliteration of the Japanese city's name. A few of the many possibilities follow:

מ י ש ו ר י ה (8 Letters)

ע מ י ש ו ר ה (7 Letters)

א מ ש ו ר ה (6 Letters)

ה מ ש ר ה (5 Letters)

There is no absolutely uniform method of producing a transliteration of a name. Sometimes we use vowel letters and sometimes we don't (substituting understood or implied vowel signs under, to the side of or above Hebrew letters). The longer the spelling, the less likely one is to find the city encoded at that specific skip. I only found Hiroshima at skip -1,945 when it was spelled with five letters. If this spelling is used, and if we search 200 skips – intervals +1,901 to +2,000 and –1,901 to –2000, which includes –1,945, then we find 133 hits (multiple hits at many skips). So, a majority of skips searched will have a hit. This makes the find far less significant than it would be if -1,945 were the *only* skip where Hiroshima is encoded. Less than fully candid claims like this have, unfortunately, given the field of Torah Codes study a black eye in the view of many scholars who have not taken the time to examine the more serious studies out there.

(4) If the Ark is where the Codes suggest, we must pay attention to threats that are military or natural in nature. A problem here is that it is usually difficult to know what key words to search for before an event occurs. It is probably true that the more significant an event for humanity in general and for Israel specifically, the more it will be encoded.

(5) The more people act upon Codes data and alter their plans, the less accurate that the Code is likely to be. This process may have already begun. I sailed to the Middle East because of a prediction of a plane crash. I also provided Codes-information to the Egyptian Government that *might* have been acted upon. Prime Minister Netanyahu may have altered his travel plans to Amman, Jordan in 1994 due to a Codes-based warning about his possible murder there. He canceled his trip with the excuse that "King Hussein had a cold that day." Further, Drosnin (*Bible Code II*, p. 99-105) met with Yassir Arafat on April 13, 2001, to warn him that in accordance with the Codes, the Arab terrorist group Hamas would assassinate Arafat. He claims that Arafat took the warning seriously. Even if the Codes are bogus, this warning might have kept Arafat from resuming efforts to find a peaceful solution to his dispute with Israel. He may have feared that such a deal would have forced Hamas to kill him. Thus, it is conceivable that Drosnin bears some responsibility for protracting the Israeli-Palestinian conflict.

(6) There will be a certain degree of cultural shock if it is discovered that we do not have the degree of free will previously envisioned. If I find the Ark, will it be because I'm smart enough to crack the Code, or will it be because I am a preprogrammed robot with the right software *installed* genetically? I'd like to think that the first reason is the case, but the Torah says that God would harden Pharaoh's heart to show His signs and wonders, so just how much free will do we have?

The above are just a small sampling of problems to be expected if the Code is validated through a fully funded expedition in the future. And what if there is no Ark find and the Code is *not* validated? Then the following must be considered:

(1) We must stress that a negative Codes find doesn't negate the value or the Authorship of the Torah. It only shows us that an ELS Maps line of

interpretation might not be justified.

(2) We must explain why so much data is meaningless. The answer will probably be related to a question of degrees of freedom, or to too much wiggle room, or to a focus on what *was* found for each plot rather than what was *not* found. The more things that one will accept as a *hit* on a plot, the more likely one will be to find one or some of them. It may turn out that the things *missing* on a plot are more important than the things present. This is why, as a sanity check, an expedition and hard physical evidence are essential.

(3) There are those who will tell you that Noah's Ark has been found on top of Mount Ararat in Turkey or that the Shroud of Turin is the burial cloth of Jesus. Based on carbon-14 tests and other evidence, both claims are highly questionable, but there are many all too ready to overlook this fact. As such, I am certain that there still will be many that will try to use the Torah Codes to back all sorts of ideas.

As was said before, there are two ways of approaching reality. There is the reality that we *want* to believe exists, and there is the reality that *does* exist. Before setting sail, I heard a Reform rabbi tell an audience of children that, "God did not kill the firstborn children of Egypt as the tenth plague. God is much too loving to do that." I never did hear him say *why* he thought the holiday that he was describing is called *Passover*. But his statement, totally in contradiction to the teachings of the Bible, is typical of those who want a *designer god*. That is, *If you don't like the God of the Torah, invent another one!* The Bible often mocks those who create gods with their own hands, yet there are many who seek to mold God into their own creation rather than just accept Him as He is. Poor scientific methods can allow a Code user to back all sorts of religious claims. *Caveat emptor*. Let the buyer beware.

Ark of the Covenant crossing the Jordan River.

CHAPTER 6

THE QUESTION OF BAAL ZEPHON

On January 18th, 1998 I attended a lecture on the Torah Codes given at the Florida Atlantic University campus by Dr. Leon Weissberg, the Director for Jewish Education in South Palm Beach County, Florida. Dr. Weissberg was gracious enough to allow me to address his audience for the last 20 minutes, where I presented my initial findings about the suspected coordinates of the Ark.

When I finished, Weissberg informed me that he had read about underwater fortresses in the general area cited. He reminded me that the area in question (Lake Bardawil) was suspected by some to be the *Yam Suf* (an *a posteriori* find on Figure 1C). The Yam Suf (Sea of Reeds) was crossed by the Israelites in miraculous fashion when the sea was parted.

Several months after meeting Dr. Weissberg, I became curious about the name of any fortress that might be in the area (submerged). When I called him about the name, he searched for and faxed me a map that showed the site as *Baal Zephon* .

Map 6 – Baal Zephon in the MacMillan Bible Atlas

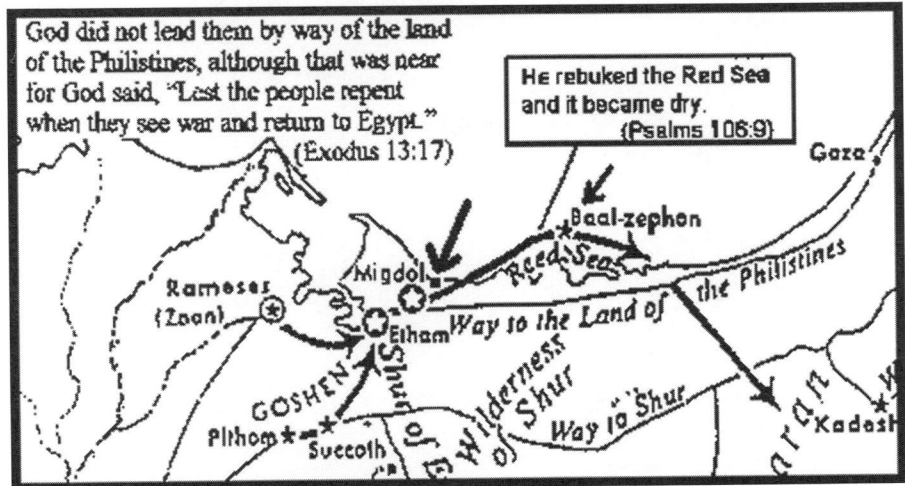

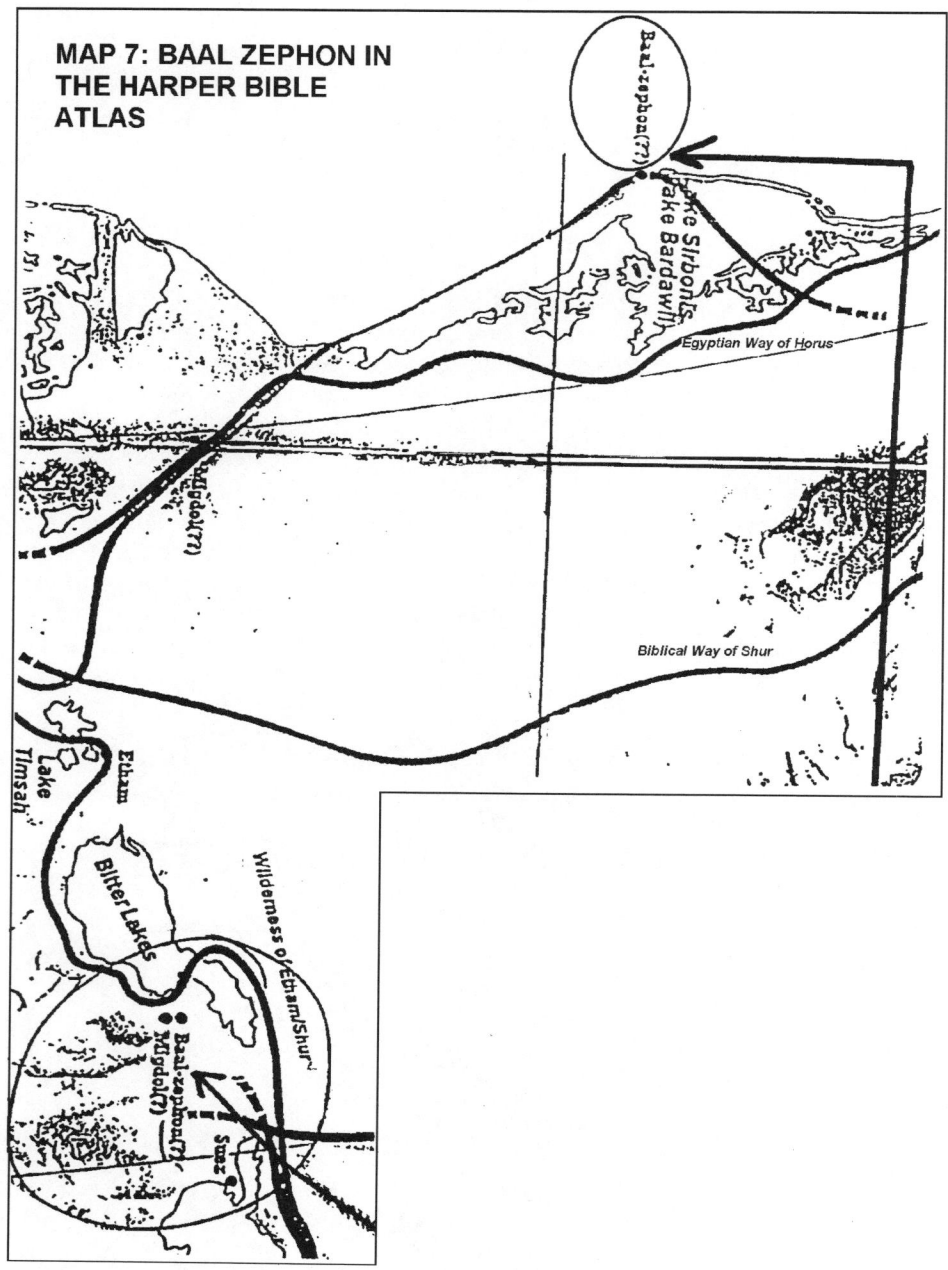

The MacMillan Bible Atlas (Map 6) did show the fortress of Baal Zephon at the suspect coordinates. However, the Harper Atlas of the Bible (Map 7) listed two suspect sites for Baal Zephon – one at the previous suspect coordinates, and the other at approximately 30 degrees 14 minutes North, 32 Degrees 30 Minutes East. Harper stated a preference for the latter site. Baal Zephon's exact location remains unresolved. Further, Weissberg was never able to locate anything in print that identified any fortress in the area as being underwater.

My first reaction to Weissberg's map was to type in Baal Zephon (בעל צפון) and start a search at skips +1 to +1,000 over the entire length of the Torah. There was just one hit with the name spelled *bet ayin lamed tsadeh feh vav nun* and it was *not* encoded at ELS. Baal Zephon was found in the open text at Numbers 33:7, within the span of *Ark of the Covenant's* encoding (at skip –306) and three verses after the key coordinate letter at 33:4. The smallest matrix to show both terms here requires 390 letters (see Figure 10). This closeness was somewhat surprising. What was even more surprising was the fact that Baal Zephon occurs twice in Exodus (at Ex. 14:2 and 14:9) as בעל צפן without the letter vav.

What's the significance of no letter vav? Quite simple. *If Baal Zephon were to be spelled the same in Numbers as it is in Exodus, there would be no encoding of Ark of the Covenant in Numbers* (at a skip of -306). The additional letter (vav) is essential for each letter in ארון ברית to be exactly 306 letters from the next letter of the term. Without that extra letter my experiment would never have advanced past the first night's investigation in 1997.

Figure 10 – Baal Zephon and Ark of the Covenant

Terms on Figure 10	Translation	Symbol	Skip	Start	End
ארון ברית	Ark of Covenant	◯	-306	Numbers 34 V8 L13	Numbers 33 V4 L14
בעל צפון	Baal Zephon	☐	1	Numbers 33 V7 L31	Numbers 33 V7 L37

For Figure 10 the ELS reference is 153 characters between rows. There are 2 displayed terms in the matrix. The matrix starts at Numbers 33 V3 L70 and ends at Numbers 34 V8 L13. The matrix spans 2168 characters of the surface text. The matrix has 15 rows, is 26 columns wide and contains a total of 390 characters.

לעיניכלמצרימומקברימאת
בעלצפונןויחנולפנימגדליסעומ
מויחנועלימסופויסעומימסופו
ברסיניויחנוובקברתהתאוהויסעו
ומקהלתהויחנוובהרשפרויסעומה
ובמסרותויסעוממסרותויחנוובנ
ואקדשויסעומקדשויחנוובהרההר
ישמעהכנענימלכערדוהואישבבנג
חנוובדיבנגדויסעומדייבנגדויח
מואבוידבריהוהאלמשהבערבתמוא
לבמותתשמידוורשתמאתהארצ
לוואמלאתורישואתישביהארצמפנ
ראלואמרתאלהמכיאתמבאימאלהא
רצנהוהיהתצאתיומנגבלקדשברנ
לתתאולכמהרההרמההרההרתאולבא

Figure 10

The -306 ELS of *Ark of the Covenant* has an even closer meeting with Baal Zephon in Figure 11.

Figure 11 – Baal Zephon, Zuqba, and Ark of the Covenant

תאשרה
יחנוב
רשפרו
בקצהא
נובעל
וישבת
רצכנע
אחמתו

Terms	Translation	Symbol	Skip	Start	End
ארון ברית	Ark of Covenant	○	-306	Numbers 34 V8 L13	Numbers 33 V4 L14
בעל	Baal	☐	1	Numbers 33 V46 L18	Numbers 33 V46 L20
צפן	Zephon	◯	-306	Numbers 33 V37 L23	Numbers 33 V11 L15
צקב	Zuqba	◯	-1	Numbers 33 V37 L23	Numbers 33 V37 L21

For Figure 11 the ELS reference is 306 characters between rows. There are 4 displayed terms in the matrix. The matrix starts at Numbers 33 V4 L14 and ends at Numbers 34 V8 L17. The matrix spans 2147 characters of the surface The matrix has 8 2*ows, is 5 columns wide and contains a total of 40 characters text.

In Figure 11, (see also Figure 1D in Chapter 1) the fortress name is divided into the two words/terms that make it up: Baal (בעל) and Zephon (צפן). Zephon appears at the same skip as Ark of the Covenant, just two columns left of the *bet resh yud* (ברי of my first name, Barry) in *Ark of the Covenant* (ארון ברית) and parallel to it.

Figure 12
Ark of the Covenant at Skip 3,102 and Baal Zephon

Terms	Translation	Symbol	Skip	Start	End
ארון ברית	Ark of Covenant	◯	3102	Exodus 15 V8 L6	Exodus 29 V24 L35
בעל צפן	Baal Zephon	▢	1	Exodus 14 V2 L53	Exodus 14 V2 L58
מצרים	Egypt	▢	1	Exodus 16 V1 L84	Exodus 16 V1 L88
מבצר	Fortress	▢	2066	Exodus 13 V6 L8	Exodus 17 V2 L17

For Figure 12 the ELS reference is 1034 characters between rows. There are 4 displayed terms in the matrix. The matrix starts at Exodus 13 V6 L2 and ends at Exodus 29 V24 L44. The matrix spans 24826 characters of the surface text. The matrix has 25 rows, is 10 columns wide and contains a total of 250 characters, however only 240 characters are needed to show Ark of the Covenant with Baal Zephon.

As for *Baal* at a skip of +1, it begins immediately below *Zephon* with the bet (ב) of *Baal* touching the *tsadeh* (צ) of *Zephon*. In this 40-letter box with the Ark, you could read vertically an abbreviated *B. Zephon* (ב צפן) with the meaning of the ב made clear in the open text with the letters *ayin* (ע) and *lamed* (ל) that follow the ב. Odds against this were at least 654 to 1.

Let's examine a second *Ark of the Covenant* encoding on Figure 12 (at skip +3,102). It's fair to ask if *Baal Zephon* is close to *Ark of the Covenant* again. It not only is, but it's actually a good bit closer than it was in Figure 10. While Figure 10 required 390 letters in the matrix to plot the Ark and an open text *Baal Zephon*, Figure 12 requires only 240 letters to include the finding of *Baal Zephon* at Exodus 14:2 with the encoding of the Ark at the skip of +3,102.

Map 8 – Extract of British Admiralty Chart 56100

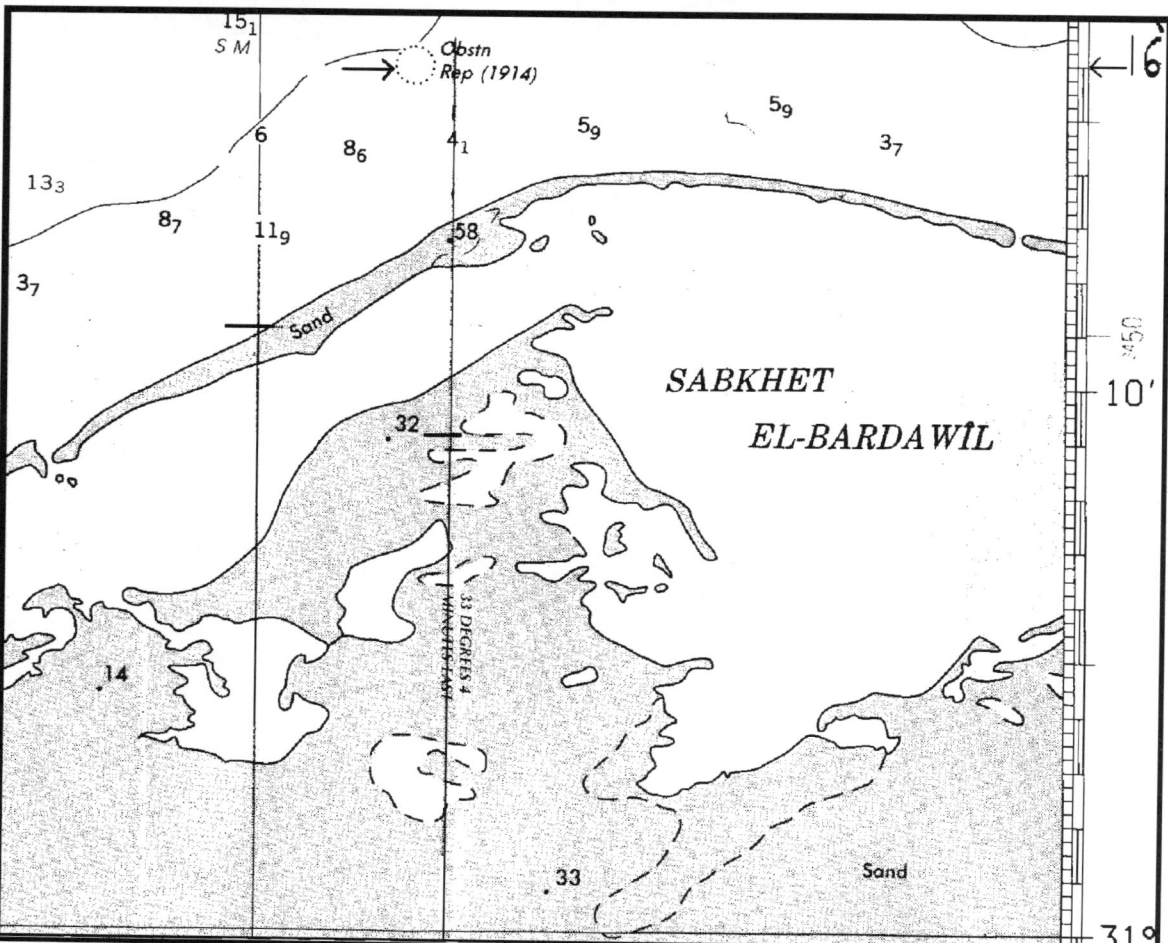

```
ש פ ח ת ה
ו ה ח ר ט
מ צ ר י ם
כ ו נ ט ה
י א מ ר ל
ר ו א ת ה
ר מ צ ב ת
י ו ת א ם
א ה ר נ א
כ ל י ו ו
ת נ ו ו י
ב ת א ח ת
מ ש ו ז ר
ת א ז כ ר
ה ח ט א ת
ג ר א ת מ
ש ר ל ו ס
ר א ש ו ג
ו ט מ א ע
ב ג ר ו כ
ל ט ה ד ו
ת ה מ ע ם
מ י ש כ י
ה ה ש נ י
ל ו ה י ו
ל פ י ה
```

Dr. Weissberg spoke of an underwater fortress in the Bardawil area. However, an obstruction just offshore must also be examined, since sea level has risen by nearly 20 feet and moved the current coast south by about three miles in places, from its Biblical location since the Ark was lost. This change is due to continual melting of ice from the last ice age.

There are two ways to spell the *16 of 31-16*. Jewish writers normally use *tet zayin* (9+7 = **טז**) to avoid using letters *yud vav* (10+6=**יו**) in God's name. Figure 13 shows my preferred (i.e., much harder to find) spelling of **לאטז** (*lamed alef tet zayin*), touching *Ark of the Covenant*'s encoding at skip -8,752. At 31°16' North, 33°3.5' East, British Admiralty Chart 56100 (Map 8) indicates the presence of a shallow-water obstruction in the Mediterranean Sea 2.9 miles off the Egyptian coast. This position is matched on Figure 13 by a word for *obstruction* (**מכשול**). The odds of finding **לא-טז** with this word for obstruction in this 130-letter box with the Ark were one chance in 84,494. However the plot also includes prime suspect latitude 31° 9' again (**לאט**).

Figure 13
Ark of the Covenant at Skip -8,752
and Obstruction at 31° 16'N

Terms	Translation	Skip	Symbol	Start	End
ארון ברית	Ark of Covenant	-8752	◯	Leviticus 5 V12 L64	Exodus 6 V19 L25
מכשול	Obstruction	4375	▢	Leviticus 23 V29 L37	Numbers 4 V49 L2
מצרים	Egypt	1	◯	Exodus 12 V12 L11	Exodus 12 V12 L15
לא טז	31-16 (Latitude of the obstruction)	-4376	▢	Leviticus 11 V9 L25	Leviticus 2 V2 L69
לא ט	31-9 (Latitude of the obstruction)	-4376	▢	Leviticus 11 V9 L25	Leviticus 5 V12 L63

For Figure 13 the ELS reference is 4376 characters between rows. There are 5 displayed terms in the matrix. The matrix starts at Exodus 6 V19 L22 and ends at Numbers 4 V49 L6. The matrix spans 109405 characters of the surface text. The matrix has 26 rows, is 5 columns wide and contains a total of 130 characters.

Bir El Qals is at 31° 13' North, 33° 5' East, just over 4 nautical miles North-North East of the 31° 9' North, 33° 4' East prime suspect site. It is one of the named features that are closest to the area scholars believe to be the former Baal Zephon. Figure 14 shows that the two words that make up *Baal Zephon* at skip +1 could be placed in a 36-letter box with *Bir El Qals* (בר אל קלס) at skip –1,775 (again, the minimum ELS for this term). Also in this box was the key word used for longitude (ארב) at a similar interval to Bir El Qals (+1,775), a special case for calculation purposes. The probability for finding *Baal + Zephon + longitude* at a special case skip so close together was one in 840,998. On Figure 14, *Ark* does not appear, but the word *Zephon* on the plot appears at Exodus 25:11 which describes the construction of the Ark of the Covenant.

Figure 14
Bir El Qals and
Baal Zephon

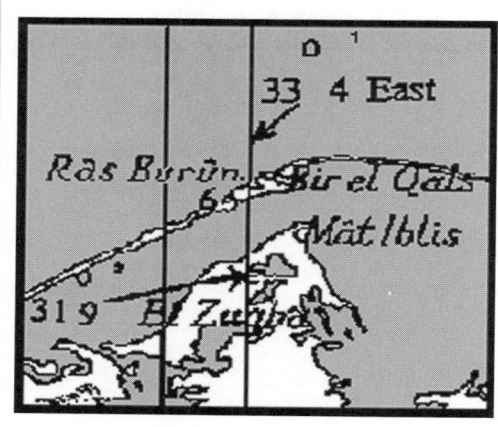

Bir El Qals and
El Zuqba

Terms on Figure 14	Translation	Symbol	Skip	Start	End
בר אל קלס	Bir El Qals	○	-1775	Exodus 22 V10 L45	Exodus 14 V27 L45
בעל	Baal	☐	1	Exodus 22 V10 L45	Exodus 22 V10 L47
צפנ	Zephon	⬭	1	Exodus 25 V11 L26	Exodus 25 V11 L28
ארב	Longitude	⬭	1775	Exodus 18 V15 L29	Exodus 21 V8 L45

For Figure 14 the ELS reference is 1775 characters between rows. There are 4 displayed terms in the matrix. The matrix starts at Exodus 14 V27 L44 and ends at Exodus 25 V11 L29. The matrix spans 14204 characters of the surface text. The matrix has 9 rows, is 4 columns wide and contains a total of 36 characters.

There were a number of interesting plots produced when Baal Zephon was used as the first term sought (conditional axis term) but none of them were ELS map figures. With Figure 15 an effort was first made to see if the suspect Ark longitude coordinate (33-4) could be found in sequence with *Ark*. At skip -3,903 (the term's lowest ELS), the required seven letters (ארון ל-גד) were not only found, but they were there just five rows directly below *Baal Zephon*'s appearance at Numbers 33:7. *ARK 33-4* and *Baal Zephon* were together in a 12 row by 7 column (84 letter) matrix against odds of 1,210 to 1. With the matrix expanded to 12 rows by 16 columns, the suspect latitude coordinate for Baal Zephon *(31-16)* spelled לא-יו appeared at special case skip +1 just seven letters left of the letter *resh* (ר) in *ARK 33-4*.

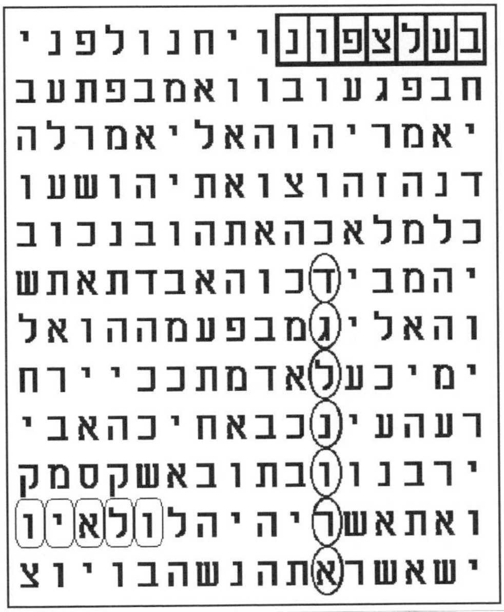

Figure 15
Ark 33-4 and Baal Zephon

Terms	Translation	Symbol	Skip	Start	End
ארון ל-גד	Ark 33-4	◯	-3903	Deuteronomy 24 V11 L17	Deuteronomy 7 V24 L13
בעל צפון	Baal Zephon	▢	1	Numbers 33 V7 L31	Numbers 33 V7 L37
לא-יו	31-16	▢	1	Deuteronomy 21 V16 L32	Deuteronomy 21 V16 L35

For Figure 15 the ELS reference is 3903 characters between rows. There are 3 displayed terms in the matrix. The matrix starts at Numbers 33 V7 L31 and ends at Deuteronomy 24 V11 L27. The matrix spans 42949 characters of the surface text. The matrix has 12 rows, is 16 columns wide and contains a total of 192 characters.

When I sailed for Israel in 1999 I had altered my initial impression that the Ark was at 31-9 North, 33-4 East. At the time I thought the Ark was at Baal Zephon, seven nautical miles due north of my beginning and current opinion. With time, I returned to my original belief because the ELS Maps all pointed to the more southerly site, and because Baal Zephon was not at the intersection of major question terms used as ELS axis terms. When I used the term *WHERE IS THE ARK* seen on Figure 4 in Chapter 3, in exploring beyond the minimum ELS of the term seen on that plot, I could place it in a 198-letter matrix with Baal Zephon with the axis term at skip 21,187. I could also put it in a 220-letter matrix with Baal Zephon when the question was at skip 18,830 on a rounded torus matrix. But those matrices only involved the 4th and 5th shortest ELSs for the axis term question. Often Baal Zephon was close to the Ark in the matrices observed, never did it intersect the Ark or the axis term. It is important to discover the location of this fortress. In doing so we will have found the route of the Israelites on their Exodus from Egypt. What we will probably not discover, however, is the Ark itself at the site. To find the Ark, we must go south for seven miles along the same line of longitude.

Chapter 7

ZUABA AND TREASURES IN THE SAND

We visited St. Thomas as our first port of call on our transatlantic passage, on Saturday April 24, 1999. Unfortunately, it was the Jewish Sabbath. This meant that as an Orthodox Jew I couldn't drive unless there was a medical emergency or a matter of national defense. Neither occurred while we were in port, so the best our family could do was stretch the law of walking limits just a little by climbing the mountain that immediately adjoins the port. The view was terrific at the top, but I must tell you it's a lot more work hiking up a mountain than driving up (or taking the gondola that was just over our heads). Still, I have no problem in following rabbinical edicts in matters other than experimental protocol.

"We won't see land for six days," the captain announced as we left port. With so much time on my hands I did a search, and when the sun set I found Figure 16.

Figure 16
Ark Position at Skip 2,698

Terms	Translation	Symbol	Skip	Start	End
ארון מקום	Ark Position	◯	2698	Numbers 5 V29 L11	Numbers 16 V9 L28
זאבה	Zuaba	▢	2698	Numbers 4 V28 L1	Numbers 7 V88 L10
ארון	Ark	∪	2698	Leviticus 26 V22 L11	Numbers 3 V27 L39
מקום	Position	▭	1	Numbers 13 V24 L2	Numbers 13 V24 L5

For Figure 16 the ELS reference is 2698 characters between rows. There are 4 displayed terms in the matrix. The matrix starts at Leviticus 26 V22 L11 and ends at Numbers 16 V9 L37. The matrix spans 32399 characters of the surface text. The matrix has 13 rows, is 23 columns wide and contains a total of 299 characters.

As was discussed earlier with ELS Map Figure 10, I sailed to the Middle East believing the peninsula jutting into Lake Bardawil was named *El Zuaba* rather than *El Zuqba*. On Figure 16, there are three key terms at the same skip (+2,698). They are *Ark Position*, *Ark* (separately) and *Zuaba* with the four-letter transliteration (from Figure 1H) used until my trip to Egypt in 1999 (two letters can be rendered as a Z in transliteration, zayin ז and tsadeh צ). *Position* in the open text crosses *Position* in *Ark Position*. The word for *Position* (מקום) is, curiously enough, one of God's names when preceded by the letter *hey* that normally means *the*.

Could Figure 16 be a map figure? There is a triangle (shown) with an X/Y ratio of 22/7 (3.14) that yields a course of 252.35° True from the first letter of the top of *Ark* to the last letter of *Zuaba*. That's only 0.45 ° off the 251.9° course from Jerusalem to the peninsula prime site coordinates provided by the Java Course Calculator. But to qualify as a map figure the course line really needs to be drawn from a site name like Jerusalem or Temple, not from a mobile object like the Ark. Further, the vertical *Ark* in *Ark Position* is closer to *Zuaba* and that does not yield anything within a degree of the 251.9° course (it yields a course of 257.47°, a 5.57° error). The Ark should be at the end of the course line, not at the beginning.

One of the more curious plots was found when the term *coordinate* was sought (see Figures 17A and 17B below). The correct word in Hebrew is *coordiniTAH* (קואורדניטה), a Hebrewized version of the English word *coordinate*. The spelling is *kuf vav alef vav resh dalet nun yud TET HEY*. *CoordiniTAH* wasn't found at any skip in the Torah. I then sought *coordini* with a spelling of the first eight letters of *Coordinitah*. When this was done the eight letters popped just once in the Torah and they were followed by the other Hebrew letter to have a "t" sound, *tav*. Reading vertically back from Exodus 37:26, 11th word, 1st letter is the English word *coordinate* (קואורדנית)!

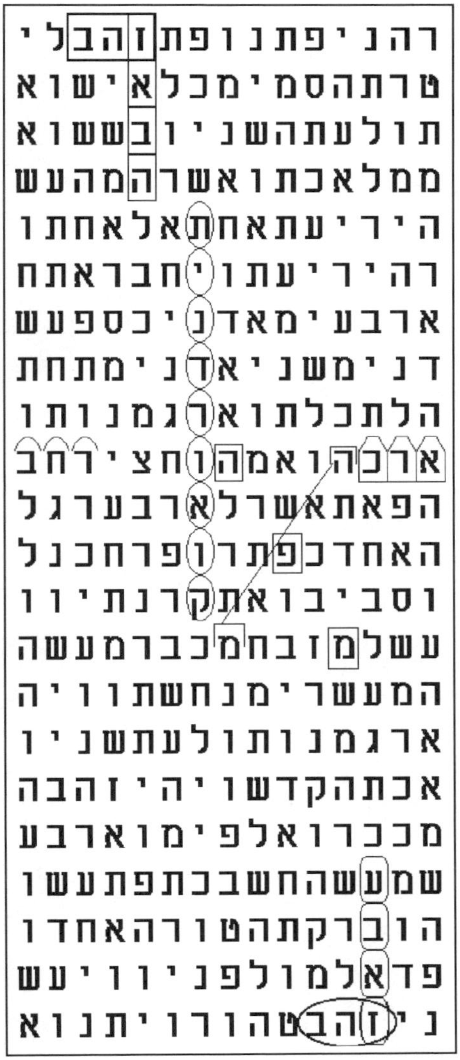

Figure 17A

Terms	Translation	Symbol	Skip	Start	End
קואורדנית	Coordinate	○	-337	Exodus 37 V26 L36	Exodus 36 V10 L19
זאבה	Zuaba	□	337	Exodus 35 V22 L74	Exodus 36 V4 L48
זאבע	Zuaba	⬭	-337	Exodus 39 V25 L11	Exodus 39 V3 L73
זהב	Gold	▭	1	Exodus 35 V22 L74	Exodus 35 V22 L76
זהב	Gold	⬯	1	Exodus 39 V25 L11	Exodus 39 V25 L13
רחב	Latitude	⌒	1	Exodus 37 V6 L37	Exodus 37 V6 L39
ארכ	Longitude	⬭	1	Exodus 37 V6 L25	Exodus 37 V6 L27
מפה	Map	⌐	-676	Exodus 38 V4 L10	Exodus 37 V6 L28
מפה	Map	⌐	-676	Exodus 38 V4 L14	Exodus 37 V6 L32
מפה	Map	□	-672	Exodus 38 V4 L6	Exodus 37 V6 L32

Matrix Figure 17A was most exciting while I thought the name of the peninsula in question was *Zuaba*, but it is still of great interest even if *Zuqba* is the correct term to seek. For starters, the word for *longitude*, (ארכ) is in the open text six letters right of the second *vav* (ו) in *coordinate*. The word for *latitude* (רחב) is four letters left of the same *vav* in *coordinate*. These words are identical with the words *length* and *width*. What is being described in this passage? The length and width of the Ark of the Covenant!

The word *chart* (מפה - *mapah*) appears three times on the plot. One of two *charts* at skip –676 touches both the words *coordinate* and *longitude*.

What about *Zuaba*? We saw *Zuaba* parallel to and at the same skip as *Ark Position* on Figure 16. In Figure 17A there are two transliterations for Zuaba at the same skip and parallel to *Coordinate*. In each case the letter *zayin* (ז) of *Zuaba* is identical with the first letter of the unencoded key word *gold* (זהב). The odds of finding the top transliteration of *Zuaba* in the 15 columns and top 14 rows with

Figure 17B – Coordinate Plot with Zuqba

Terms	Translation	Symbol	Skip	Start	End
קואורדנית	Coordinate	◯	-337	Exodus 37 V26 L36	Exodus 36 V10 L19
צקבה	Zuqba	◯	683	Exodus 37 V6 L35	Exodus 38 V18 L61
צקב	Zuqba	☐	337	Exodus 38 V4 L41	Exodus 38 V18 L62
זהב	Gold	⬭	1	Exodus 39 V25 L11	Exodus 39 V25 L13
רחב	Latitude	◯	1	Exodus 37 V6 L37	Exodus 37 V6 L39
רחב	Latitude	☐	1	Exodus 37 V6 L37	Exodus 37 V6 L39
ארכ	Longitude	⌐	1	Exodus 37 V6 L25	Exodus 37 V6 L27

Coordinate, one of the two *chart* finds, one *gold, longitude,* and *latitude* with key words *gold, longitude,* and *latitude* at skip +1 were one chance in 5,245,033. If one argues that Zuqba is the correct name, then the odds for the rest of the data are one chance in 21,637. This is still significant, but it leaves us with a need to look for Zuqba near the axis term, *Coordinate.* This is done in Figure 17B.

There are two *Zuqba* finds on Figure 17B. One is the three-letter spelling version of Figure 1B, and ELS Maps 1 and 2 - צקב. This Zuqba on Figure 17B is at the same skip as *coordinate.* The other *Zuqba* is צקבה (a better transliteration). The last letter of the second *Zuqba* (ה) touches the last letter of the shorter first *Zuqba* (ב - *bet*). This same *bet* of the smaller *Zuqba* is directly followed by the word *latitude* (רחב), it is six letters after *longitude* (ארך), and it is directly below *gold* (זהב). As such it was only natural to look to see if the angle from the top letter in *coordinate* to the top letter in Zuqba is anything close to the 251.9° course from Jerusalem to Zuqba even if *coordinate* is not a site. The 30 columns and 9 rows between the two correspond to a course of 253.3 degrees. The difference is 1.4°. However, while the 251.9° course is the approximate course from Jerusalem to the prime suspect Ark site at 31° 9' North, 33° 4' East, the northern most point of land on Zuqba is at 31 degrees 11 minutes 40 seconds North, 33 degrees 6 minutes 30 seconds East. The course from Jerusalem to that point on Zuqba is 252.8 degrees by Java calculator. Using this destination the difference in course is only 0.5°. Thus the course given on this figure works for the peninsula itself, but not for the suspect site on it. Why not include it in the map figure section? Again, the course is drawn from the term *coordinate,* not from a geographic site. We may be looking at a clue, but there's too much wiggle room to say more.

The last portion of the Torah is *Vezos HaBerachah,* "This is the Blessing..." In it each tribe of Israel is blessed by Moses just before he dies. Included in the blessing of Zebulun and Issachar in Deuteronomy 33:19 is the statement, *"For by the riches of the sea they will be nourished, and by the treasures concealed in the sand."* Upon reading these words on Simchat Torah in 1998, it seemed obvious that this was a place that the Ark coordinates *had to be* if the Code was to be taken seriously. Figures 18 shows findings consistent with 33-4 East, but meaningful results for determining a latitude are clouded by the fact that as the column width varies all sorts of key words can be made to appear on the related matrix.

The longitude coordinate (לג-ד, *33-4*) is found two letters after *sand* (חול), and for the first time in this experiment it is found at skip +1. It is especially interesting because the coordinate *33-4* follows a letter *vav* (ו) which could be read *and.* If so, שפני טמוני חול ולג-ד reads, *treasures concealed in the sand and 33-4!*

Figure 18 – Treasures Concealed in the Sand

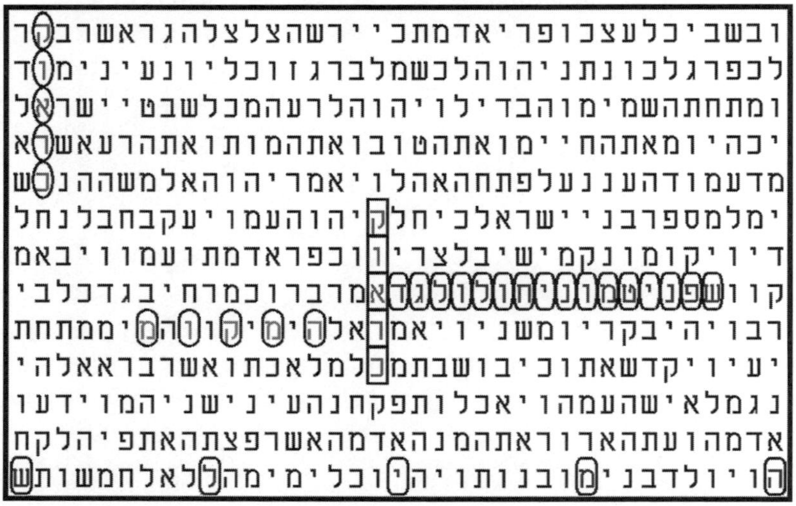

Terms	Translation	Symbol	Skip	Start	End
שפני טמוני חול ולג-ד	Treasures concealed in the sand and 33-4	◯	1	Deuteronomy 33 V19 L41	Deuteronomy 33 V20 L4
קו ארכ	Line of Longitude	◯	1442	Deuteronomy 32 V9 L5	Genesis 2 V3 L38
קו ארכ	Line of Longitude	☐	1442	Deuteronomy 28 V43 L8	Deuteronomy 31 V16 L17
שלימה	Selima	◯	-9	Genesis 5 V17 L22	Genesis 5 V16 L45
המקום	The position	◯	2	Genesis 1 V9 L8	Genesis 1 V9 L16

For Figure 18 The ELS reference is 1442 characters between rows. There are 5 displayed terms in the matrix. The matrix starts at Deuteronomy 28 V41 L29 and ends at Genesis 5 V17 L22. The matrix spans 17341 characters of the surface text. The matrix has 13 rows, is 37 columns wide and contains a total of 481 characters.

Other items of interest on Figure 18 (a wrapped plot) are the dual appearances of the term *Line of longitude*, *Position* and *Selima* (recall that Ugret Selima is the salt marsh found about 600 meters from the prime suspect site). However, as was just explained, these terms could easily be replaced by a slew of other items. This is because we are trying to match terms with a set of words that are found in the open text at skip +1. Whenever this is the case with an axis term, you can pair it with almost anything you please. Meaningful matches for other key words can only be made when the axis term is at skips above 10 and when it is arranged in vertical fashion. The sole exception to this rule is when we find the *a priori* key word or term immediately before or after the horizontal axis term, as with *The riches of the sea and treasures concealed in the sand.* There are 304,805 letters in Torah. Only six of them can be read in sequence as *and 33-4.* Is it just a coincidence that we find these letters immediately follow such a critical phrase? We'll only know when we start digging for treasures concealed in the sand at longitude 33-4.

Small model of the Ark of the Covenant.

Chapter 8

ALTERING TIME LINES
AND DESTINY

While sailing to the Middle East, we stopped at the spectacular island of Tenerife in the Canary Islands on April 30, 1999. The perfectly conical 12,198 foot Mount Pico de Teide volcano there last erupted in 1909 leaving a three-mile stream of brittle black lava. There were also fields of tephra (volcanic ash) to romp around in, and abundant micro-climates to marvel at as we ascended the mountain (which sports a gondola ride to the top that is available when wind speeds are under 40 kilometers per hour). Yet, more ominous than the volcano in my thoughts, was the airport. Two Boeing 747's had once collided there on the runway in heavy fog. Some 583 people had died that day in aviation's worst disaster. The place was a stark reminder of why I chose to sail over; and it caused some of my followers and I to discuss the sticky questions of altering time lines and destiny.

A numbers of Torah Codes *experts* have stated that the Torah Codes can't be used to predict the future. They're concerned about the subjective nature of the selection of key words that cannot usually be known before an event occurs. They're probably right most times, especially when one is looking for particulars about an individual's future. But what happens if one stumbles across what seems to be a specific warning ahead of time?

A prediction might be attempted based on data gleaned *a posteriori, a priori,* or through some combination of these two. On Figure 19 to the left of *Ark of the Covenant* (ארון ברית), at its minimum ELS, we find the word *airplane* (אוירון). Airplane touches the word for fire (אש). It also touches the word for *explosion* (נפצ). The letters used to spell *explosion* are precisely the same letters (read in reverse) as those used for *Zephon* in *Baal Zephon* as shown earlier on Figure 1D in Chapter 1. The chance to have both airplane and explosion this close to Ark of the Covenant was one in 29,903.

If Figure 19 were expanded to 646 letters, it would reveal *Bardawil* (ברדול) touching *airplane,* and show that Baal Zephon's suspect latitude coordinate *31-16* (לא-יי) shares three letters with *airplane*. It would also include an open-text reference to Baal Zephon at Numbers 33:7.

What's the nature of the aircraft explosion warning if real? There are many possibilities, but it might be a warning to avoid transporting the Ark by aircraft (the

Torah requires that when the Ark must be moved, members of the Hebrew tribe of Levi should carry it). Or it may be that the Ark is really, as many believe, an electrical capacitor that might discharge and detonate aircraft fuel. This is what I warned Egyptian officials about when we discussed the possible recovery of the Ark.

Figure 19 – Aircraft Explosion					
Terms	Translation	Symbol	Skip	Start	End
ארון ברית	Ark of Covenant	○	-306	Numbers 34 V8 L13	Numbers 33 V4 L14
בעל	Baal	☐	1	Numbers 33 V46 L18	Numbers 33 V46 L20
צפן	Zephon	○	-306	Numbers 33 V37 L23	Numbers 33 V11 L15
נפץ	Explosion	⌐	306	Numbers 33 V11 L15	Numbers 33 V37 L23
אוירון	Airplane	○	-154	Numbers 33 V37 L28	Numbers 33 V8 L8
אש	Fire	☐	1	Numbers 33 V4 L15	Numbers 33 V4 L16

For Figure 19 the ELS reference is 153 characters between rows. There are 8 displayed terms in the matrix. The matrix starts at Numbers 33 V4 L14 and ends at Numbers 34 V8 L20. The matrix spans 2150 characters of the surface text. The matrix has 15 rows, is 8 columns wide and contains a total of 120 characters.

SLIDERS – Has Drosnin or Rips already altered the time line?

I'm not the first person to attempt to alter a time line. Drosnin has that honor. His first attempt failed when he warned Prime Minister Rabin on September 1, 1994 that the only time Yitzhak Rabin came up in the Bible, a*ssassin will assassinate* crossed his name in the Code (see Figure 20). Rabin told him that he wasn't a mystic, blew off the warning, and was assassinated where, when and by whom the Codes seemed to indicate.

Drosnin then warned the father of Benjamin Netanyahu of his son's impending assassination in Amman, Jordan on Tish B'Av (July 25, 1996). The Code said Netanyahu would be there that day, and he was indeed scheduled to travel there then. Netanyahu cancelled his trip, using King Hussein's cold as an excuse. Dr. Rips thereafter found the word *delayed* immediately above and touching the phrase *July to Amman* which was two letters left of the conditional axis letters for *Prime Minister Netanyahu*.

Figure 20 – Assassin and Rabin

Terms	Translation	Symbol	Skip	Start	End
יצחק רבין	Yitzhak Rabin	◯	4772	Deuteronomy 2 V33 L2	Deuteronomy 24 V16 L15
רוצח אשר ירצח	assassin will assassinate	▢	1	Deuteronomy 4 V42 L7	Deuteronomy 4 V42 L17

For Figure 20 the ELS reference is 4772 characters between rows. There are 2 displayed terms in the matrix. The matrix starts at Deuteronomy 2 V32 L27 and ends at Deuteronomy 24 V16 L16. The matrix spans 33415 characters of the surface text. The matrix has 8 rows, is 11 columns wide and contains a total of 88 characters.

When Drosnin's first predicted year for an atomic holocaust in the Middle East passed peacefully on September 13, 1996, on the last day of the Hebrew year 5756, he stated, "One last word, and I'm out of the fortune-telling business . . . On several occasions I have seen things happen as predicted, but not *when* predicted. I urge you to remain alert to what is almost certainly a real danger."

One of Drosnin's plots has *another will die, Av* (a Hebrew month), *Prime Minister*. The phrase *another will die, Av, Prime Minister* was obviously found *a posteriori*. It appears one row above and 13 columns right of the conditional axis words *the next war*. On Figure 21, Prime Minister Netanyahu intersects the phrase *surely he will be killed* and touches the phrase *his soul was cut off*.

So what happened? Was the Code wrong? Did it not happen because of Torah

Codes-based intervention? Or is the above prediction one that was delayed by the Barak and Sharon elections; one that will be fulfilled during a future term for Netanyahu? My gut feeling is that if the Code is real, and if we can at all control our destinies, a war was prevented or at least put off because of the Drosnin/Rips Torah Codes intervention. When Netanyahu put off his trip, this set up a new time line that began at that point. The concept was well portrayed in the television series called *Sliders*. Yet, with the passage of time it is becoming more apparent that Israelis will recycle Netanyahu the way they have previous prime ministers, and he will serve again. In short, it's too soon to tell.

If time lines can be altered, what are the limits? This is hard to answer. Each alteration theoretically sets up a parallel dimension or world according to Hugh Everett of Princeton University. Communication is probably not possible between each of these worlds, but even if it were, the number of alterations to a timeline may be limited by the number of alterations made based upon the Codes.

Figure 21
Prime Minister Netanyahu to Die

Terms	Translation	Symbol	Skip	Start	End
רהם נתניהו	Prime Minister Netanyahu	○	-19129	Deuteronomy 4 V47 L43	Exodus 19 V12 L54
מות יומת	Surely he will be killed	☐	1	Exodus 19 V12 L 53	Exodus 19 V12 L59
נכרתה הנפש	His soul will be cut off	◖	1	Exodus 31 V14 L 53	Exodus 31 V14 L61

For Figure 21 the ELS reference is 19129 characters between rows. There are 3 displayed terms in the matrix. The matrix starts at Exodus 19 V12 L45 and ends at Deuteronomy 4 V47 L48. The matrix spans 153047 characters of the surface text. The matrix has 9 rows, is 15 columns wide and contains a total of 135 characters.

Drosnin cites a plot on page 164 of *The Bible Code* book that has, in conjunction with the threat of a Netanyahu assassination, the phrase *five futures, five roads*. He does not identify the source of this phrase, but I found it at Numbers 7:23 along with at least ten repetitions of the same phrase in the same chapter that deals with sacrifices in the open text.

I don't know that the limit of possible futures is indeed five. But at some point it would seem that the general usefulness of the Torah Codes (from a predictive point of view) begins to break down and eventually become completely lost as too many actions and outcomes are altered as a result of Codes findings. Certainly political actions and war plans would be first to be altered and first to see this effect. Something like an inbound comet would seem to be the last type of event to be affected by Codes actions, though the Codes could be used for an early warning of such an event if the Codes can be validated by way of Ark find or some physical mechanism.

Those of us who excel at finding predictions of possible things to come need to exercise extreme caution before acting. Frankly, while in a retired status from the Coast Guard, I did conduct talks with members of the Egyptian Government in 1999 that were designed to head off a nuclear conflict in the area. But I would feel better about my actions if the U. S. State Department supervised them. The fear here is that independent researchers can act as loose cannons that might do more harm than good. Thus when I discovered a matrix for a possible future terrorist attack on a southern U.S. city, I called the matrix to the attention of certain high-ranking officials and to the attention of the group that appeared to be targeted.

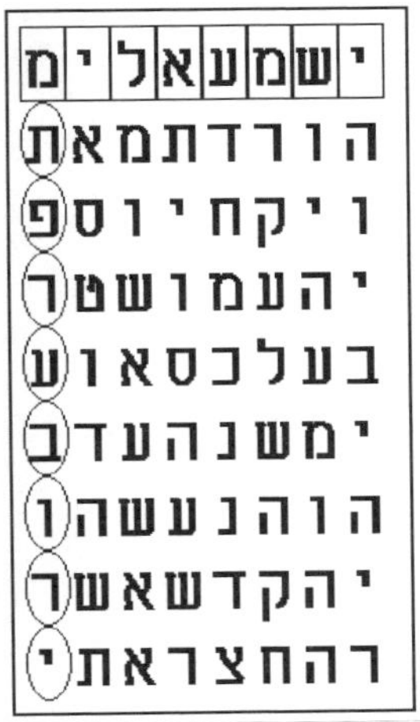

Figure 22
Ishmaelites (Arabs) ... they shot Arafat

Terms	Translation	Symbol	Skip	Start	End
ירוב ערפת	They shot Arafat	◯	-9526	Exodus 35 V18 L3	Genesis 42 V38 L69
ישמעאלים	Ishmaelites (Arabs)	☐	1	Genesis 37 V2 L12	Genesis 37 V2 L19

For Figure 22 the ELS reference is 9526 characters between rows. There are 2 displayed terms in the matrix. The matrix starts at Genesis 37 V27 L12 and ends at Exodus 35 V18 L3. The matrix spans 76216 characters of the surface text. The matrix has 9 rows, is 8 columns wide and contains a total of 72 characters.

But I will not publish it, name the city, or the means of attack here. Such a matrix could cause some sick mind to act in a way that he thought was fulfilling Bible prophecy. The officials were not notified with the hope that they would take action – especially because there was no date on the matrix. They were notified simply because they then would be made aware of the Code's prediction ability if the attack occurred during their tenure in office. I am a Coast Guard officer. My tasking is to help thwart attacks on my country, to save lives, and to protect the environment. If the Code can facilitate these tasks, then we need to know about it. This was the original reason that I got into Codes research.

I am most concerned about Mr. Drosnin's actions with respect to the meeting he had with Yassir Arafat on April 13, 2001, to warn him Hamas would assassinate him. As I wrote earlier, even if the Codes are not yet fully proven, this warning might have kept Arafat from resuming efforts to find a peaceful solution to his dispute with Israel. Thus Drosnin may bear indirect responsibility for many of the subsequent terrorist attacks. Whereas Drosnin did not include supporting data for his Arafat predictions made on pages 103-104 of *Bible Code II*, the information is shown in Figure 22. The phrase *All in Hamas* in figure 23 is an expansion of Drosnin's *Hamas* find. There was one chance in 1058 for *Ishmaelites* in the open text to be a 72-letter matrix with *They shot Arafat* in Figure 22. Figure 23 mentions *Shooters of Yassir Arafat . . . all in Hamas.*

Figure 23 – Shooters ... all in Hamas

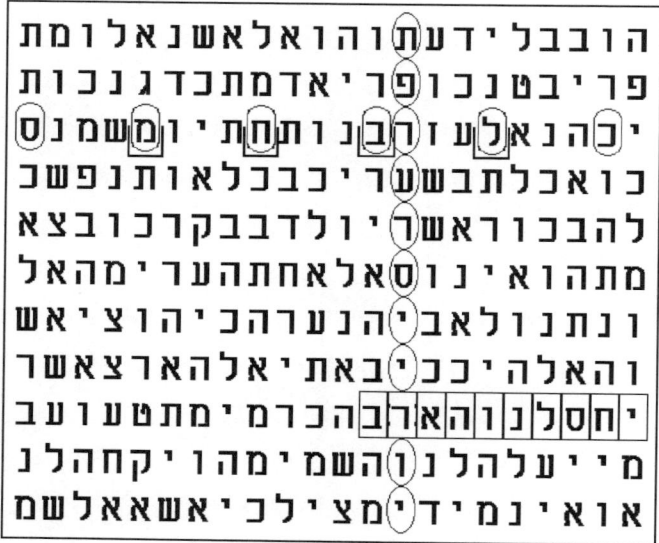

Terms	Translation	Symbol	Skip	Start	End
יורי יסר ערפת	Shooters of Yassir Arafat	○	-4307	Deuteronomy 32 V39 L63	Deuteronomy 4 V42 L30
יחסלנו הארב	The ambusher will kill (eliminate) him	□	1	Deuteronomy 28 V38 L25	Deuteronomy 28 V38 L34
מחבל	Terrorist	⊔	-4	Deuteronomy 10 V6 L52	Deuteronomy 10 V7 L5
כל בחמס	All in Hamas	◡	4	Deuteronomy 10 V6 L52	Deuteronomy 10 V7 L5

For Figure 23 the ELS reference is 4307 characters between rows. There are 3 displayed terms in the matrix. The matrix starts at Deuteronomy 4 V42 L22 and ends at Deuteronomy 32 V40 L9. The matrix spans 43092 characters of the surface text. The matrix has 11 rows, is 22 columns wide and contains a total of 242 characters.

For the phrase *All in Hamas*, there was only one chance in 1,260 to be in the matrix. For *terrorist* (which Arafat certainly is), the chance to find the 4-letter word found here is .1722 (about one chance is six). The crossing term is also of interest, but it's an *a posteriori* term which is hard to compute for true significance. There are many terms in the Torah that deal with murder, and none of those open-text terms cross the axis term. What does the surface text crossing term here really say? The verse reads, *You will take abundant seed out of the field, but you will harvest little, for the locust will devour it.* Thus there is no open-text discussion of anyone getting killed. We only get the death threat when we play with word breaks, which is an acceptable codes methodology.

In Figures 22 and 23, the idea that Arafat will be killed by fellow Arabs makes sense. He has created a lot of enemies. It is possible that Hamas may do him in; it's also possible that Palestinians may tire of his corruption, his $600,000,000 in private bank accounts, and his payments of $150,000 per month to his wife in Europe, all skimmed from Palestinians who suffer from extremely high unemployment as a result of his policies. Thus Drosnin may cause Arafat to avoid a reasonable settlement with Israel by fostering fear of Hamas, yet bring about his assassination by frustrating those who want a state with financial security sooner rather than later (or never).

If we knew about the Japanese attack on Pearl Harbor before it occurred in December 1941, but nothing else, should we have prevented it? The knee-jerk response is yes. The more thoughtful answer is that if we prevented the attack and the war with Japan and nothing else, Hitler could have won the war in Europe. Remember, it was only after the Pearl Harbor attack that we declared war on Japan, and Germany (as Japan's ally) declared war on us. Only then did we declare war on Germany. Without the Japanese hook in our jaw to enter the war, Hitler would have had time to develop nuclear weapons and the V-3 rocket to deliver nuclear warheads to New York and Washington. The extra time he would have gained might well have been enough for him to develop the means needed to conquer the entire world. In summary, we must be very careful in trying to affect world events. Nuclear wars are probably good things to avoid. Assassinations of terrorists are probably events that we might not want to prevent. Sometimes it's just best to trust in God's grand design.

Chapter 9

DROSNIN'S ATOMIC HOLOCAUST PREDICTION

A major purpose of the Ark Search experiment has always been to determine if Michael Drosnin's drastic predictions for the future need to be taken seriously. We now turn to the issue of the atomic holocaust prediction. How good is it mathematically? Let it be said up front that I have reservations about a number of Mr. Drosnin's findings. As will be shown in this chapter, some of his terms look dramatic, but have no real statistical significance at all. Further, supposedly related finds do not show up on plots at related skips with common column width. Where encoded material shares no more than a single letter from one plot to another, a *three-dimensional* plot would be required to compactly show the true relationship of letters to each other. Such a plot does not, of course, lend itself well to a two-dimensional book page. Even if we could build such a complex model with new computer software, the possibility of finding desired key words increases greatly with the addition of a third dimension. This, of course, implies a proportional decrease in the statistical significance of such a plot.

Probability calculations in this chapter will generally focus on the chance of finding individual items seen on the plots examined rather than combined probabilities as is the case in the rest of my Ark Search experiment. This is because the specification of key words in the Ark search was simpler. Words like *latitude, longitude, position,* and the Arabic site names closely linked with the coordinates were all natural and logical key words to seek *a priori*. On the other hand, while a year or phrases like *The End of days* or *Ninth of Av is the Day of the Third* are interesting, there was no way of knowing whether or not they are correct key words to search for *a priori*. These findings (at least the first time seen) are *a posteriori*. Thus, we will give a measure of their expected probability based upon observed frequencies in the Torah, but a combined probability is often inappropriate.

So how good are Drosnin's Atomic Holocaust findings? We begin with my Figure 24, a composite of plots found on pages 87, 124, and 163 of *THE BIBLE CODE*. It shows *World War* (מלחמת עלם) encoded vertically at skip +2,839. Figure 24 shows the Hebrew year *5760* (1999-2000 CE) not far from *World War*, but page 124-125 of Drosnin's book also portrays the Hebrew year *5766* (2005-2006 CE) connect his World War plot with an Atomic Holocaust plot. The way that the *World War* and *Atomic Holocaust* plots are arranged in his book, one might easily get the impression that one plot is a continuation of the next. This is a false impression because *Atomic Holocaust* is encoded at a skip of 3,133. The World War and Atomic Holocaust plots can only be properly related in three dimensions because the base skips are not compatible for a small two-dimensional plot.

Also on Figure 24 are the words *Ninth of Av is the day of the Third, In the End of Days* and *Ariel* (which in the Book of Isaiah is used to mean *Jerusalem*). That Drosnin had to hunt for *Ariel* means that he could not find *Jerusalem* on the matrix using either the older 6-letter spelling, or the more modern 7-letter spelling. Jerusalem is not that hard to find when one is not restricted to a specific course angle. It occurs 7,397 times at an ELS in a single pass through the Torah.

In the 714-letter box the chance for *The Ninth of Av is the Date of the Third* to be there was about one in 427. As such, it's the most significant aspect of the find. This is so because of the low probability, the fact that the Ninth of Av has long been a day of dread for Israel (both Temples in Jerusalem were destroyed on this day) and because it includes *The Third* which may refer to the Third World War.

Ariel is at the special case skip of -1. The probability that a form of *Jerusalem* or *Ariel* would appear somewhere on Figure 24 at such a special case is about one in 31. The least significant part of the plot is with the year 5760 (which passed without a world war anyway). It had better than one chance in four of being somewhere on the plot.

Figure 24 – Drosnin's World War Three Prediction

Terms	Translation	Symbol	Skip	Start	End
מלחמת עלם	World War	○	2839	Deuteronomy 4 V28 L14	Deuteronomy 17 V4 L9
ט אב יום השלישי	9th of Av is the day of the Third	□	1	Numbers 19 V12 L44	Numbers 19 V12 L55
באחרית הימים	In the End of Times	▢	1	Numbers 24 V14 L42	Numbers 24 V14 L52
התשס	5760 (year 2000)	∩	6	Numbers 28 V5 L40	Numbers 28 V6 L16
אריאל	Ariel	⬯	-1	Deuteronomy 4 V28 L37	Deuteronomy 4 V28 L33

For Figure 24 the ELS reference is 2839 characters between rows with 5 displayed terms. It starts at Numbers 19 V12 L15 and ends at Deuteronomy 17 V4 L42. The matrix spans 56821 characters of the surface text, has 21 rows, is 41 columns wide and contains 861 characters.

On Figures 25 and 26 *Atomic Holocaust* is encoded at skip -3,133. On Figure 25 the data is presented with column width set at 1,044 as it was on Page 125 of *THE BIBLE CODE*. Items of note on Figure 25 include *Ramallah,* a hotbed of the Palestinian uprising and Yasser Arafat's headquarters. This city's name shares a letter (מ) with *Atomic Holocaust*. Like *Ramallah*, the phrase *Fulfills a prophecy* is also at a skip of −1 (a special case). *Libya* is also shown on Figure 25 with a skip of −1 and it too shares a letter (ו) with *Atomic Holocaust*. The phrase *in Egypt* (במצרים) touches a letter (א) in *Atomic Holocaust*. The same exact phrase *In the End of Days* (באחרית הימים) as was seen on Figure 24 encoded with *World War* appears here too.

Finally, the phrase *Code will rescue* (Drosnin translates קוד ימשה as *Code* will save) appears at skip +1 with its letter *shin* (ש) in sequence with *Atomic Holocaust*. This same phrase is shown forming a perpendicular with *Atomic Holocaust* in a plot presented as Figure 26 with column width set at 3,133.

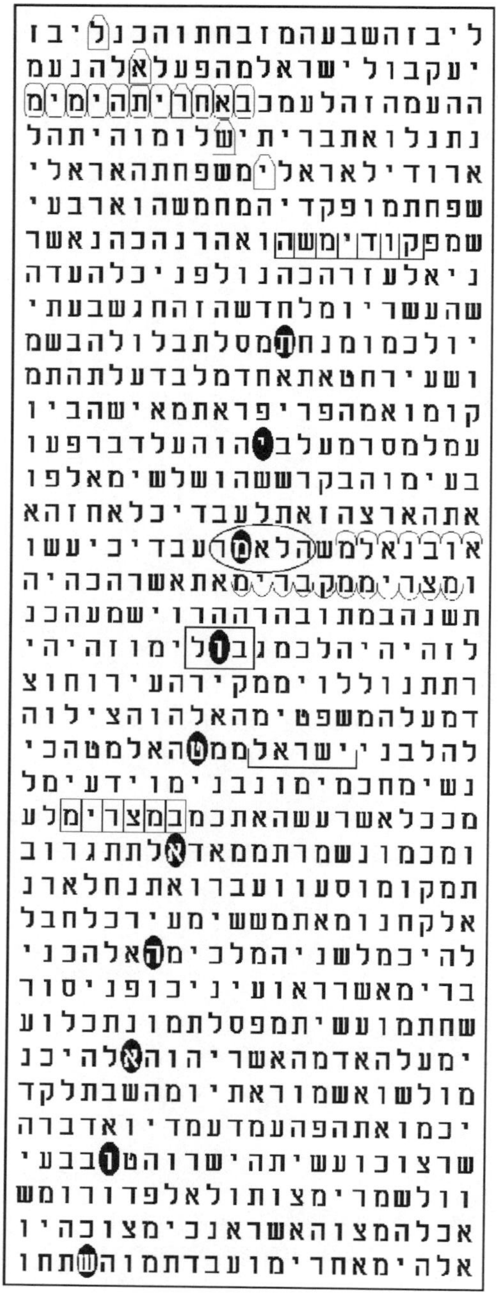

Figure 25
Atomic Holocaust Participants

Terms	Translation	Symbol	Skip	Start	End
שואה אטומית	Atomic holocaust	●	-3133	Deut. 8 V19 L52	Numbers 29 V9 L5
במצרים	In Egypt		1	Deut. 1 V30 L44	Deut. 1 V30 L49
באחרית הימים	In the end of days		1	Numbers 24 V14 L42	Numbers 24 V14 L52
ישראל	Israel		1	Numbers 36 V7 L15	Numbers 36 V7 L19
ישראל	Israel		-1042	Numbers 26 V17 L22	Numbers 23 V1 L36
מצרים מקברים	Egyptians were burying		1	Numbers 33 V4 L2	Numbers 33 V4 L12
קוד ימשה	Code will rescue		1	Numbers 26 V64 L16	Numbers 26 V64 L22
רמאלה	Ramallah		-1	Numbers 32 V25 L28	Numbers 32 V25 L24
מלא נבוא	Fulfills a prophecy		-1	Numbers 32 V25 L22	Numbers 32 V25 L16
לוב	Libya		-1	Numbers 34 V6 L38	Numbers 34 V6 L40

For Figure 25 the ELS reference is 1044 characters between rows. There are 11 displayed terms in the matrix. The matrix starts at Numbers 23 V1 L18 and ends at Deuteronomy 8 V19 L55. The matrix spans 37606 characters of the surface text. The matrix has 37 rows, is 22 columns wide and contains a total of 814 characters.

Of particular note on Figure 25 is that the exact same single occurrence phrase that started my search for the Ark of the Covenant, *Egyptians were burying* (את

מצרים מקברים), and the last letter of the encoding of *Ark of the Covenant* at skip –306 (ת) at Numbers 33:4 are on the plot with the *tav* (ת) of *Ark of the Covenant* (ארון ברית) less than three letters away from the letters *mem* (מ) and *vav* (ו) of *Atomic Holocaust*. However, a three-dimensional plot would be needed to show the full *Ark of the Covenant*.

Although the phrase *In the End of Days* (באחרית הימים) is vague, because it was also on Figure 24, I used a spreadsheet to check on its significance. I also checked on *Israel* (ישראל), *Egypt* (מצרים), and *Code will rescue* (קוד ימשה) only at skip +1. For *Libya* (לוב), *Ramallah* (רמאלה), and *Fulfills a prophecy* (נבוא מלא) I ran calculations for what I call "special case skips" +1, -1, "N," and "-N" with N here a column width of 1,044.

	A	B	C	D	E	F	G	H
	ATOMIC HOLOCAUST	SKIPS	NUMBER	DIVIDE BY	THE	E QUOTIENT	POISSON	EACH WORD
	MEETS	USED	IN	304805	QUOTIENT	X 792	EQUATION	OR PHRASE
	EGYPTIANS WERE	ON	CONTROL	LETTERS	EQUALS	LETTERS	PROBABILITY	HAS 1 CHANCE
	BURYING	FIGURE		IN THE	FREQUENCY	EQUALS	FOR WORD	IN THE
	(FIGURE 25)	25		CONTROL	PER LETTER	WORD	APPEARING	FOLLOWING OF
						EXPECTANCY	1+ TIMES	BEING HERE
	IN THE END OF DAYS	1	4	304805	1.31231E-05	0.01039353	0.010339704	96.71456562
	CODE WILL RESCUE	1	2	304805	6.56157E-06	0.005196765	0.00518 3285	192.9278321
	EGYPTIANS WERE BURYING	1	1	304805	3.28079E-06	0.002598383	0.00259501	385.3550145
	RAMALLAH AT SKIPS	-1	121	304805	0.000396975	0.314404291	0.269776255	3.706775459
	-1, +1, N (1044) AND -N							
	ISRAEL @ SKIP +1	1	589	304805	0.001932383	1.530447335	0.783561175	1.27622454
	EGYPT @ SKIP +1	1	364	304805	0.001194206	0.945811256	0.61163562	1.634960371
	LIBYA @ SKIPS +1,	-1	433	304805	0.00142058	1.125099654	0.675379884	1.480648186
	-1, N (1044) AND -N						COMBINED	
							PROBABILITY =	
							1.39076E-07	
							THE ABOVE IS 1	
							CHANCE IN	
							7190312.809	
	ATOMIC HOLOCAUST MEET	SKIPS	NUMBER	DIVIDE BY	THE QUOTIENT	E QUOTIENT	POISSON	EACH WORD
	LIBYA ON FIGURE 26	USED	IN	304805	EQUALS	X 30 LETTERS	EQUATION	OR PHRASE
		ON	CONTROL	LETTERS	FREQUENCY	EQUALS	PROBABILITY	HAS 1 CHANCE
		FIGURE		IN THE	PER LETTER	WORD	THE WORD	IN THE
		26		CONTROL		EXPECTANCY	APPEARING	FOLLOWING OF
							AT LEAST ON	BEING HERE
	LIBYA @ SKIPS = +1,	-1	402	304805	0.001318876	0.03956628	0.038793757	
	-1, N (1044) AND -N						THIS IS 1	25.77734354
							CHANCE IN 25.7	

None of the locations shown on the plot were statistically significant. The odds were better than one chance in two that *Israel, Egypt,* and *Libya* would appear on the plot (but on Figure 26 the odds that *Libya* at skips +1, -1, "N," or "-N" would be in a 30-letter box with *Atomic Holocaust* were about one in 25.8). Even *Ramallah* had a surprisingly high probability – about one chance in 3.7 that it would be there. This is so because the open text here includes the commonly found words "Moses saying" (*Ramallah* at skip –1 is made of the four letters of *saying* and the last letter of *Moses*). Three items were statistically significant – the phrases *In the End of Days, Code will Rescue,* and *Egyptians were burying.*

The chance that one of the four Torah findings of *In the End of Days* would be there was about 1 in 97. The probability for *Code will rescue* to be on the plot was one chance in 193, while the probability for *Egyptians were burying* was about one in 385. The combined chance that all three phrases would be this close to *Atomic Holocaust* would have been about one in 7,190,313 if these three phrases were the only phrases sought *a priori.* But I have no way of knowing what was *a priori,* what was *a posteriori,* and what was sought but not found. Only Mr. Drosnin can address these issues. Further, the phrase *Egyptians were burying* is significant in my research, but was not mentioned by Drosnin even though it obviously is a topic related to any potential nuclear war.

On Figure 26 (from *The Bible Code*, p. 64), the words *Atomic Holocaust* run into the phrase that Drosnin translates as *Code will save* (קוד ימשה). The term is better translated as *Code will rescue* or *Code will draw out of water* (the actual open-text discussion is about Moses counting). It is possible that the Code will draw the Ark out of water because the prime suspect site at 31° 9' North, 33 °4' East is approximately 110 meters north of an unnamed salt marsh shown on the vintage 1935 Qatia chart (Map 3). On British Admiralty Chart 56100 (Map 8) the prime site appears to be around 500 meters north of a merged set salt marshes (Mallahet Ugret Selima being the northern one and Mallahet El Mapia the southern one). Marsh areas vary with rainfall. During the rainy season, the suspect site may even be under water itself. The secondary site, however, is definitely underwater. It's the obstruction at 31°16' North, 33° 3.5' East, the site that I favored when I made my presentation in Jerusalem in 1999.

On page 132 of his book, Drosnin has a plot based on a finding of *Atomic Weapon* intersecting *Jerusalem* where it appears in the open text. If this plot were based on Torah, it would be truly astounding, but it isn't. Although it's never found in the open-text of the Torah, Jerusalem with its most common, six-letter Biblical spelling (ירושלם) appears 49 times in the book of Isaiah and 664 times in the Tenach (Old Testament) outside the Torah. In this case *Jerusalem* and *atomic weapon* (כלי אטום) can both be placed in a 42-letter box. A spreadsheet revealed that the probability to have *Jerusalem* in the 42-letter box with *atomic weapon* is about one in 33. But when I attempted to reproduce this plot on my own computer, the attempt failed due to a difference in spelling in Isaiah from Drosnin's software to my own. There were many other similar plots that did turn up.

Figure 26 – Drosnin's Atomic Holocaust Matrix

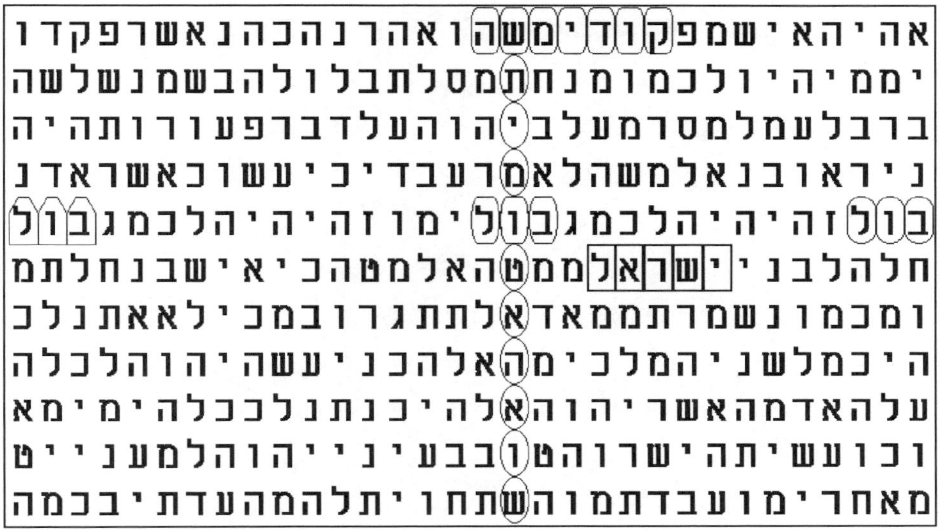

Terms	Translation	Symbol	Skip	Start	End
שואה אטומית	Atomic holocaust	◯	-3133	Deuteronomy 8 V19 L52	Numbers 29 V9 L5
קוד ימשה	Code will rescue	☐	1	Numbers 26 V64 L16	Numbers 26 V64 L22
ישראל	Israel	☐	1	Numbers 36 V7 L15	Numbers 36 V7 L19
לוב	Libya	◯	-1	Numbers 34 V6 L27	Numbers 34 V6 L25
לוב	Libya	◯	-1	Numbers 34 V6 L40	Numbers 34 V6 L38
לוב	Libya	⌂	-1	Numbers 34 V7 L14	Numbers 34 V7 L12

For Figure 26 the ELS reference is 3133 characters between rows. There are 6 displayed terms in the matrix. The matrix starts at Numbers 26 V64 L7 and ends at Deuteronomy 8 V19 L69. The matrix spans 31369 characters of the surface text. The matrix has 11 rows, is 32 columns wide and contains a total of 352 characters.

Figure 27 shows one of them found in Jeremiah with *Libya* also on the plot at the same interval and column as *atomic weapon*. None are very significant from a statistical point, but all were consistent with the concern expressed earlier.

```
י ר ו ש ל מ
מ ס ב י ב ה
ת ב ו א ת ה
ב כ ל ה מ ק
ה ו ה ה ח ד
ה נ ב י א א
ו א ל י ה ו
ת י ל מ ק ט
ב כ ל נ פ ש
ו ה א ת מ ל
מ ל כ א ת כ
ו א ל ה ב ו
פ נ י כ ב ל
א ל א ש ר ש
מ ק ט ר ו ת
י ו ו א ח ר
ק י מ ז ב ע
```

Figure 27
Jerusalem, Libya and Atomic Weapon in Jeremiah

Terms	Translation	Symbol	Skip	Start	End
כלי אטום	Atomic weapon	○	3084	Jeremiah 36 V16 L56	Jeremiah 49 V4 L14
ירושלם	Jerusalem	☐	1	Jeremiah 17 V27 L47	Jeremiah 17 V27 L52
לוב	Libya	☐	-3084	Jeremiah 24 V9 L53	Jeremiah 20 V10 L21

For Figure 27 the ELS reference is 3084 characters between rows. There are 4 displayed terms in the matrix. The matrix starts at Jeremiah 17 V27 L47 and ends at Jeremiah 49 V4 L17. The matrix spans 49350 characters of the surface text. The matrix has 17 rows, is 6 columns wide and contains a total of 102 characters.

On page 134 of Drosnin's book, *Armageddon, Asad,* and *Holocaust* appear in sequence. Figure 28 shows the three words are composed of 13 letters, a relatively rare find in terms of ELS length. I assume Mr. Drosnin searched just for *Armageddon* (a term only found in the open text of the New Testament). If so, he probably noticed *a posteriori* the words *Asad* (אסד) and *Holocaust* (שאה). We call this technique of looking immediately before or after an *a priori* term "snooping." The chance that *Asad* and *Holocaust* would be in a 13-letter box with *Armageddon* (הר מגידו), is about one in 23,447. Further, touching the 13-letter ELS for Armageddon/Asad/Holocaust (שאה אסד הר מגידו) is, in direct sequence at skip +1, *Libya/Egypt* (לוב מצרים). This is the only time in the entire Tenach (Old Testament) that these two countries appear together in this manner.

What do the codes appear to be telling us? If the message is deliberately encoded, my guess is that at some point the Libyans might first try to decapitate the Israeli government and military Command and Control with a small-yield nuclear strike aimed at the Knesset. This would be followed up with a Syrian assault over the Golan Heights and into Northern Israel. Then the surviving Israelis lash out at the Arabs. They use neutron bombs to obliterate the Syrian forces as they sweep through the area around Meggido, then possibly up the ante with a nuclear strike directed against Egypt.

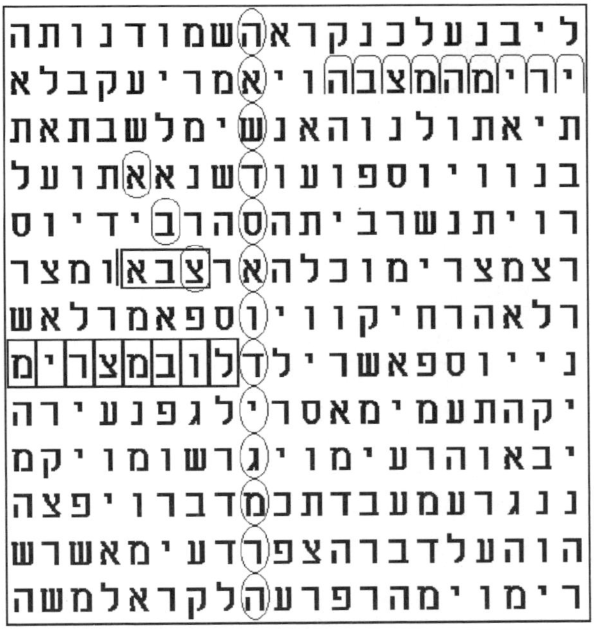

Figure 28
Armageddon-Asad-Holocaust

Terms	Translation	Symbol	Skip	Start	End
הר מגידו אסד שאה	Armageddon, Asad, Holocaust	◯	-4240	Exodus 10 V16 L9	Genesis 30 V6 L43
ירים המצבה	Shooting from the Post	⌂	1	Genesis 31 V45 L13	Genesis 31 V45 L21
לוב מצרים	Libya, Egypt	▢	1	Genesis 46 V27 L15	Genesis 46 V27 L22
צבא	Army	▭	1	Genesis 41 V57 L7	Genesis 41 V57 L9
צבא	Army	◯	-4239	Genesis 41 V57 L7	Genesis 37 V8 L51

For Figure 28 the ELS reference is 4240 characters between rows. There are 5 displayed terms in the matrix. The matrix starts at Genesis 30 V6 L32 and ends at Exodus 10 V16 L17. The matrix spans 50900 characters of the surface text. The matrix has 13 rows, is 20 columns wide and contains a total of 260 characters.

On Figure 29 there is a suggestion that we are rapidly coming to the culmination of history. Taken from Page 17 of Drosnin's *Bible Code II* we find a "DNA-type" plot with the sugar-phosphate-sugar-phosphate component presented by two findings of *End of Days*. The first find (in the open text at Deuteronomy 4:30) is Hebrew. The encoded find is Aramaic and matches the last two words of the book of Daniel. The first of the two *nucleotide bases* for the plot, *Arafat* (ערפאת) is at skip +1. The second, *A. Barak* (א ברק - Prime Minister of Israel from May, 1999 until March, 2001), is at skip -1 and shares the letter *kuf* (ק) with the

Aramaic expression for *End of Days, ketz hayamin* (קץ הימין). Thus *Arafat* touched one *End of Days* expression at five letters, and *A. Barak* intersected the other.

Figure 29
Arafat, Barak, and End of Days

Terms	Translation	Symbol	Skip	Start	End
קץ הימין	End of Days	◯	-7551	Deuteronomy 19 V10 L14	Numbers 28 V9 L36
ערפאת	Arafat	⌒	1	Deuteronomy 9 V6 L57	Deuteronomy 9 V6 L61
באחרית הימים	In the End of Days	▢	1	Deuteronomy 4 V30 L24	Deuteronomy 4 V30 L34
א ברק	A. Barak	◡	-1	Deuteronomy 19 V10 L17	Deuteronomy 19 V10 L14

For Figure 29 the ELS reference is 7551 characters between rows. There are 4 displayed terms in the matrix. The matrix starts at Numbers 28 V9 L36 and ends at Deuteronomy 19 V10 L30. The matrix spans 45323 characters of the surface text. The matrix has 7 rows, is 17 columns wide and contains a total of 119 characters.

The chance for *Arafat* to meet *A. Barak* in conjunction with two *End of Days* terms was about one in 55,754,246. The term *End of Days* does not necessarily mean *End of the World*. In Judaism, it is used to denote the end of pre-messianic times and the arrival of a messiah who will end war. This messiah will usher in a new era of life in accordance with God's Plan. He will also induce the *Shechinah* (the Presence of God) to return to Jerusalem as we saw described in Jeremiah 3:17-18 (see Chapter 3 of this book, page 32). How seriously should we take the above matrix? Again, only something like an Ark find is likely to quickly answer that question.

A	B	C	D	E	F	G	H
	SKIPS	NUMBER	DIVIDE BY	THE	E QUOTIENT	POISSON	CHANCE
FIGURE 29 - ARAFAT AND	USED	IN	304805	QUOTIENT	LETTERS	EQUATION	FOR
THE END OF DAYS:	ON	CONTROL	LETTERS	EQUALS	LETTERS	PROBABILITY	EACH
CONDITIONAL AXIS TERM IS	ARAFAT		IN THE	FREQUENCY	EQUALS	FOR THE	TERM
ARAMAIC END OF DAYS	PLOT		CONTROL	PER LETTER	WORD	WORD	TO BE
PHRASE.					EXPECTANCY	APPEARING	ON
N = -7,551						AT LEAST	THE
						ONCE	PLOT
ARAFAT ONLY @ SKIP +1	1	2	304805	6.5616E-06	0.000780827	0.000780522	1281.193342
A. BARAK @ N, -1, +1, AND	-1	38	304805	0.00012467	0.014835715	0.014726208	67.90614564
SKIPS; END OF DAYS @	1	4	304805	1.3123E-05	0.001561654	0.001560435	640.8467688
SKIP +1 ONLY #						COMBINED	
#NOTE: THE CONTROL WAS						PROBABILITY	
SEARCHED FOR						IS	
BOTH HEBREW AND						1.79359E-08	
AND						THIS EQUALS 1	
ARAMAIC END OF						CHANCE IN	
DAYS PHRASES.						55754246.73	

Small model of the Ark of the Covenant.

Chapter 10

TREE OF LIFE—THE BLESSING?

As was the case when we arrived in St. Thomas on our voyage to the Middle East, we docked at Madeira, another beautiful island, on the Sabbath (May 1st, 1999). The voyage was free, so I couldn't complain about the itinerary, but it would have been nice to see more of the island than we did on foot. The walk into the town of Funchal took a half hour, and it was charming. Lots of flowers everywhere and we saw one of the weirdest soccer games I've ever seen. That's because the hillside playing field was about as far from level as one could imagine.

A few hours after we sailed it dawned on me that many folks on our ship expected me to be some kind of a saint. I'm not, even though I do my best to keep the Law. If I ever *appear* to become one, it's likely to be because the Ark is found through my work and I'll have to live up to a circumstance-imposed image. When not in uniform, my hat is brown, and has (since about 1981) been of Indiana Jones style, not the black hat of many of my Orthodox compatriots.

If you want a black-hatted saint, go see Rabbi Glixman who converted my wife and older son from a previous marriage. The man drives around all night long visiting the sick in hospitals, doing all in his power to help every single human that he meets. It's an addiction with him. I like doing good deeds, but if I'm addicted to anything, it's high adventure. My ethic is shaped as much by U.S. military standards as it is by Orthodox Jewish values (which is why I was absolutely thrilled to be called back to active duty after over seven years in retirement). After Moses, the biblical heroes I most admire would be Joshua and Caleb, two *can do* military style guys with the guts to tell Moses that the Israelites could take those bigger guys in Canaan. In the end, these two were the only men of their generation that God saw fit to admit into the Promised Land.

The night we sailed from Madeira a nice Christian lady in the ship's library asked me, "If the Jews find that the code says *Jesus is the Messiah,* will they finally accept him as such?" I politely told her "No."

"Why are we so stubborn?" you ask. Christianity teaches that the Messiah had to die to take on the sins of the world. Judaism generally rejects this concept of vicarious atonement, preferring instead to stress the concept of individual responsibility. Judaism was first to coin the title *Messiah,* so how does it define the term? There's an old cliché that sums it up best: *Where there are ten Jews there are eleven opinions.*

To Orthodox Judaism the basic requirements of a messiah are probably (in decreasing order of importance):

(1) End war on Earth *permanently*,
(2) Make all humanity understand that there is *One* God who created us all,
(3) Restore the Temple so all 613 commandments of Torah may be fulfilled,
(4) Return all Jews to Israel, and
(5) Facilitate the resurrection of the dead.

You won't find the largest group of American Jews (Reform) agreeing with (or even aware of) the above list. They've largely sworn off the idea of a messiah altogether and now speak only at most of a *Messianic Age* where war is a thing of the past.

Orthodox or Reform, the Jewish position is that the Messiah or the Messianic Age are marked primarily by an end to war. As I *require* the Code to produce the Ark before personally accepting its validity, Jews will *require* fulfillment of at least the first two Orthodox conditions listed above before accepting a messianic candidate. I would think that at least *several hundred years* would have to pass without war anywhere on Earth for most rabbis to lend serious credence to such a claim. This caution is, to a certain extent, matched by that of Fundamental Christians who expect an *Antichrist* who will bring a false peace for three and a half years.

The Christian lady in the ship's library wanted to know why Jews would not accept Jesus if the code says *Jesus is the Messiah?* Setting aside all the preconditions listed above, it is much too easy to find the mere four letters meaning *Messiah* or five letters meaning *The Messiah* with all sorts of names (especially when one overlooks the importance of minimum or near minimum ELS). Over the past seven years I have met people who were excited about finding their own name encoded as the Messiah. In response, I produced similar plots that named Donald Duck, and a host of other characters as Messiah. So what we must look for is far more than the existence of a simple string of eight to twelve letters or chance meeting of a few terms.

Having set the above call for extreme caution, have I found anything linking the Ark to the Messiah? Certainly. The *Tree of Life* (עצ החיים) is spoken of as the key to immortality in Genesis 3:22. Figure 30 has the seven letter term at its minimum ELS. It is encoded backwards two columns left of *the Ark* (הארנ). The association here of *the Ark* with the key to immortality is particularly interesting because the Ark, the Temple it would be placed in, the Messianic Age, and immortality are linked together in the eschatology of several faiths. HaMashiach (המשיח, *the anointed* – it also means *the Messiah*) shows up on this plot too.

Baal Zephon's suspect latitude *31-16* (לא-יו) and *staff* (מטה) were a priori finds after *the Ark* and *The Messiah (the anointed)* were found a posteriori.

So what does all this mean? The linkage of the coded terms: the *Tree of Life*, *the Ark*, and *the Messiah* may indicate that if the Ark is found, something else will be found with it to not only bring on the age of the Messiah, but to prolong life. The *Stone Artscroll Chumash* states, "The staff remained in bloom for centuries. It was placed in front of the Holy Ark through most of the First Temple era, together with a flask of manna until they were hidden by King Josiah." Again, the word for *staff* is also on Figure 30, and it's in sequence with *tree* (as in *Tree of Life*) as is seen in the Hebrew מטה עץ. Thus, aside from the obvious miracle that we are told of in Numbers 17:23, there may be some powerful drug or chemical either in the Ark or on the staff that, if replicated, could retard the normal effects of aging.

Figure 30 – The Ark and the Tree of Life

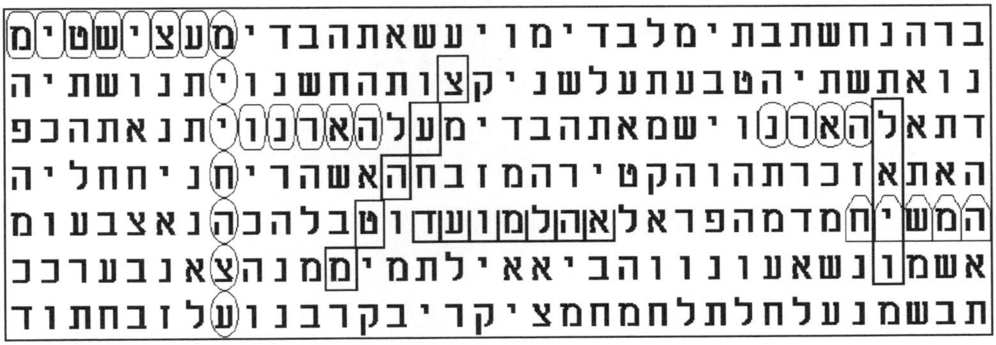

Terms	Translation	Symbol	Skip	Start	End
עץ החיים	Tree of Life	◯	-2185	Leviticus 7 V13 L22	Exodus 38 V6 L11
הארן	The Ark	◯	1	Exodus 40 V20 L17	Exodus 40 V20 L20
הארן	The Ark and	◯	1	Exodus 40 V20 L34	Exodus 40 V20 L37
מעצי שטים	From Acacia Wood	▢	1	Exodus 38 V6 L12	Exodus 38 V6 L18
מטה עץ	Staff tree	▢	-2186	Leviticus 5 V18 L12	Exodus 39 V16 L49
לא-יו	31-16	▯	2185	Exodus 40 V20 L16	Leviticus 5 V17 L53
המשיח	The Messiah	⌂	1	Leviticus 4 V16 L10	Leviticus 4 V16 L14
אהל מועד	Tent of Meeting	⊔	1	Leviticus 4 V16 L25	Leviticus 4 V16 L31

115

For Figure 30 the ELS reference is 2185 characters between rows. There are 7 displayed terms in the matrix. The matrix starts at Exodus 38 V5 L26 and ends at Leviticus 7 V13 L22. The matrix spans 13137 characters of the surface text. The matrix has 7 rows, is 27 columns wide and contains a total of 189 characters.

Figure 30 also has the phrase *from acacia wood*. It flows in the open text from the last letter of *Tree of Life*. The acacia tree was used to make the Ark of the Covenant and it is also cited in Isaiah 41:19 as a sign of the Messianic restoration in Israel. The tree has deep roots and survives throughout drought and famine. Since Biblical times, it has been a symbol of stability and resilience. It has compounds called avicins. When extracted from *Acacia victoriae*, an Australian desert tree, these chemicals inhibit inflammation and cancer in test-tube and mouse studies (Croce, C.M. 2001. How can we prevent cancer? *Proceedings of the National Academy of Sciences* 98 (Sept. 25):10986-10988). Further, the tree apparently yields drugs known as DMT (N-dimethyltryptamine) and 5-methoxy-DMT that have been used as snuff by shamans among Indian groups in Amazonian Columbia and Venezuela. It is employed for diagnosis and treatment of disease, prophecy, divination, and other "magic" or religious purposes. (*Psychedelics Encyclopedia,* by Peter Stafford).

One of the greatest mysteries of the Bible relates to the change in life expectancy. From its peak with Methuselah (969 years according to Genesis 5:27) it declined to a maximum of about 120 years (see Genesis 6:3, just 8 verses after Methuselah's age was recorded). Did people really live that long? Some trees like sequoias and bristle cone pines live many thousands of years. Perhaps there is a gene segment in these trees, or in acacia wood that would be useful to us. Further, experiments have revealed that with certain drugs, test animals (only invertebrates so far) have had life expectancies increased by a factor of six. *Acacia wood* intersects the *Tree of Life*. It has drugs associated with fighting cancer and inflammation (a factor in arthritis). When we find the Ark, we may well find the chemical required to radically improve life expectancy. If discovery of the Ark brings on the Messianic Age, we will spend far less on weapons, and far more on science. That too is likely improve overall lifespan. Worried about overpopulation? Take those trillions of dollars used to kill each other, and we can even terraform Mars (and possibly also Jupiter's ocean-covered moon, Europa). It's a big universe. Given funds freed from weaponry, the sky will be no limit to our expansion. The Ark could hold the key to all these wonders.

Chapter 11

WHO WROTE THIS CODE?

Monday, May 3rd 1999, was the most critical day of the passage to Israel. Our ship arrived in Malaga, Spain that morning and it took longer than anticipated to clear Customs. The plan was to rent a car and drive 200 miles to Alicante where we would board our train for Barcelona, then connect with another train for Milan, Rome and Bari. If we missed the Alicante train, we would have missed our ferry from Greece to Israel on May 6. That would have been disastrous. I had to make that ferry in order to deliver my speech and report in Jerusalem on May 10.

Malaga was full of surprises – and none of them were good. Slow Customs, a slower Avis car rental office, notification that the Avis office in Alicante would be closed for siesta when we arrived, and finally the realization that Alicante wasn't 200 miles away (as a Spanish tourist office had told me) – it was 300. This realization came just five hours before our train was to depart Alicante. Solution?, a 300 mile, $410, up to 110 mile per hour taxi-ride through the mountains and coastal plains of Spain.

Our driver spoke no English and I speak limited Spanish; but I was too nervous to talk much as we raced through the countryside. Better not to distract him at those speeds.

Finally, Alicante loomed on the horizon. Twenty minutes to go. The driver was unfamiliar with this city. He didn't know where to find the train station. Solution?, hire a second cab to lead the first. So we became a taxi convoy speeding toward the train station. When we arrived, the second driver wanted too much to lead the first. No time to argue. I paid the man and dragged our ten pieces of luggage toward the train as fast as possible. "What's this?" I asked. The ticket lady wanted me to go back to the check-in counter to initiate our Eurail pass before boarding! Three minutes to go. "There's no time," I pleaded. "Entonces, vaya manana (Then go tomorrow)," she said. "Impossible," I replied while dragging my bags past her. We boarded the train, pulled up the last piece of heavy luggage, and just as it cleared the door, the train began to roll. We made it!

The land of Don Quixote lay before us; and as our train sped on towards Barcelona from Alicante, I wondered whether he was out there, somewhere? Was he, perhaps, that half reflection that I saw in the window? One thing I knew for sure: while Dulcinate's virtue was a figment of Don Quixote's imagination, my wife's is not. Few women would tolerate such an unsettled lifestyle.

117

That part of the trip was filled with travel connection problems and a raging war in the Balkans. *"Was I wise in traveling over the sea and the rails, or would I be victim of an error made in the fog of war?"* I wondered. The day before, a bus was blown up by mistake when a bomb went astray, resulting in sixty dead. "Most regrettable," a British military public affairs officer stated. Ethnic cleansing has its price.

The train ride offered time to consider the Code's source for about six hours. Michael Drosnin thinks aliens who went back in time wrote it. Arthur C. Clarke believes the Code is analogous to the Monolith portrayed in his *2001 Space Odyssey* book and its sequels. My native tongue is a hybrid of science and religion. There's only one truth. Where they appear to conflict we simply haven't yet identified the source of our error.

Some have suggested future-based human time travelers wrote the Code. You're probably curious about my impressions. Based on hints seen throughout the project, one thing appears obvious. As Drosnin states, "The Code *seems to be* interactive." When I sit at my computer terminal, I feel almost certain that I am talking to Someone and that He is directly answering me. How can He know my thoughts, even my spelling mistakes? I once heard a Muslim say that Allah is closer to you than your jugular vein. The Code often tends to support this view.

Could people from our future have written it? A NOVA Time Travel show broadcast on PBS in 1999 claimed that travel into the past is theoretically possible. The program opened with discussion of a paper on Time Travel done by Kip Thorne of Cal Tech. It featured such exotic topics as *quantum foam* (proposed by John Wheeler of Princeton University) with mini-wormholes that might be enlarged to provide a passage through time. It spoke about parallel universes first outlined by Hugh Everett of Princeton. These might be indicated by experiments conducted by David Deutsch (of Oxford University) that reveal unexpected interference patterns when single photons are fired through narrow slits. The NOVA show also presented evidence by Guenter Nimtz (of the University of Cologne) that indicates microwave messages can be made to travel 1.7 to 4.7 times the speed of light through a process known as *quantum tunneling*. Einstein said that if something could go faster than light, it could go into the past. The general opinion of most physicists featured on the show, however, was that travel into the past is limited to going back to the time that a time machine would be first invented. Whereas no human on Earth had the technology to create such a device when the Torah was given, if they are right, it would appear that we can probably exclude the possible authorship of humans from the future.

What about the transmission of a signal from the future? There has been some speculation about the existence of superluminal (faster than light) particles called *tachyons*. They haven't yet been found, but according to Scott I. Chase (*Physics*, 22 March 1993), you can't use them to send information faster than light. "Doing so would require creating a message coded in a localized tachyon field, and sending it off toward the intended receiver. "But", Chase claims, "You can't have it both ways – localized tachyon disturbances are subluminal and superluminal disturbances are nonlocal." Further, how would Moses pick up such a signal? Even if the Ark was some kind of receiver, the Ark wasn't yet made when he initially heard from his Source.

Could aliens from the future have written the Code? They could have developed appropriate technology in time to bring it to Earth and so apply it thousands of years ago. If they are the source of the Code, then what might be waiting at my prime suspect site is evidence of their presence on Earth. Someone who must remain anonymous has shown me photographs allegedly taken in the area that would seem to support this possibility (and/or show a fortress ruin [Baal Zephon?] at the site), but the images are suspect as is the source. For now, all I can reasonably say is that I lack the kind of evidence required to say that aliens are the authors of the Code.

On December 24th 1997, I met a formerly high-ranking, retired NASA official (not the source of the images referred to above) who confided to me in private that in 1964 he had, as required by his job, been shown an alien spacecraft. I didn't ask him if it was the one supposedly recovered from outside Roswell, New Mexico, though that was the topic before his remark. He might have been referring to an alleged landing at Holloman Air Force Base on April 25th 1964.

When I asked the retired official if they were friendly or hostile, his response was, "You don't know what your neighbor is thinking." He claimed that there was ongoing contact between our government and these creatures. The man said he never told his wife about his experience, because he didn't want to upset her.

A non-Codes experiment that I conducted (when not on active duty) in 2001 provided strong support for my NASA friend's assertions. I sent an e-mail to Codes research associates describing the particulars of the above incident (minus the name of the official involved), plus a link with the Kennedy assassination, and a discussion of possible underground alien research sites that are mentioned on the internet. The hypothesis was that if any of these things were based on reality, one of two things would happen – my phone would be tapped or my computer would be hacked. Within a few hours, my computer and those of several research associates were indeed hacked into. My phone was tapped, and so was that of an associate. In the case of my associate (within a few minutes) when his wife picked up the phone after I transmitted the message, an unknown voice came on and said, "You are in the house across the street from the green and white house." The speaker then hung up, but the implication seemed clear enough. *We know where you live and we can come and get you whenever we choose. Back off!*

I have the Zone Alarm firewall software on my computer that allows me to get an IP address of any hacker. I mailed the address of the hacker to an expert who ran a trace on the source. He concluded that the hacker was probably working for a government agency. The hacking and phone tapping do *not* prove that there really are aliens here. It might just be evidence that the government is merely looking for misguided nut cases that might pose a threat of some sort. However, we can't overlook the second possibility that the government (or a shadow government operating outside the bounds of the U.S. Constitution) wants to know who knows what with respect to a real alien presence here.

As for why my e-mail experiment was sent to Codes research associates, the answer is quite simple. Three of us have personally seen UFOs, another had one fly a few feet over his wife's car a mile from his home, and one has missing time after a UFO encounter. Missing time (according Budd Hopkins and other UFO researchers) is associated with abductions by aliens. The man with the missing time is the husband of the woman who received the phone call identifying their house immediately after my e-mail experiment.

In science, we list any observations that might influence our results. The many UFO related experiences of Codes researchers may be coincidence, or they might not be. There is more along these lines than I care to relate because of threats received, and because I don't want to damage anyone's reputation. While I believe the Codes (if confirmed by an Ark find or some other means) can most probably be associated with God, if aliens are the authors, they might in some unknown way try to influence the findings of Codes researchers. The above information is offered here to ensure that this possible influence isn't overlooked.

The reality (or lack thereof) for an alien presence on Earth can not be established through use of the Codes, as the Codes have yet to be fully validated in my mind. However, (to satisfy my curiosity) I made a few attempts to explore the issue with the *CodeFinder* codes software. In the first query (Figure 31), I searched for ELS terms about the Roswell incident. I simply searched for Roswell spelled *resh vav samech vav lamed* (**רוסול**). The minimum skip for this spelling in the Book of Genesis is +40 (but there are four shorter ELS hits in all Torah). Where it occurs, it crosses the surface text where God told Abraham in Genesis 15:5 to *"(Look please to the heavens,) and count the stars if you are able to number them."* (**וספר הכוכבים אם תוכל לספר אתם**).

Figure 31 Roswell and the Stars

והנהדבריהואליולאמרלאיי
עיכהואירשכויוצאאתוהחוצ
וספרהכוכבימאמתוכללספראת
כוהאמנביהוהויחשבהלוצדקה
שרהוצאתיכמאורכשדימלתתלכ

Terms on Figure 31	Translation	Symbol	Skip	Start	End
רוסול	Roswell	☐	40	Genesis 15 V4 L19	Genesis 15 V7 L36
וספר הכוכבים אם תוכל לספר אתם	Count the stars if you are able to number them.	◯	1	Genesis 15 V5 L30	Genesis 15 V5 L53

For Figure 31 the ELS reference is 40 characters between rows. It starts at Genesis 15 V4 L1 and ends at Genesis 15 V7 L41 spanning 184 characters of the surface text. The matrix has 5 rows, 24 columns, and contains 120 characters.

This passage rang true for a personal reason. For thirty years whenever I began teaching astronomy, I'd first draw a picture of the Milky Way on the blackboard. Then I'd write the number 400,000,000,000, an estimate of the number of stars in our galaxy. Next, I'd point out that it takes light 100,000 years to cross our galaxy at 186,282 miles per second and ask the kids how many galaxies they thought we could see through our telescopes on Earth. Some would say one, others 100, but few if any would answer 10,000,000,000 and/or know this was only 10 to 20 percent of the total estimated.

Based on what we see in our own solar system, I'd ask my students to multiply that above number of stars by ten to estimate the number of planets and large moons. The product of the galaxies we see, times stars in each, times planetary objects is 40,000,000,000,000,000,000,000. Now suppose that one out of a thousand worlds has an ocean for life to evolve in, even though in our own solar system Jupiter's moon Europa has an ocean just under its ice (as may Ganymede and Callisto). Indeed, we suspect that Mars (and possibly Venus) also once had oceans. Now suppose that only one out of a thousand of these worlds has a proper atmosphere. That still leaves 40,000,000,000,000,000 worlds something like ours. Again suppose that primitive life evolved in just one out of a thousand of those worlds, and that over billions of years of time it evolved to an intelligent state on one out of a thousand of those. That still leaves us forty billion worlds with intelligent life.

So when the word Roswell is met by an order to go count stars, the implication could be, "*What do you think I am? Impotent? Let me tell you something. I'm God Almighty! Do you really think that I could get my act together on just one planet, and fail on so many trillions? No friends, I love all My children, but you're just part of the family, not the whole show!*"

Did aliens write the Code? Its Author seems to know my thoughts. I searched for *saucer* (**תחת ית**) as in *flying saucer*, and found it at its second smallest Genesis ELS (+25) in Genesis 35:2-3. When I checked the crossprint (Figure 32A), it read **הסרו את אלהי הנכר** which means *Rid thyself of thy alien gods!* The *King James Version* translates the word **נכר** not as *alien* (as in seen in the *Stone Artscroll Chumash*), but as *strange* or *foreign*, however, the first translation seemed clear enough. God may have made millions of species of aliens, and some may have visited Earth. But (if this find isn't a fluke) the message seems to be that God isn't an alien, He is the Creator of all life – human *and* alien. On Figure 32B when I searched for *Roswell UFO* (**רוסול עבמ**) immediately above its minimum ELS (at the same interval, opposite direction) was a transliteration for *Zuaba*. Touching *Roswell UFO was* the a-prior phrase *Before Baal Zephon* (**לפני בעל צפון**). While these terms suggest alien involvement in the Code and the area of concern, nearby is what seems to be a warning similar to that found in below in Figure 32A – *Do not set up an alien man over you* (**לא תוכל לתת עליכ איש נכרי**).

הסרואתאלהיהנכר
הרווהחליפושמלת
עלהביתאלואעשהש
האתיביומצרתיוי
שרהלכתיויתנואל

Figure 32A
Rid Thyself of Thy Alien Gods

Terms on Figure 32A	Translation	Symbol	Skip	Start	End
תחתית	Saucer	◯	25	Genesis 35 V2 L32	Genesis 35 V3 L64
הסרו את-אלהי הנכר	Rid thyself of thy alien gods!	▯	1	Genesis 35 V2 L27	Genesis 35 V2 L40

For Figure 32A the ELS reference is 25 characters between rows. The matrix starts at Genesis 35 V2 L27 and ends at Genesis 35 V4 L7. It spans 114 characters of surface text, has 5 rows, 14 columns and contains 70 characters.

So what does it all mean? It seems that whenever God reveals his power, He also provides a cause for doubt. When Moses began to bring the plagues to Egypt, Pharaoh's magicians managed to replicate the first few. The Bible is full of similar stories where prophets had their moments of doubt. Always, there seems to be conflicting thoughts for the believer to choose between. And so it is with the Code; and indeed with the entire story given to us in the book of Exodus. Are we really looking at the story of God's power, or one of alien intervention in the development of our species? In Second Kings Chapter 2, Verse 11 we read:

> *And it came to pass, as they still went on, and talked, that, behold, there appeared a chariot of fire, and horse of fire, which parted them both asunder; and Elijah went up by a whirlwind into heaven.*

Figure 32B Roswell UFO

```
ז ר ע כ א ת כ ל ד ר ש ת כ א ת כ א ת א ר צ מ ג ר י כ א ש ר נ
א ד מ ת נ ו ק נ ה א ת נ ו ו א ת א ד מ ת נ ו ב ל ח מ
ב י ע י ש ב ת ל י ה ו ה א ל ה י כ ל א ת ה ע ש ה כ ל מ
א ל י ו מ א ה ל מ ו ע ד ל א מ ר ד ב ר א ל ב נ י י ש
מ ת ח ת א מ ו ו מ י ו מ ה ש מ י נ י ו ה ל א ה י ר צ
ב ל ב א ח מ ת ו י ע ל ו ב נ ג ב ו י ב א ע ד ח ב ר ו
ע ל פ נ י ב ע ל צ פ ו נ ו י ח נ ו ל פ נ י מ ג ד ל ו
ל י כ מ ל כ ל א ת ו כ ל ל ת ת ע ל י כ א י ש נ כ ר י
ו ה מ ב ו ל ה י ה מ י מ ע ל ה א ר צ ו י ב א נ ח ו ב
ס פ א ל ה י מ א ת ח ר פ ת י ו ת ק ר א א ת ש מ ו י ו
ו מ י ע ב ר ו י מ י ב כ י ת ו י ד ב ר י ו ס פ א
ר י ב ו כ י ת פ ג ע ש ו ר א י ב כ א ו ח מ ד ר ו ת ע ה
```

Terms on Figure 32B	Translation	Symbol	Skip	Start	End
רוסול עבמ	Roswell UFO	◯	-34281	Exodus 23 V3 L11	Leviticus 22 V27 L30
לפני בעל צפון	Before Baal Zephon	▢	1	Numbers 33 V7 L27	Numbers 33 V7 L37
לא תוכל לתת עליכ איש נכרי	Do not set an alien man over you	▢	1	Deuteronomy 17 V15 L52	Deuteronomy 17 V15 L71
זאבא	Zuaba	∪	34281	Leviticus 1 V1 L20	Genesis 28 V4 L22

For Figure 32B the ELS reference is 34281 characters between rows. It starts at Genesis 28 V4 L22 and ends at Exodus 23 V4 L22, spanning 377117 letters of surface text. The matrix has 12 rows, 26 columns and 312 letters.

Chapter 1 of Ezekiel describes wheels seen coming out the heavens. Are we reading about a chariot of fire or a rocket in Second Kings, an ascension or an abduction; the Merkabah – or a UFO in Ezekiel? As a scientist, I suspect we may obtain the final answer with a properly funded expedition to check out the area of concern – assuming that the Egyptian government gives us access to the site.

As a religious Jew, I believe the Bible codes are from God. Figure 32B is thus particularly disturbing to me because of the aerial photos mentioned previously, that were purportedly taken of the area of concern. What these photos show are ruins that may be Baal Zephon. However, there are aspects of the ruins that make no sense, because the number of apparent doubled-humped battlements on the north and west walls changed from one frame to the next (these structures have no apparent east or south walls – only sloping sand running into what looks like pits). The area of concern for four fortress-like structures ran from approximately 31 degrees 9.3 minutes North, 33 degrees 5.1 minutes East down toward the southwest terminating at 31 degrees 7.8 minutes North, 33 degrees 4.05 minutes East. When these coordinates are matched with the coordinates for the Temple Mount, the results are quite interesting. The average course from Jerusalem is shown in the table below to be 251.65°. Recall that the redundant course seen on ELS Map Figures 1, 2, 3, 4, 5 and 7 was 251.565°. The difference between the redundant ELS map course and this average is 0.085° (less than a tenth of a degree). It is worth noting that the 251.565° course from Jerusalem would pass through some of these structures.

Object Imaged	Latitude	Longitude	Distance from Temple Mount	Course from Temple Mount by Java Course Calculator, Temple Coordinates: 31° 46' 39.7" North, 35° 14' 4.4" East
Northeast Ruin-like Structure	31° 9.3' North	33° 5.1' East	116.45 Nautical Miles	251.9°
Southwest Ruin-like Structure	31° 7.8' North	33° 4.05' East	117.8 Nautical Miles	251.4°
				AVERAGE COURSE 251.65°

Further, there are objects seen on some (but not all) frames that resembled UFOs (circular objects that appear to be about 65 feet in diameter). I will not publish the photos because I doubt their authenticity, and because the source wishes to remain anonymous. However, what if the photos of UFOs are real objects rather than distortions or effects caused by reflections off salt crystals (as I believe)? Then the message of Figures 32A and 32B may be that we may encounter aliens at the site in question who attempt to turn us from God to a belief that aliens have played the deciding role in our evolution. This concern is openly expressed today on a number of Christian web sites that link aliens and UFOs with dark forces. An event of this nature would have dire consequences with respect to general morality and social order. Further, such a claim would still not answer the question of who created the aliens. If these creatures exist and have elected to capitalize on Codes findings to further their own agenda, the consequences for mankind could be catastrophic. This does not imply that we should greet them with a predisposition towards hostile behavior; but it does mean that we should exercise extreme caution with respect to following their lead. As the NASA official discussed earlier once told me, when asked if they were friendly or hostile, "You don't know what you neighbor is thinking." *Caveat Emptor.*

Chapter 12

CODE RELIABILITY
AND STRUCTURE

Turning now to a more mundane but central question: Is the Torah text as we find it now, the original? Do we really have the original Code, if a Code exists at all?

Bible Review magazine has published a number of academic articles arguing that today's Torah differs from the original, in that vowel letters may have been added. This argument is, however, quite dubious based on variations of spelling found within the Torah itself. We have seen with *Baal Zephon* that it is written in the Torah without the vowel letter *vav* and with the vowel letter *vav*. As was pointed out before, the significance of this here is that if *Baal Zephon* was spelled the same in Numbers as it is in Exodus, there would be no encoding of *Ark of the Covenant* in Numbers (at a skip of -306). The additional letter is essential for each letter in the Ark term to be exactly 306 letters from the next letter of the term. My experiment would never have gotten past the first night's search if *Baal Zephon* had no *vav* on all three of its open-text appearances.

Many, of course, will argue that the Torah of today is the same as that which Moses received because one wrong letter renders it *pasul* (unfit to be read from until repaired by a scribe at a cost of something like $200 per letter). I am *not* of the opinion that there is one wrong letter in the Torah, but if there were it would not necessarily invalidate any particular Torah Code find. Let us, for example suppose that there was an extra vowel added to the first book of the Torah. This would not affect the encoding of *Ark of the Covenant* in Numbers or Deuteronomy. It would, however, possibly invalidate the encoding of Clinton on Figure 9 at a skip of +33,720 because the first two letters of Clinton's name are found encoded in Genesis. Thus the site of the error is relevant to whether or not an error or even a few errors in the Torah would affect any particular encodings. A letter for letter swap (i.e., *tet* for *tav,* or *samech* for *sin*) would also not necessarily negate encoding of words that do not contain the swapped letters.

Any alteration of the original Torah would seem more likely to destroy encoding than to produce it. This is especially true with respect to long plot axis words. These words are assigned probabilities of 1.0 throughout my Experimental Report and, as such, are only deemed of interest when they are accompanied by auxiliary key words that are low in probability. One would not expect a false encoding due to an error in the text to be accompanied by numerous topically related low probability key words that are close together, though I have seen a few plots where this has occurred when I spelled an axis search term incorrectly.

Code Structure

Experience dictates that four models be considered to describe the manner of Code construction: The DNA Model, the Schwarztman Dialog Mode, Map Figures, and Rounded Torus or Wrapped Plots.

1. The DNA Model. The Code is based not on the two dimensional plots shown throughout this book; it is based on a three dimensional spiral down a cylinder. DNA, the molecule of life which makes up our genes, has mirror image symmetry on the outside of the spiraling molecule with a repetitive pattern of sugar-(deoxyribose) phosphate-sugar-phosphate, etc. The significant data is encoded in the center of the molecule and is based on the arrangement of four nucleotide bases: adenine, thymine, cytosine and guanine.

Figure 4 (axis term: *Where is the Ark?)* had *Tent of Meeting* three times. The words *Tent of Meeting* (אהל מועד) there serve as sugar-phosphate. The codons are the terms *Where is the Ark?* (איפה הארן), and possibly *Fortress* (מצד). All terms there either touch or share common letters.

We saw on Figure 16 (*Ark Position* at skip +2,698) and for the encoding of *Position Ark* at skip +1,337 that *Position* in the open text crosses and shares a letter *kuf* (ק) with the vertical encoded *Position*. Here the sugar-phosphate-sugar-phosphate role is filled by the words *Ark* and *Position* that are both found twice. This dual finding of two or more key words is the structure that most often catches my eye. That both *Ark* finds are at skip "N" (equal to column width) and both *Position* words cross each other serve to highlight the find all the more.

On Figure 17A there was a fascinating, almost mirror image plot seen. The words *Zuaba, Gold,* and *Chart* were each seen on opposite sides of *Coordinate* with *Zuaba* and *Gold* connected in each case. This was somewhat reminiscent of the sugar-phosphate repetition on the outside of the DNA molecule. The different data here, corresponding to the nucleotide bases of DNA, are the words *Coordinate, Longitude,* and *Latitude* which are encoded over the descriptions of the dimensions of the Ark of the Covenant. But is this type pattern repeated elsewhere?

On Figure 21, the vertical Prime Minister Netanyahu term is intersected once by the phrase *Surely he will be killed* and on the line under it by *His Soul will be cut off*. These two phrases have similar meaning even though each line is 19,129 letters away from the next in the surface text.

Figure 29 with two *End of Days* finds plus *Arafat* and *Barak* is also noteworthy. On Figure 30, we found references to the Tree of Life, Acacia wood (from the acacia tree) and staff tree. The trees there represent the sugar-phosphate aspects of the plot, with *the Ark* representing a connecting codon.

Without DNA encoding the Torah often appears to be redundant in the open text. With it everything appears to make sense.

What does Dr. Rips think about DNA encoding? By e-mail, he had the following to say:

Dear Mr. Roffman,
First, let me say that I like very much the idea of DNA type encoding. I think that it is well worthwhile to collect together all the findings that support it or allude to it. If it turns out to be a systematic structural feature, I can only congratulate you. (Another important structural feature is Leib Schwarztman's dialog mode – see www.ma.huji.ac.il/~rips/dialog.html

With my best regards, Eliyahu Rips

2. The Schwarztman Dialog Mode. You type in a question as a search term and the answer appears in the crossprint where the question is found. Figure 4 is also an example of this type plot. The Dialogue Mode can be modified from a question to a command. This was shown on Figure 5 with *Find the Ark* and Figure 6 with *Find Ark*. Figures 5 and 6 can be combined as is shown with Figure 33 below. On this matrix both commands occur entirely in chapter 9 of Leviticus. The second letter (צ) of the command, *Find Ark* (מצא ארון), is at Leviticus 9:5. The sixth letter (ד) of the command *Find the Ark* (מצא הארד) is also at Leviticus 9:5. How does this compare with the minimum ELS (+2,101) of the question, *Where is the Ark* (הארד איפה) on Figure 4? The question *Where is the Ark* begins at Leviticus 6:23 and ends at Leviticus 14:23. However, the third letter of the question (פ) is also at Leviticus 9:5.

By itself, the fact that the three phrases, *Find Ark, Find the Ark,* and *Where is the Ark* all pretty much crossed in Leviticus 9:5 was intriguing. In navigation (and I am approaching this Code like a navigator) when three lines cross we have a fix - that is, a position. Figure 33 also shows how the *Tent of Meeting* (also at Leviticus 9:5 and featured in Figure 4) relates to each command and to *Bardawil*. On Figure 33 there is also a DNA-type double encoding with the sugar-phosphate analogy represented by the two similar commands.

Figure 33 – Find the Ark, Find Ark, and Bardawil

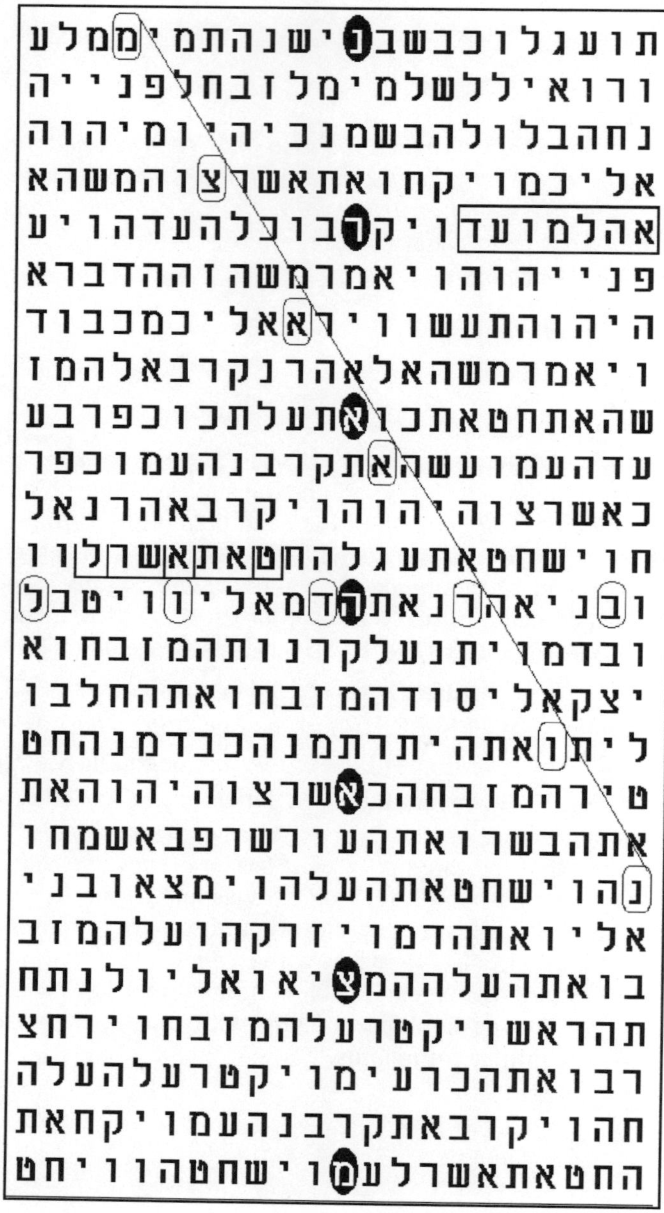

```
תועגלוכבשבנישנהתמיממלע
ורואיללשלמימלזבחלפנייה
נחהבלולהבשמנכיהיומיהוה
אליכמויקחואתאשרצוההמשהא
אהלמועדויקהבוכלהעדהויע
פנייהוהויאמרמשהזההדברא
היהוהתעשוויראאליכמכבוד
ויאמרמשהאלאהרנקרבאלהמז
שהאתחטאתכואתעלתכוכפרבע
עדהעמועשהאתקרבנהעמוכפר
כאשרצוהיהוהיקרבאהרנאל
חוישחטאתעגלהחטאתאשרלוו
ובניאהרנאתהדמאליווויטבל
ובדמויתנעלקרנותהמזבחוא
יצקאליסודהמזבחואתהחלבו
ליתואתהיתרתמנהכבדמנהחט
טירהמזבחהכאשרצוהיהוהאת
אתהבשרואתהעורשרפבאשמחו
נהוישחטאתהעלהוימצאובני
אליואתהדמויזרקהועלהמזב
בואתהעלההמציאואליולנתח
תהראשויקטרעלהמזבחוירחצ
רבואתהכרעימויקטרעלהעלה
חהויקרבאתקרבנהעמויקחאת
החטאתאשרלעמוישחטהויחט
```

Terms	Translation	Symbol	Skip	Start	End
מצא הארנ	Find the Ark	●	-104	Leviticus 9 V15 L35	Leviticus 9 V3 L45
מצא ארונ	Find Ark	◯	75	Leviticus 9 V3 L53	Leviticus 9 V11 L28
ברדול	Bardawil	◯	5	Leviticus 9 V9 L7	Leviticus 9 V9 L27
אהל מועד	Tent of Meeting	▭	1	Leviticus 9 V5 L22	Leviticus 9 V5 L28
לא-ט	31-9 (suspect latitude)	⊔	-3	Leviticus 9 V8 L35	Leviticus 9 V8 L29

For Figure 33 the ELS reference is 26 characters between rows. There are 4 displayed terms in the matrix. The matrix starts at Leviticus 9 V3 L35 and ends at Leviticus 9 V15 L46. The matrix spans 646 characters of the surface text. The matrix has 25 rows, is 22 columns wide and contains a total of 550 characters.

I notified Dr. Rips about these findings on January 23, 2000, pointing out that I was unable to locate Jerusalem on the Figure 5, 6, or 33 plots, but two days later I found Figure 34 and sent him the following e-mail:

Dear Dr. Rips,

While I'm not yet ready to say that the rabbis are correct about the Ark's location, I did stumble upon one very dramatic plot this evening to back their contention that the Ark remains in Jerusalem. The command FIND ARK is encoded at skip -8,634. Jerusalem with its biblical six-letter spelling is encoded at skip +43,170. This is not only exactly 5 times the preceding value of 8,634, but the two terms overlap, share the letter resh and are found together in a matrix measuring ONE COLUMN BY 26 ROWS! Still, if not just a fluke, this may represent what WAS the case rather than what IS the case. Or we may be seeing evidence that there were indeed two arks, one for the broken tablets and one for the unbroken, second copy. I would urge you to carefully examine the Hebrew to see if anything else is of value here.

Barry

With respect to two arks, The Stone Edition Art Scroll text, *The Chumash* (Scherman, 787, 1994), states of Numbers 10:33, "And the Ark…journeyed before them. The commentators raise the difficulty that the Ark traveled after the formations of Judah and Reuben, not at the forefront of the camp. Rashi cites Sifri that this was not the Ark that contained the Tablets, but a second Ark, which contained the broken pieces of the First Tablets which Moses had shattered."

Figure 34 Find Ark & Jerusalem

Terms on Figure 34	Translation	Symbol	Skip	Start	End
מצא ארון	Find Ark	◯	-8634	Exodus 12 V20 L25	Genesis 30 V39 L9
ירושלם	Jerusalem	▢	43170	Genesis 15 V3 L2	Numbers 26 V52 L17

For Figure 34 the ELS reference is 8634 characters between rows. There are 2 displayed terms in the matrix. The matrix starts at Genesis 15 V3 L2 and ends at Numbers 26 V52 L17. The matrix spans 215851 characters of the surface text. The matrix has 26 rows, is 1 columns wide and contains a total of 26 characters.

Dr. Rips has maintained a practice of not responding to matrices that imply a move of the Ark out of Jerusalem. However, since the above *Find Ark-Jerusalem* message backed his personal belief, on February 4, 2000, he wrote:

Dear Mr. Roffman,
I returned recently to Nashville. I considered your finding; I think it is remarkable. Both expressions are clearly a- priori. Probably we can state that there is a new category of findings in which the skips are just multiples of a given number. I know several such examples. This new plot considerably adds to them.

With my best regards, Eliyahu Rips

Figure 34 may prove the rabbis right, but there are other ways to interpret the find *if* it's not just due to chance alone. Chance is indeed a very possible explanation as the skips are very large and far from minimum. In fact, there are 3,119 ELS finds for *Jerusalem* with this spelling that have a lower skip. There are also 12 ELS hits for *Find Ark* with a lower skip. However, if not due to chance, the Torah Code might contain all the homes of the Ark. We've seen *Tent of Meeting* found encoded with the Ark. So Jerusalem's appearance might be what was meant both for another time in our past and for its future home.

3. ELS Map Figures. Here the crossprint yields not only key positional site names or cities, but they are displayed at angles that correspond precisely to their positions and connecting courses on Earth. This structure was thoroughly covered in Chapter 1.

4. Rounded Torus or Wrapped Plots. Here the computer program makes more than one pass through the Torah to search for an axis term and/or related terms.

Kevin Acres, programmer of the *CodeFinder* program, points out, "The length of the Torah is only divisible by two numbers. One of these is the number 5, the number of books, and the other is 60961. Both of these are prime numbers." He further states, "The possible number of ELSs are higher in a toroidal search, and the chances of an ELS re-covering its own ground are limited." The disadvantage of accepting such a protocol is that it cheapens the statistical value of any related calculation for simpler matrices. It increases the chance to find whatever you want if your terms are short. If you can't find your key target word in the first Torah pass, you might well get it in additional passes. On the other hand, this method of encoding increases the data carrying capacity of the Code and makes it easier for the Encoder to incorporate desired information.

Other codes researchers are using toroidal searches of the Torah with great success and developing complex and statistically significant matrices. These findings bode well in answering the initial questions on whether the Torah we have today is accurate. The answer seems to be *yes* for accuracy as it relates to additions or subtractions of letters from the original, and leaves open the minor question of individual letter substitutions. However, that minor question is constrained by the necessity of having a surface text of the Torah that makes sense when you read it.

Tabernacle in the wilderness with pillar of fire.

Chapter 13

FROM ROME TO ISRAEL

We arrived in Rome on Tuesday May 4th 1999. Every time I go there, I find the hotel rooms cost two to three times what they do in America, and their quality is about one fifth of what's offered at home. I asked our hotel manager about it when we arrived. He pointed out that we were paying so much ($150 per day for a dump) because the city was founded in 735 BCE, and *like a fine wine, its value increases with age.* Perhaps, but the leaky plumbing and lumpy mattresses don't really need to be that old too to serve as an excuse for price gouging.

Rome provided us with a chance to restock our kosher food supplies. We'd been eating airline-type food all the way across the Atlantic and the ship was kind enough to provide us with additional meals to get us as far as Rome, but no farther. There wouldn't be another opportunity until we reached Israel.

I took my family to see the Coliseum, then headed for the Vatican, intending to deliver a copy of my Experimental Report to a Vatican representative. The actual meeting took place at Gregorian University in Rome.

As I told father Robert O'Toole there, it's important for the Ark to be found by a joint-faith expedition. This will decrease doubt and skepticism about the Ark's authenticity should the Code prove as productive in the field as it has on a statistical basis alone. I invited O'Toole to attend our conference in Jerusalem, but that was only five days away, not enough time for his associates to absorb what I had found (which at the time included only one ELS map figure). O'Toole understood that my project was designed to bring us together, but he informed me the Church never worked that fast. We shook hands as I left. I have a hard handshake – instilled by my military training. His hand was like warm butter.

There is a slower pace throughout Europe and the Middle East than Americans are used to dealing with. This method of doing business must be planned for in any serious, full-blown expedition. Time to get approval for decisions equates to money required. A serious expedition would probably require at least a year's worth of funding.

There are no limits to how much energy I'm willing to expend to see this project through. But there is a limit to how much I can put on my credit cards to finance the operation. Rome was expensive, a reminder that it will take more than my research alone to make this investigation a success. Planning, Operations, Logistics, Finance, and Public Relations all will be necessary to successfully conclude the project. I'm going to need help with all these things. I'm concerned, but know that if God wills something to happen, it will.

We took the train to Bari, Italy on Wednesday afternoon, May 5th. As our *Superfast Ferry* got underway that evening, we passed a NATO cruiser. While cruise ships had all cancelled their passages into the Adriatic due to the war in Kosovo, Bosnia, and Serbia; ferries had not (thankfully) and we were concerned about how safe it would be. I did, however, come within an inch of being killed in Rome earlier that day. While crossing a street, the light changed. When I turned to go back to the curb, a car sped by close enough to graze my open jacket, but it left my body untouched. If He really wanted me that bad, He could have had me then. That thought provided some measure of confidence as we sailed.

Wednesday night the lifeboat drill was of great interest; but by Thursday morning we were snuggled safely in the bosom of Greek coastal islands – getting further from the madness of war by the minute. All the connections had been made save two – a bus from Patras to Athens and the car ferry from the port there in Piraeas to Rhodes, Cyprus, and at long last Israel.

Rome provided us with some kosher food supplies; but not the desired quantity and the ice in our ice chest was quickly exhausted. Israel's *all you can eat and it's kosher* restaurants and supermarkets began to look pretty good by the time we made our last connection in Piraeas, Greece.

I used to think that it was just the Israeli attitude toward bureaucracy that can drive an American Jew nuts, but after crossing Southern Europe, I realized that it's the Mediterranean mindset that permeates the place that's so hard for an American to get acclimated to. When I lived in Israel for two months in 1992, I found myself saying at least twice per day, "This is not how it's done in America." The response was always the same of course. "This is not America." That may be so, but if Israelis had developed the manners and sense of fair play that Americans have, it seems likely that the Intifada might never have occurred. You don't win friends by bulldozing their homes when they don't get building permits, because you don't want their kind to build homes on *your* land.

God told the Jews to throw out the non-Jewish inhabitants of Canaan *not* because they were Muslim, but because 3,200 years ago the previous occupants were pagan folk who sacrificed their own children to a false god named Moloch. It was not, in-other-words, our virtue that earned us the land. Rather, it was simply that *we were not as bad as the previous occupants*. As ill-mannered bureaucrats are clearly not as bad as suicide bombers or their proud parents, the Jews still hold the upper hand.

Islamic Jihad? Jihad (holy war) is today is an oxymoron. Allah of Islam, Adonai of Judaism, and the Father of Christianity are all the same. It's never holy to take the life of another believer just because he or she has a slightly different understanding of God. Such a war can only be an unholy war. There's an interesting section in the Muslim Koran that backs this idea:

...To each among you We prescribed a Law and an Open Way. If God had so willed, He would have made you a single People, but (His plan is) to test you in what He has given you: so strive as in a race in all virtues. The goal is to God; it is He that will show you the truth of all matters in which you dispute;
(Koran, Ali translation, The Table 5:51)

If you've guessed by now that I'm an idealist, you're quite correct. This doesn't mean I'm always an optimist. Each of the major monotheistic faiths have an abundance of people who have memorized their Scriptures, but who focus only on the divisive aspects of the texts while missing entirely the overall main message that was delivered. God derives more pleasure from kindness to each other than He does from worship. Abraham demonstrated his understanding of this concept. In Genesis 18:1 God appeared to him in the plains of Mamre. In the following verse the patriarch noticed three men and he ran to them to provide water, rest beneath a tree, and a meal. The Talmud (Shevuos 35b; Shabbos 127a) instructs us that his actions were not disrespectful to God because he knew that by serving God's creatures he was serving God Himself. How tragic, then, that the descendants of Abraham must spend about a trillion dollars or more in the world each year for arms to kill each other. Many of our wars are religious in nature. Indeed, the cause of war has always been attributable to a very few causes – disputes over territory, natural resources, and economic/political systems (capitalism vs. communism) or religion. If we could divert just a small fraction of these funds we could buy the Brazilian rain forest and save the lungs of the world. Make the place a world park. An Ark find and religious reawakening might make such a thing possible.

The problem, of course, is that it is the nature of many to be shortsighted. As I looked around on the ferry lounge almost everyone was smoking. If they don't care about their own lungs, why should they care about rain forests? Indeed, Europeans, Israelis and Egyptians are addicted to the evil weed at an incredible rate. They also seem oblivious to signs posted that forbid its use. I once stood in line (an hour long with pushing and shoving) in an Israeli bank. I nearly died there from the thick smoke. When it was finally my turn to step up to the window, I noticed that behind each teller was a sign that forbid smoking in the bank; yet every single teller was smoking.

So much to do, so little time. Friends, every minute of life is ever so precious. Use your time wisely. Perhaps if we do, God will extend our lives considerably as was hinted at in the Tree of Life plot (Figure 30) presented earlier.

God undoubtedly has worked hard to give us such a beautiful world. He did, He told us, need a rest from His work on the seventh day. Let's stop fighting not only ourselves, but Him. Let's bring Him out of hiding around El Zuqba or wherever He is – with or without an Ark find, and help complete the task of making this world the paradise it was designed to be.

After rough seas from Piraeus to Rhodes, and a Sabbath in Cyprus, we arrived in Israel on Sunday, May 9th. Normally the thing to say would be, "We arrived safely in Israel." We did, but after our ship pulled into Haifa, we were told at the luggage claim area that we'd have to leave our baggage there and then follow an agent. At first I was afraid they finally had me. I never did pay the real estate tax on my property in Karkom, but did request the bill from the village council after I left Israel in 1992. They hadn't forwarded it because they wanted someone else to get my prize lot overlooking the Jordan River, the Sea of Galilee, and the Golan Heights. So on arrival in 1999 I was sure that my debt had shown up on the agent's computer. That's what the council had warned me about when they asked me to sign the property over to them. I almost said something to the agent, but decided to keep quiet. Good thing I did. Nothing to worry about. Nothing at all… just a bomb scare. That's a daily (or is it hourly?) event. Welcome to Israel.

Chapter 14

THE INTERNATIONAL TORAH CODES SOCIETY (ITCS)

I presented my Experimental Report before Dr. Rips and the Torah Codes Society on Monday, May 10th 1999. I'd never met or heard him before, and was struck by the similarity between his voice and mannerisms and those of Albert Einstein.

I didn't come to Jerusalem with any delusions that Rips would publicly endorse my findings, and was pleased enough to learn that he found my statistical approach to Codes analysis "promising" even if he was troubled by my findings about the Ark's location which ran counter to rabbinical understanding. He's an Orthodox Jew living in a city dominated by rabbis.

In 1979 I once got onto a bus in this city, looked around and thought, *How very odd these people look.* All the men had black hats, white shirts, black suits and peiachs (side locks of hair). I had on a cowboy hat. This was during a period of broken service between the Navy and Coast Guard and also before the first Indiana Jones movie. It was also five years before I became a *modern* Orthodox Jew. After a while, I noticed that the men on the bus were staring at me dressed as I was. *How very odd*, they must have thought. *What kind of mishuganuh* (crazy person) *is this? Can he be a Jew?* I'm certain, as I sat around the room full of black hats at the ITCS, they didn't think too much more of my *Indiana Jones* hat. I was always proud to wear a military uniform, but see no reason to lose my individuality when not serving my country. When civilians succumb to peer pressure to dress in one manner only, and to think in one manner only, creativity will likely suffer.

The final handshake at the Vatican had been a friendly one. There was a wide gulf between our faiths, but recent momentum to start to close the gap and the priest appreciated what I was attempting to do. The ITCS in Jerusalem was something else.

Dr. Haralick informed me that my presentation had been nearly cancelled by Rabbi Silman of the religious court in B'Nei Brak. A meeting with the rabbi had been requested by "the committee" which was represented by Dr. Moshe Katz. He was concerned by my belief that the Ark was no longer in Jerusalem. While I was at sea without a clue as to what was going on, Haralick tried to argue forcefully on my behalf. Rabbi Silman spoke little English, so my opponent, Dr. Katz, had to translate Haralick's arguments for him. The cards were therefore stacked against me and the rabbi ruled likewise. Dr. Haralick then pointed out that the original "call for scientific papers" made no mention of the need to follow *halacha* (Jewish religious law). The rabbi agreed that this was true, and informed Dr. Haralick, "Then you must do something clever." In the end, a compromise had been reached which allowed me to present my paper, but under the somewhat insulting heading of "Controversy: Use and Misuse of Codes, The Roffman Paper, Ark of the Covenant." While I was allotted a mere 45 minutes to sum up nearly two years of work, the discussion about the paper occupied the bulk of the afternoon and actually took up about 20% of the two day conference. The schedule of speakers read as follows:

First Congress of the
International Torah Codes Society
Program
Monday May 10, 1999

Technical Sessions

Hilton, 7 King David St., Jerusalem, Israel

9:00 - 9:20 AM	Opening Ceremony and Blessing	
	Statistical Methodology	
9:20 - 10:10 AM	Computing ELS Joint Placement Probabilities	Prof. Robert M. Haralick
10:10 - 10:40 AM	Hybrid Measurement Schemes	Prof. Ilya Rips
10:40 - 11:00 AM	*Coffee Break*	
	Exploratory Methodologies	
11:00 - 11:30 AM	The Death of Diana	Dr. Moshe Katz
11:30 AM - 12:00 PM	Elokim-Din	Nachum Bombach
12:00 - 1:45 PM	*Lunch*	
	Controversy:	
	Use and Misuse of Codes - The Roffman Paper	
1:45 - 2:30 PM	Ark of the Covenant	Barry Roffman
2:30 - 3:15 PM	Panel Discussion	
	Codes and Halacha	
	Predictions	
	Involving Anything Unknown	
	Counter-examples	
3:15 - 3:30 PM	*Coffee Break*	

New Experiments

3:30 - 4:15 PM	Replication of the Famous Rabbis' Experiment	Doron Witztum
4:15 - 4:45 PM	Rabbis and Cities	Harold Gans and Nachum Bombach
4:15 - 5:15 PM	Sons of Hamen	Dr. Alex Rotenberg
5:15 - 5:45 PM	Mishnayot	Dr. Moshe Katz
5:45 – 7:30 PM	*Dinner*	

Tuesday, May 11, 1999

Technical Sessions – Hilton

Statistical Methodology

9:00 - 9:45 AM	Best Star Team Methodology	Prof. Robert M. Haralick
9:45 - 10:15 AM	Evaluation of Long Expressions	Dr. Alex Rotenberg
10:15 – 10:45 AM	The Misleading Statistics in the Torah Codes Opponents' Experiments-Nachum Bombach	
10:45 - 11:00 AM	*Coffee Break*	

Exploratory Methodologies

11:00 – 11:45 AM	The Clustering and Dialogue Mode	Dr. Leib Schwartzman
11:45 AM – 12:15 PM	Goral HaGra	Dr. Moshe Katz
12:15 PM - 1:45 PM	*Lunch*	
1:45 - 3:00 PM	**Open Discussion**	
	New Software Tools	
	New Experiments	
	Negative Results	
	Finding Structures in Codes	
3:00 - 3:15 PM	*Coffee Break*	

New Experiments

3:15 - 4:15 PM	Sons of Yaakov	Prof. Ilya Rips
4:15 - 4:30 PM	The Encampments of the Exodus	Art Levitt
4:30 - 5:00 PM	New Experiment Specifications	Prof. Robert M. Haralick
5:00 - 7:30 PM	*Dinner*	

Public Session - Hilton

7:00 - 7:15 PM	Opening and Blessings	
7:15 - 8:15 PM	Historical Perspective	Dr. Moshe Katz
8:15 - 8:45 PM	The Torah Code Controversy	Prof. Robert M. Haralick
8:45 - 9:00 PM	*Break*	
9:00 - 9:30 PM	Summary and Highlights	Prof. Ilya Rips
9:30 - 10:30 PM	Questions and Answers	Prof. Paul Eidelberg

After my presentation, the ITCS informally voted to exclude consideration of any matters not in accordance with *halacha*. This unfortunate decision moved the Society out of the function of a scientific body and placed it squarely in the realm of a religious forum dressed in quasi or pseudo-scientific garb.

The apprehension of what they had just witnessed was more than apparent. It was audibly expressed: "We fear that while you will prove the Codes right if you succeed, you will bring great damage to our cause if you fail to locate the Ark. We must focus on a much more restricted use of the Codes than what you advocate." They voted (while I was out of the room being interviewed by Elli Wohlgelernter of the *Jerusalem Post*) to exclude my Report from the official proceedings even though they could not attack my math.

Only Dr. Katz attempted a feeble excuse for not including my paper in the conference report. "We can only accept papers based on Torah Codes, and your paper adds the concept of chapters and verses rather than limit its scope just to the 304,805 letters of the Torah." What he forgot, of course, were the following words in his own COMPUTORAH book published in 1996: "Moses was like a scribe, copying what he had seen onto parchment, while God's voice taught him the spacing of words, *verses,* and paragraphs…"

One of the papers by Dr. Alex Rotenberg dealt with the sons of Haman. Haman is the man spoken of in the Book of Esther who tried to exterminate all the Jews in the Persian Empire. His plan fell apart when the King learned that his wife (Queen Esther) was Jewish. Haman was hung as were all his sons. It was shown that when the date of this incident showed up at an ELS in Torah, the next five letters in sequence spelled *Purim* which is the holiday that recalls this incident. The find was *a posteriori*. If I heard right, (and this was later disputed) it was then argued that this was such a special case, that a probability should be run on it. While this is probably fair, some went on to argue that there were many other things that would also work for calculation purposes here including all the sons of Haman, their wives, and any number of other items. Once we start accepting this line of logic, however, the probability of finding *something good* increases rapidly and the significance of the find drops proportionally. As Harold Gans once pointed out, if you are researching the Holocaust and you will accept anything found relating to it – any of the German characters, or the concentration camp names, or any of the years associated with it, or any of the people executed during it – such an open list renders findings meaningless. The key words must be specified *a priori* and the field should be somewhat limited. This reminds me of another concern with the meaning of Torah Codes findings. At just what point do the things *not* found begin to become more significant than the things found?

Dr. Haralick is a wonderful man who has done much to assist me with my research and who has even worked hard to develop computer software to standardize my probability calculation techniques. This is flattering, and I know that he stuck his neck out to get my paper onto the agenda at the conference, and returned in 2002 to push my enhanced findings again. At the 1999 conference, he acknowledged that the ITCS moved out of the realm of pure science when it voted to proceed only in accordance with Jewish law. I was, however, troubled in 1999 by his Best Star Team Methodology presentation on the second day of the conference.

The archenemy of the conference was a man named Professor Brendan McKay. He claimed to have found similar encoding in a non-religious book. He also believed the original WRR study was selective in a biased manner with respect to findings included for publication – a fatal experimental flaw. Therefore he had concluded that the Torah Codes were bogus. McKay wasn't at the conference, but he was at the focus of Haralick's concerns (see Foreword for further discussion of this issue).

Dr. Haralick was of the opinion that McKay had also manipulated his data to make encoding seem to appear in what should have been only a statistical control book. He was quite concerned by McKay's charge that the original WRR study had also manipulated data. From what I've observed of McKay's work, Haralick is correct about McKay manipulating data. McKay uses two primary tricks to produce matrices from books like *Moby Dick* or *War and Peace*. First, he does not pay attention to minimum ELS or near minimum ELS requirements. Second, he employs large row skips to bring an open text phrase like *He will be killed* in line with a name like *Kennedy*. If you don't control both of these items very carefully, you can come up with all kinds of impressive findings that are meaningless.

There were obviously strong and bitter feelings between the two opposing camps of thought, and Dr. Haralick spoke in terms of *our team* vs. *their team*. There were also comments to remind everyone that statistics could be found to back either case. When taken with repeated comments about how some statistical measures were more favorable than others, this only served to underscore the necessity of hard, physical evidence. While the ITCS voted to bar predictive reports in the future, without such tests, as I informed them, nobody is going to take the Codes seriously – nor should they. *"Snake Oil,"* I reminded Harold Gans, "was the charge leveled against the Codes by some critics, and *snake oil* they would seem if the so-called experts could not agree amongst themselves, let alone others, as to appropriate and extraordinarily clear measures of success."

When it became clear that the purpose of most of the ITCS (with the primary notable exception of Dr. Haralick) was no longer to investigate the truth of the phenomena, but to promote the certainty of its existence, I bid the group a fond farewell and headed for the Egyptian Embassy. The meeting there in Tel Aviv with Yasser Abed and Amin Mohsen was a very friendly one. They were fascinated by what they saw and optimistic about capitalizing on the tourist aspects of the search and its notoriety; but both were concerned about Egypt's involvement in the nuclear holocaust prediction. They wanted to know what was required of their government for the search to proceed. I requested noninterference as minimum, but stated my preference for Egyptian Coast Guard participation. Contrary to Douglas Haldane's warning from the Institute of Underwater Archeology in Alexandria, I was informed that the decision would require about six days, not six months. The delay was due primarily to the Embassy's preoccupation following the Israeli election set for May 17, 1999.

Simple model of the Ark of the Covenant.

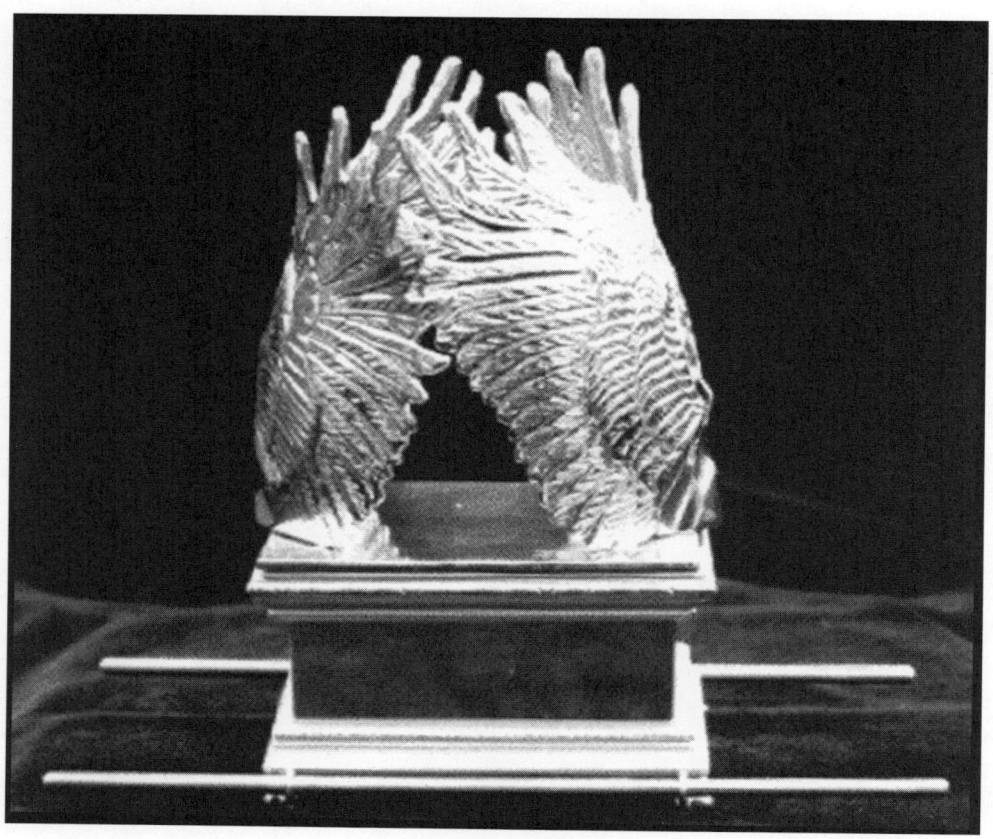

Chapter 15

ADOLPH HITLER

I am the Lord and there is no other. I formed the light and create darkness; I make peace and create evil; I the Lord do all these things. Isaiah 45:6-7

Michael Drosnin states that Adolph Eichmann (the man who arranged transportation of Jews to extermination camps) is encoded with Zyklon B, the gas used to kill the Jews, and that the Holocaust is found in the Codes in great detail.

As discussed earlier, I met Dr. Moshe Katz at the Torah Codes Society conference in Jerusalem. He gave me a copy of his book *COMPUTORAH: On Hidden Codes in the Torah* (1996). Dr. Katz's book deals at length with the Holocaust and in more detail than Drosnin's books. A brief summary of Dr. Katz's Holocaust plots follow:

Page	Key Words (Letters)	Skip	First Letter	Rows *Columns = Area
84	Germany (6),	507	Leviticus 25:47	26R * 60C = 1,560
	Vengeance of the Covenant (7)	99	Leviticus 26:22	
	Vengeance of the Covenant (7)	1	Leviticus 26:25	
	Amalekites (6)	8	Leviticus 26:24	
91	Germany (6),	-933	Deuteronomy 33:28	36R * 76C = 2,736
	Crematorium for my sons (8),	134	Deuteronomy 31:28	
	Auschwitz (6),	536	Deuteronomy 33:24	
	Plagues (5),	-134	Deuteronomy 32:32	
	Eichmann (6)	-670	Deuteronomy 32:52	
92	Auschwitz (6),	536	Deuteronomy 33:24	26R * 23C = 598
	In Poland (6)	-107	Deuteronomy32:22	
	I will make My arrows			
	drunk with blood			
	As My sword devours flesh			
	(23 – open text)	1	Deuteronomy 32:42	
93	Hitler (5)	22	Deuteronomy 10:17	16R * 9C = 144
	Auschwitz (6),	-13	Deuteronomy 10:21	
	Holocaust (4)	13	Deuteronomy 10:20	

93	Hitler (5), Mein Kampf (7)	-3 7,832	Numbers 19:13	33R*16C = 528
94	King of the Nazis (8), Genocide (5), "shall say, Destroy them" (9 – open text)	-246 -22 1	Deuteronomy 33:16 Deuteronomy 33:21 Deuteronomy 33:27	10R * 89C = 890
95	The Fuhrer (5) Samael(4) King of the Nazis (8)	5 5 -246	Deuteronomy 32:50 Deuteronomy 32:50 Deuteronomy 33:16	19R * 52C = 988

The first thing noticed about the Katz plots is that they tend to be quite large. The above seven plots have an average of 1,063 letters. By comparison, the Experimental Report that I presented to the ITCS in 1999 had an average matrix size of 236 letters. That's less than a quarter of what Dr. Katz requires to show supposedly related material. The ten ELS map figures presented in Chapter One of this book average 847 letters in size, but larger plots may be necessary to generate the *a priori* angles required for such plots. For ELS Map Figures 1 through 5 with a course angle of 251.565 degrees True from Jerusalem to the prime suspect site, the average number of letters required was only 577. For ELS Map Figure 7 there were 1,887 letters required, but the matrix has not only the rough course angle from Jerusalem to Katib El Qals, but the correct course angle from the fort to the suspect Ark site four miles south.

A year after the 1999 ITCS conference, Dr. McKay read the above criticism and argued (with respect to his unsuccessful attempts to replicate ELS map figures in War and Peace), "Sorry, but I don't accept you as rule master. It would be just as reasonable to allow larger plots, but require more words in them." To the good Doctor, I replied, "There are some serious considerations that must go into deciding how many more words would be required as well as what type (high or low frequency) words would be required. Dr. Haralick confirmed the Skip Formula (presented in Appendix A at the end of this book) that I developed. It indicates that a six-letter word is 24 times more likely to be found on a 20 * 20 matrix than on a 10 * 10 matrix. That's why I insist on small windows. It's also why I would be leery of accepting results based on larger windows with more words." McKay never challenged this reasoning. Indeed, he praised the ELS map figures and went on to rate my research as some of the best he had seen.

Only one Katz-derived Nazi-era plot, from page 43 of his book, was less than the average size of the matrices in my Experimental Report. On my Figure 35 it's expanded by three columns to show the *a posteriori* word *terrible*. If we assume *Auschwitz* (אושויץ) was the conditional axis word, the chance that *Hitler* (היטלר) would appear in a 144-letter box with it (and *Holocaust*) is one in 1,058. Ignore *Holocaust* and the chance for *Hitler* to be in a 135-letter box with *Auschwitz* is one in 1,129. If Katz chose *Hitler* as the axis term here and *Auschwitz* and *Holocaust* (שואה) were sought *a priori*, then the chance for those two terms to be in the 144-letter matrix with *Hitler* was about one chance in 8,191. Only *Auschwitz,* however, was really statistically significant. There was about 1 chance in 2,117 that it would be encoded this closely with *Hitler*, but there was more than one chance in four that *Holocaust* would appear on the plot. The word *terrible* (נורא) on the bottom row appears in standard open text form touching *Holocaust*. It is also shown on the second and third rows touching letter hey (ה) of *Hitler*. The word is split between two rows due to column width being set at just 12 letters. It must be remembered that each two-dimensional matrix really represents a three-dimensional spiraling cylinder.

Figure 35
Hitler, Auschwitz and Holocaust

Terms	Translation	Symbol	Skip	Start	End
היטלר	Hitler	⊔	22	Deut. 10 V17 L37	Deut. 10 V19 L15
שואה	Holocaust	○	13	Deut. 10 V20 L36	Deut. 10 V21 L37
אושויץ	Auschwitz	▢	-13	Deut. 10 V21 L24	Deut. 10 V19 L28
נורא	Terrible	◯	1	Deut. 10 V17 L50	Deut. 10 V17 L53
נורא	Terrible	◯	1	Deut. 10 V21 L38	Deut. 10 V21 L41

For Figure 35 the ELS reference is 12 letters between rows. There are 5 terms in the matrix which starts at Deuteronomy 10 V17 L29 and ends at Deuteronomy 10 V21 L41. The matrix spans 192 characters of the surface text. It has 16 rows, is 12 columns wide and contains a total of 192 characters.

Dr. Katz uses three spellings for Germany. All started with *gimel resh mem* (גרם), but they finish with *mem yud alef* (מיא); *nun yud hey* (ניה); or *nun yud alef* (ניא). This allowance, of course, decreases the statistical significance of any particular finding with *Germany* in it. Likewise, he uses two different spellings for *Auschwitz*, one with a *vav* (ו) for the 4th letter, the other with a *vet* (ב). Multiple spelling possibilities for transliteration of names are a problem for everyone (myself included – as with Zuqba and Zuaba) in the field of Torah Codes research. Dr. McKay points out in an article entitled "A Quick lesson in Hebrew Spelling," that there are on the Rabbi Abulafia synagogue in Tiberias, Israel, **four different Hebrew spellings of the name (Abulafia) on the same building (אבולעפיה, אבולעפייה , אבולעאפיה and אבולעפיא)**!

I checked briefly, and found a few poignant clues to also suggest that the *Holocaust* is encoded. The most striking is the location of *Hitler* at a skip of 44 in the 5th chapter of Exodus (Figure 36).

**Figure 36
A Sword in Hitler's Hand**

Terms	Translation	Symbol	Skip	Start	End
היטלר	Hitler	○	-44	Exodus 5 V22 L36	Exodus 5 V19 L32
לתת חרב בידם להרגנו	To put a sword in their hands to slay us.	□	1	Exodus 5 V21 L64	Exodus 5 V21 L79
למה הרעתה לעם הזה	Why did you bring harm to this people?	∪	1	Exodus 5 V22 L23	Exodus 5 V22 L36
הרע לעם הזה	Evil to this people	∩	1	Exodus 5 V23 L23	Exodus 5 V23 L31

For Figure 36 the ELS reference is 44 characters between rows. There are 4 displayed terms in the matrix. The matrix starts at Exodus 5 V9 L19 and ends at Exodus 5 V23 L42. The matrix spans 243 characters of the surface text. The matrix has 6 rows, is 23 columns wide and contains a total of 138 characters.

Figure 36 is an *a posteriori* set of finds. In my standard protocol, a probability can not be assigned to words around the conditional axis word (here *Hitler*) unless they are specified *a priori*. In this Torah section the Israelites complain that Moses has made them loathsome to the Pharaoh and his courtiers, and that Moses has put a sword in the hand of the Egyptians to slay them. Moses then asks God why He has brought evil to this people. He complains that God has done nothing to alleviate their suffering.

There is an obvious similarity to the Holocaust. Rather than assign the conditional axis word a probability of 1.0, let's assign this probability to the *a posteriori* items like *Why do you harm this people*, *put a sword in their hands to slay us*, and *evil to this people*. Then let's ask, "What are the chances that *Hitler* would be encoded here?" Hitler is encoded in reverse from Exodus 5:22 back through 5:19. He can be placed together in an 85-letter box with the above

Holocaust-related material. The odds that he would be in such a box are one chance in 1,793.

I found several similar matrices that are left out of this book for the sake of brevity. The question must, of course, be asked. Why would God encode such a thing, and not stop it? Surely He could have spared at least one lightning bolt to take out such evil, but chose not to. Even when German generals attempted to assassinate their leader, though their bomb detonated under Hitler's table, he survived! The extermination then continued at an even more furious rate. Why?

Katz cites numerous open-text Bible passages (like Leviticus 20:26, 26:25, Ezekiel 2:32 and Daniel 12:1) to support his view that the Holocaust was brought about as a punishment for Jews becoming like other nations. The implication is that when the Reform Jewish movement began in Germany, it sowed the seeds for the Holocaust to follow which was brought about by Germans, the modern Amalekites.

Frankly, this makes God out to be quite cruel. Yes, Judaism does teach of an aspect of God that denotes judgment, but it also speaks of one with mercy. Traditionally the God of the first chapter of Genesis (אלהים – pronounced *Elohim*) was one of judgment, but He learned that the world could not survive through judgment alone. The 4-letter Tetragramatton (יהוה - *yud hey vav hey*) of the second chapter of Genesis was dominated by mercy. This same four-letter name of God is used in the *Shema* and *V'yahavta* prayers where *He commands us to love Him*. It is not pronounced out loud by Jews, but is referred to with the names *HaShem* (*the Name*) or *Adonay* (*My Lord*).

After delivering my Experimental Report to the ITCS in Jerusalem, I spent ten days in Tel Aviv waiting for clearance from the Egyptians to enter Egypt under their supervision to begin the Ark search. I also remained in Israel trying to clear up a problem that dated back to 1992. I brought over a sailboat from San Francisco then, and sold it; but the buyer in Tel Aviv never finished paying for it. The Israeli government never responded to my numerous pleas for help. I did find my letters in the file at the Ministry of Transport when I arrived in Haifa, so I know that they were received, but the attitude was, *He's in America, we already have his $5,000 in duty for the boat, so who cares if he was cheated?*

I was also deceived by the Israeli government, and by a builder with respect to the home that I tried to construct in the northern town of Karkom (near Tiberias) in 1992. In fact, I actually found somebody else's new house sitting on the parcel of land that I had a deed for when I arrived there on the 1999 trip (the homeowner said he sensed something was wrong about the deal that led to construction of his home). The attitude was similar to that described with the boat transaction above. I don't want to go into details of these nightmares here, but I will state that any Jew who would treat a non-Jew in this manner would be quite likely to contribute to the ranks of the world's anti-Semites.

Where prejudice exists, who deserves the blame? I know that it will upset my fellow Jews that I place *some* of the guilt for the Holocaust at our own feet too. Yes, most Jews are highly ethical. Our crime rate is also extremely low. But those few who cheat others do incredible damage to our image.

We are the ones that the Bible lists as God's chosen people. If *we* don't bend over backward to behave morally, why shouldn't we expect those not so honored in Scripture to express resentment and outrage? We've got to do a better job of policing ourselves. In my Tel Aviv hotel room I found that when I turned on the television to look for news about the election, I had to switch it off quickly before my six-year old would be exposed to an advertisement for a pornographic film. No wonder many of my Orthodox colleagues prohibit television in their homes! Nothing was left to the imagination. This is the Holy Land? Would the Muslims permit this on family television if they controlled the station? What message does this send to religious Christians who are making a pilgrimage to the Holy Land?

A Muslim once told me of his admiration for the great intelligence of the Jews. But there is, I told him, a classic joke about our smarts and Jewish Law (the Torah).

The Creator came down to Earth and tried to find a taker for His Laws. When he went to the first nation the people were interested until they learned they couldn't murder anyone. A second nation didn't want them because you couldn't work, drive, or spend money on the Sabbath. A third nation almost bought them until they found they couldn't eat pork, lobster, or cheeseburgers, and had to wait for seven days after their wives stopped bleeding before having sex. Then the Creator came to the Jews.

"Do you want my Ten Commandments?" He asked.

"How much do they cost?" was the cautious reply.

"They're free! And just for you today, I've got 603 more I'll throw in at no extra cost!"

"Such a deal," they replied. "Nasah v'nishma," the Jews said. "We will do, and we will hear." Thus it was that our ancestors agreed to obey a complex set of laws before even hearing them. These laws would require them to be a kingdom of priests to the nations of the world. But today, while the vast majority of Jews live moral lives, few know most of the laws. Nor do they feel a calling to set the example and teach the world the difference between right and wrong. "So," I asked my Muslim friend. "How smart were we to take on such awesome responsibility so quickly?"

Why did the Holocaust happen? It was probably due to some combination of God's wrath and the wrath of people some of us have wronged. In Isaiah 42:6 we were told:

> *I the Lord have called you in righteousness, and will hold your hand, and will keep you, and give you for a covenant of the people, for a light of the nations.*

Figure 37
Crematorium for my Son

Terms	Translation	Symbol	Skip	Start	End
כבשן לבני	Crematorium for my son	◯	134	Deut. 31 V28 L29	Deut. 32 V17 L50
מצד ארון ברית	Fortress of the Ark of the Covenant	▭	1	Deut. 31 V26 L25	Deut. 31 V26 L35
אושביץ	Auschwitz	▮	-536	Deut. 33 V24 L28	Deut. 32 V18 L1
זאבה	Zuaba	◖	-1	Deut. 31 V28 L39	Deut. 31 V28 L36

For Figure 37 the ELS reference is 134 characters between rows. There are 4 displayed terms in the matrix. The matrix starts at Deuteronomy 31 V26 L25 and ends at Deuteronomy 33 V24 L35. The matrix spans 3763 characters of the surface text. The matrix has 29 rows, is 11 columns wide and contains a total of 319 characters.

You can't be a light unto the nations if you don't live up to Biblically-prescribed laws of general morality. Israel, we must do much better than this.

One last thought in reference to a figure found on page 91 of the Katz book. Part of that matrix is shown in Figure 37 above. The phrase "Crematorium for my sons" (כבשנ לבני) begins one letter below the first letter of מצד ארונ ברית that can be translated as *Fortress of the Ark of the Covenant*. The four letters directly under and all touching the four letters of ברית *(Covenant)* are (at skip −1) זאבה *(Zuaba at my original spelling)*. *Fortress of the Ark of the Covenant, Zuaba,* and *Crematorium for my sons* all fit into a 99-letter matrix. If we include Auschwitz (אושביצ), the matrix is 330 letters.

Should I encounter the Creator in the *Zuaba/Zuqba* area, one of my first questions would be, "why He allowed the Holocaust to proceed? Indeed, why did He write it into His blueprint for our world?"

Chapter 16

THE JERUSALEM POST

Press is vital to my research. This isn't because I've got an ego. It's because Press generates interest that in turn generates funding that's essential to mounting a successful operation. Successful, by the way, does not necessarily imply recovery of the Ark. It merely implies here that the search conducted was thorough enough to draw a valid conclusion about the hypothesis that the coordinates of the Ark could be deciphered through the Code.

On May 20th, Elli Wohlgelernter of the Jerusalem Post published his article entitled *All that was, is and will be is in the Torah*. It was (with pictures) a full page spread, in which one-third was devoted to my experiment.

My *spin* on the article is that it probably did two things. It seemed to establish me as one of the few serious scientists other than Dr. Haralick present at the Congress, while portraying most of the rest of the field present as subservient to the demands of Rabbi Silman and Jewish law (*Halacha*). Again, his permission had to be obtained before I was permitted to speak under the somewhat insulting title of *Controversy: Use and Misuse of Codes, The Roffman Paper, Ark of the Covenant*.

Frankly, the Catholic Church had once attacked Galileo, Darwin, and other scientists on religious grounds, though under John Paul II it retreated from all these attacks. Today the Church allows its members to believe in Divinely inspired evolution. I'd like to see the ITCS adapt a similar willingness to accept hard evidence for what it is. While my research is something that would naturally be of interest to religion, religion has absolutely no right to interfere in the experimental process. The relevant portion of the Post article follows:

THAT THE members of this believing society are just as critical of suppositions as any of their opponents was made clear following the presentation of one startling paper on the Ark of the Covenant.

The Ark was a wooden chest that held the Tablets Moses received from God 3,311 years ago tomorrow, and was the most sacred ritual possession of the Jewish nation. It was last seen in Solomon's Temple, and tradition says it may have been hidden in Jerusalem by Jeremiah or could have been taken to Babylon after the First Temple was destroyed.

But according to Barry Roffman, who worked for the US Coast Guard for 23 years as a disaster-response planner, a search of the Torah via ELS has revealed to him the longitude/latitude coordinates of the Ark's final resting place: 31 degrees 16 minutes north, 33 degrees four minutes east, which places it in the Mediterranean 4.6 km. north of the Egyptian coast.

For Roffman, who is seeking permission from Egypt to dive and explore off the coast next week, his search could definitively prove the existence of the codes.

"If the Ark is where the code indicates, if I can pick a spot on the bottom of the ocean floor against all the rabbinical opinions, and dig up the Ark from the ocean floor based on Torah codes, I think we have a legitimate code," Roffman said.

The rabbis have always said everything's in the Torah. It's one thing to say it, another thing to prove it – and actually have physical evidence. That's what I'm attempting to do, get physical evidence."

As convincing as Roffman sounded in his 40-minute presentation, the members of the Torah Codes society would have none of it, denouncing in no uncertain terms the methodology of Roffman's research, as well as his conclusions.

"His paper is different in the following way," said Dr. Haralick, general chairman of the congress and professor of electrical engineering, specializing in the area of artificial intelligence known as pattern recognition at the University of Washington.

"He started from the premise that if ELSes can be found which are close together, that implies there's some kind of logical relationship in reality.

"All the other Torah code experiments start with some kind of certain logical relation that we know of in reality, and then you look to see if you have the ELSes. So going one way is not the same as going the other way.

Moreover, Haralick said, such a search is prohibited on the basis of Jewish law because it starts to use the Torah like a crystal ball.

"When you start out from a certain position of what you know and then look, this seems to be something that is permitted in Halacha (Jewish law)," he said. "Going from a place where you're not certain and looking, this is beginning to go almost like a prediction, and so the rabbis say it's not permitted."

IT MIGHT seem strange – even downright contradictory – for noted scientists to be surrendering to rabbinic rulings as guidelines in their scientific work. But for these men the worlds of science and religion are at once disconnected and fused.

"This is basically an observant group of people, and so they will have to stand by how the rabbis say one must use the Torah code to explore [Torah], " said Haralick. "If it was done in an academic setting, it couldn't be done with religious criteria: but what we heard this afternoon is that the Torah Codes Society wants to keep itself entirely within Halacha, so its scientific investigation must be done in accordance with Halacha."

"At the same time," Haralick said, "experiments performed by the members can only be done using the same criteria as all other scientific probes. The mathematics stand in their domain, and the experimental protocol, and the a priori nature, and all that – stands in its own domain. It's just the nature of the investigation [that is restricted]."

"In the end, you cannot use Torah to try to ascertain that which you do not know, or to prove anything which you do not already know, whether it be a prediction in the future or whether it will be something uncertain now."

These men of science know that a lot more work is needed, but they are unfazed either by that or by the criticism thrown their way. Interestingly enough, no opponents of the codes presented any papers at the congress, though they had been invited to do so.

With respect to the lack of Torah Codes opponents, Professor Brendan McKay would (a year later) write me that:

> *...the attitude of the ITCS to criticism was adequately displayed last time I was in Israel. They (through Katz) made a serious effort to prevent me speaking in public, by leaning on the director of the institute that had invited me. To the director's credit, he did not cave into the pressure. The real reason I got a formal invitation this time was because last time they made a big deal about us not going despite being invited, but ended with egg on their faces because in fact we had not been invited.*

> *Brendan.*

So it appears that Dr. Haralick (the ITCS Director) had stood up for Dr. McKay just as he'd stood up for me. In doing so he once again proved to be fit to lead a serious study group. My fear, however, is that his *troops* in the ITCS are not so willing to follow his able direction. As for the Post article, there's something positive about rejection that's plainly stated in the press to be based on unscientific grounds. These *men of science* couldn't fault my math. Indeed, Rips liked my math, just not my opinion about where the Ark was hidden.

I didn't go to the Middle East to win approval of the rabbis or a scholarship to a yeshiva (rabbinical college). I went there as part of a scientific experiment. Besides, if the Code *is* real, then its Creator went to a great deal of trouble to produce it. If it's meant to bring humanity closer to Him, or to prevent wars and suffering, then it would seem to me that we're duty bound to decipher it.

With respect to the issue of fortune-telling, if Drosnin has remembered his first encounter with Rips correctly, the professor began to prove the Code's reality by showing him the controversial plot that correctly predicted the date (January 18, 1991) of the first Scud attack fired by Iraq against Israel. Rips conceded this to me at the conference, but spoke of many bitter lessons learned since then.

There is also a question about who first correctly predicted the death of an Israeli police officer named Toledano. Drosnin claims this honor for himself in *THE BIBLE CODE* (pages 112-113); but so does Dr. Katz - the very man who argued before Rabbi Silman against my use of Torah Codes for similar purposes – finding out about the unknown. The Katz claim can be found on page 158 of his *COMPUTORAH* book.

Michael Drosnin says, "I was flying to Tel Aviv in 1992 when the stewardess handed me the Jerusalem Post. On the front page was a banner headline, '*Border*

Policeman Kidnapped.' I immediately ran his name, *'Toledano,'* on the search program in my lap top computer…. *'Captivity of Toledano'* stated the full sequence. The code also said, *'He will die.'"*

Dr. Katz, likewise, claims that, "I happened to be at my computer when I heard on the radio of Toledano's abduction in Lod. While listening to the report, I immediately entered his name into my computer with the hope of revealing any related information. After a few seconds the words *To the Captivity of Toledano* appeared on the screen… Attached to his name was *"He will die!"'*

If Dr. Rips did learn some bitter lessons in the first few years of his research, so did Galileo. The Church apologized for their treatment of him, but it took 350 years to do so. If the Code *is* real, how many lives can it save in the next 350 years? How dare Rabbi Silman impose his narrow-minded views on the work of science! As I reminded Dr. Rips at the Congress, "You lost your right (in this field of research) to be led by religious doctrine the moment you published your paper in *Statistical Science*, a scientific publication. When you try to prove anything scientifically, your Bible becomes only the Scientific Method. I stand by my experiment as one possible acid test of the Code's worth."

Chapter 17

SURVEY IN EGYPT

I had first been to the Egyptian Embassy in Tel Aviv on May 13, 1999. Amim Mohsen and Yasser Abed had assured me that it would take them six or seven days to get a response from Cairo. Amim also promised to call me frequently with questions about my report.

There were no calls from him, despite my unsuccessful efforts to get through many times, until May 23rd. Concerned by the difficulty of the trip on my family and by the mounting costs ($16,000 without even counting two months of lost wages), I left word at the Embassy that I would depart for Egypt the next day.

Amin finally returned my call. He informed me that he had read my report and forwarded a recommendation for government support to Cairo. He hadn't yet received a reply, but would get back to me later in the day with further information. This didn't happen.

The bus leaves for Egypt from the street that houses the Egyptian Embassy. I stopped by the next morning before our departure to see if Amin or Yasser were in yet. They weren't, so I left a Cairo contact phone number with one of the workers there. The man had on a grin that left me with an impression that the last thing on his mind was to be cooperative. I wondered whether or not this was the operator who was always so curt when I tried to get through. If so, his English vocabulary seemed to be limited to the simple phrase, "Call tomorrow at 9 AM," a demand that always translated into another $200 in waiting expenses.

My wife has more courage than I. She had the guts to ask our Egyptian bus driver to stop smoking. I don't think my son was bothered as much by the smoke as he was by all the men who kissed him. David's a cute kid and he quickly learned this is how Arab men show their appreciation of children (and each other).

You know you've arrived at the Egyptian border when the following events occur:

(1) Arab adults and children are fighting over who gets to carry your luggage into the customs building (thus earning a large tip by Egyptian standards);
(2) Perspiration starts to not just roll, but pour down your legs;
(3) The flies are all over you;
(4) The toilets in public areas generally have no seats (or toilet paper), and
(5) You are waiting for unexplained reasons and periods of time for your bus to start rolling.

After paying the exit tax on the Israeli side of the border at Rafiah, we proceeded to drive a few hundred feet to the Egyptian checkpoint. It's easy to fly into Cairo; but this border checkpoint seems deliberately designed to be as slow and uncomfortable as possible. Surely Egypt can afford to air condition a building. That it doesn't do so here sends a distinct message that visitors are not encouraged to arrive in this fashion, which mandates so much surface security.

There are supposed to be just two buses to get to Cairo. However, we found out there are more, because you have to wait for other buses to finish loading before your bus can depart the two-plus-hour waiting area. Our driver lacked the English skills to explain the reason for our delay, but it became manifestly obvious that buses from the Israeli border to Cairo still can only proceed in a convoy with border police/military stationed both at the front and at the rear of the convoy. That's because a similar busload of passengers was slaughtered by terrorists at the Suez Canal crossing a number of years back.

The last time my wife and I took this twelve-hour bus ride was on a round-the-world trip in August, 1990. We were going from Cairo to Tel Aviv when the bus suddenly stopped just past the Cairo airport. Army men sporting machine guns surrounded us as we sat there for 45 minutes without explanation. The air conditioning broke down in the summer heat while the driver pumped tobacco smoke into the stifling air. Finally we were permitted to go and told that the guards were there for our protection as Iraq had just invaded Kuwait that day.

The military escorts each led and followed us for approximately 20-mile intervals. Then a new group of guards took over for the next segment of the trip. There must be well in excess of a hundred men required to get the buses safely between the border and Cairo, and there are many roadblocks and barricades to get by along the way.

We had a fleeting glimpse of Lake Bardawil. With respect to the suspected Ark sites, the nearest good-sized town was Bir-El-Abd. The bus stopped a few miles past it, and I stepped off to chat with tourist police and military personnel about the possibility of chartering a boat around there to proceed to the suspect area. "Impossible," I was told. There were many signs along the sandstorm-swept highway that warned, "Foreigners not permitted to leave the road." This may have been for security reasons, but looking around at the huge dunes, it was also apparent that only the natives had the survival skills (and camels) necessary to successfully navigate the sands. "You must get permission from the military in Cairo to go to your destination," I was informed. Later we learned that the area still had some landmines left over from previous wars with Israel. These are all rational explanations for the prohibition; but today, I still wonder about the strange UFO and ruins photos I was shown that were allegedly taken in the area.

Entering Cairo, we passed fortress after fortress along the main highway. Each had numerous guard towers facing the road – all manned with soldiers with rifles raised and ready. This was a city poised for war or revolution at any moment. At the entrance to our hotel and restaurants nearby there were metal detectors with more tourist police to guarantee our security. Egypt was apparently still reeling from the terrorist slaughter of 58 tourists and 4 Egyptians at Luxor on November 17, 1997. From my Cairo Sheraton hotel room I could see men with bullet proof jackets standing behind metal barricades with machine guns at the ready. If the goal of the fundamentalists had been to turn Egypt into a nervous, armed camp, they'd clearly succeeded.

By Thursday May 27th in Cairo, I was beginning to ask myself, *Do I stop for now or go on*? The bills were really mounting; but the desire to finish the site survey still dominated my actions. I almost threw in the towel the night before. It was quite frustrating when I'd repeatedly call information to get the phone number of the Egyptian Navy only to be told by the operator that Egypt has no Navy (or Coast Guard)! This, I am certain, would be of great interest to the editors of *JANE'S FIGHTING SHIPS* who indicate that Egypt had quite a few destroyers and submarines (in addition to a Coast Guard). The language barrier was more of a problem than I had envisioned. We also got some initial dirty looks when I asked a hotel worker to heat up some kosher food with Hebrew lettering on the package.

We wanted to take a bus straight to Tel Aviv that day, then thought we could sail directly from Egypt to Europe on an Adriatica line ferry. The ferry idea sounded especially inviting when we were told that it would sail from Port Said, about 30 miles west of the suspect region. The idea was that I could perhaps arrange for a quick site survey before sailing for home.

In Egypt, I learned to be skeptical when told that someone can do something for you in five minutes; and be careful about believing anyone who tells you about things they only think are true. The ferry didn't start sailing from Egypt to points north until July 2nd.

I bought our Tel Aviv bus tickets that morning and had a few hours to kill before our 3:30 PM departure. Was there a good library in town that could provide better maps or charts of the area than I had so far?

I hired a taxi driver. His first two stops were a waste of time and money (conventional bookstores, not libraries). But after my second rejection he finally caught on when I stressed the chart I had. We were quickly off to a government chart office where the scene was truly reminiscent of an Indiana Jones movie. I had to temporarily surrender my passport to get into the place. Old, musty, dusty, and poorly lit, the rooms were filled with ancient charts and scribe-like workers.

To my delight, the worker pulled two (then) 64 year old, vintage 1935 charts that exquisitely covered the area from El Arish to what I though was *El Zuaba*. But not so pleasant, however, was that the prime chart (Map 3 shown earlier) spelled the area of concern as *El Zuqba* substituting a letter *"Q"* for the *"A"* sought throughout my experiment until that moment. There was a Bir El *Zuabatiya* 20 nautical miles away at 31° North, 33° 25' East so initially I had hope that there was just a spelling mistake present on the 1935 Cairo map.

It quickly became apparent that the *Bir El Qals* area would move up a notch as the suspect site for *Baal Zephon*. This is when I first learned of the fortress of Katib el Qals. There was also (in 1935) a 60 meter mount (Mons Casius) on the coast within about 200 meters of what was then a 31° 13' North, 33° 4' East suspect coordinate.

At 31° 9' North, 33° 4' East, the original entry latitude for the experiment, the site on the Zuaba (Zuqba) peninsula was seen to be only about 110 meters from a large body of water measuring approximately 1,100 meters by 100 to 200 meters in 1935. There were two much larger bodies of water on the peninsula within 400 to 600 meters of the first lake. The latter two salt marshes were marked as fordable. The northern of these two marshes is *Mallahet Ugret Selima*. Two years later, it would become the focus of my ELS Map Figures 5 and 6. The southern marsh is *Mallehet El Mapia*. No significant ELS maps were produced in conjunction with that name, and it appears that all these marshes or lakes may, at times, become connected and at other times may dry up completely. I have seen aerial photographs of *Mallehet El Mapia* that are suggestive of commercial salt extraction. As there was realistically no way to obtain the Qatia chart without having gone to Cairo, the long bus rides were well worthwhile.

There were two buses to Tel Aviv that day. We had already missed the first departure àt 5:30 AM. The second one left at 3:30 PM with an arrival time of 2 AM or later. The thought of arriving in Israel at that time with nine remaining pieces of luggage (I had thrown out my printer) and a sleeping six-year old on my shoulder wasn't a cheery one, especially because we had no hotel reservation. *Could we stop for the night in El Arish some thirty miles east of the suspect area?* The answer was yes, then no, then yes again just before the bus arrived in El Arish. The Egoth Oberoi hotel there was pleasantly located on the beach, and the trip took just five hours from Cairo. All this meant that I would mount one last personal drive to get to the sites or to learn from the military or government what they knew about them.

On Friday morning, May 28th, I explained my need to meet with Egyptian military personnel to the hotel manager, Ragab Abd El Karim. He told me everything was closed for the Muslim Sabbath, but promised to call the military for me on Sunday. I then agreed to stay a few days to give their military a chance to check me (and hopefully my coordinates) out.

If you've got to be stuck somewhere for a few days, El Arish is a wonderfully idyllic place to be. Our room was located directly on a beautiful beach. We enjoyed the gentle song of waves rolling in at night, while not missing at all the maddening blast of millions of fancy car horns that dominated the polluted Cairo air night and day. El Arish probably is (if you're not kosher) a nice place to retire. The people are friendly (even if the mosquitoes aren't) and the guns of Cairo were not as apparent there.

The hotel was almost entirely empty, but the one American that I did meet (Richard Ainsworth) had GPS equipment in his room to help him navigate the desert sands while not working at his job in Cairo. He was most helpful.

I was curious to see how his equipment matched up the prime suspect coordinates with more accurate Temple Mount coordinates that I'd received while in Jerusalem. After working through the need to convert the equipment's magnetic bearings to the True headings required, it became obvious that there was a problem with the course headings given on what was then the only map figure presented in my Experimental Report.

A marine equipment store in Florida had previously quoted the course from Jerusalem to the obstruction at 31° 16' North, 33° 3.5' East as being 261° True with a one-degree margin of error. The heading based on the positioning of the first letter of Jerusalem and the first letter of Bardawil was 260.3° (with Bardawil rather than ark of the covenant as the axis term). But according to the GPS equipment used by Ainsworth, the course from Temple Mount in Jerusalem to the coordinates of the obstruction in question was 255° True. That was is a 5.3 degree error if Ainsworth's equipment worked correctly. Further, because the obstruction was a few miles north of Bardawil, the error was even greater.

The course from the Temple Mount position to the 31° 9' North, 33° 4' East coordinates was, as stated throughout Chapter One, about 251.9° (with some small, but unknown error). I would not be able to come up with a correct ELS Map Figure 1 until four months after my return to the USA in 1999. Only then did I realize that with the צקב (*tsadeh kof bet*) spelling of Zuqba, the extension of the Figure 1 series of matrices *was* an accurate map from Jerusalem to Zuqba. It took nearly three additional years to realize that ELS Map 1 indicated a bearing of 251.565° from the *Temple Mount* to the *Ark of the Covenant,* and that this course was repeated on ELS Maps 2, 3, 4, and 5 from Jerusalem to the area of concern.

After morning prayers on Saturday May 29th, I found a previously unseen Hebrew map of Egypt (see Map 9). This new map indicated that the map located in Cairo was no fluke with respect to spellings. Where I hoped to find *Zuaba* spelled זאבה (*zayin alef bet hey),* there was *Zuqba* spelled (זקבה) *zayin kof bet hey,* though as mentioned before, transliterations of names often vary widely. There are two letters in Hebrew that may render a Z sound, the zayin (ז) shown on Map 9, and a tsadeh (צ) used on the ELS Map Figure 1.

Nobody in the area was familiar with *Zuqba* or *Zuaba*. They erroneously told me the patch of desert in question was *Zaraniq*. Although Zaraniq has ancient ruins (see Map 2), it and Lake Zaraniq are about 20 miles east of the entry coordinates for the Ark search. It's a bird sanctuary popular with nature lovers.

The discovery that 31° 9' North, 33° 4' East was probably Zuqba, not Zuaba, knocked some of the wind out of my sails at a critical time. It seemed to undo the Zuaba-related significance of Figures 16 (Ark Position @ skip 2,698), 17A (the Coordinate Plot), 32B (the Roswell UFO Plot), 37 (the Crematorium Plot) and other matrices not shown in this book for the sake of brevity. These figures formed a substantial part of my findings prior to the foray into Egypt.

Map 9 – The Hebrew Map of Northern Sinai

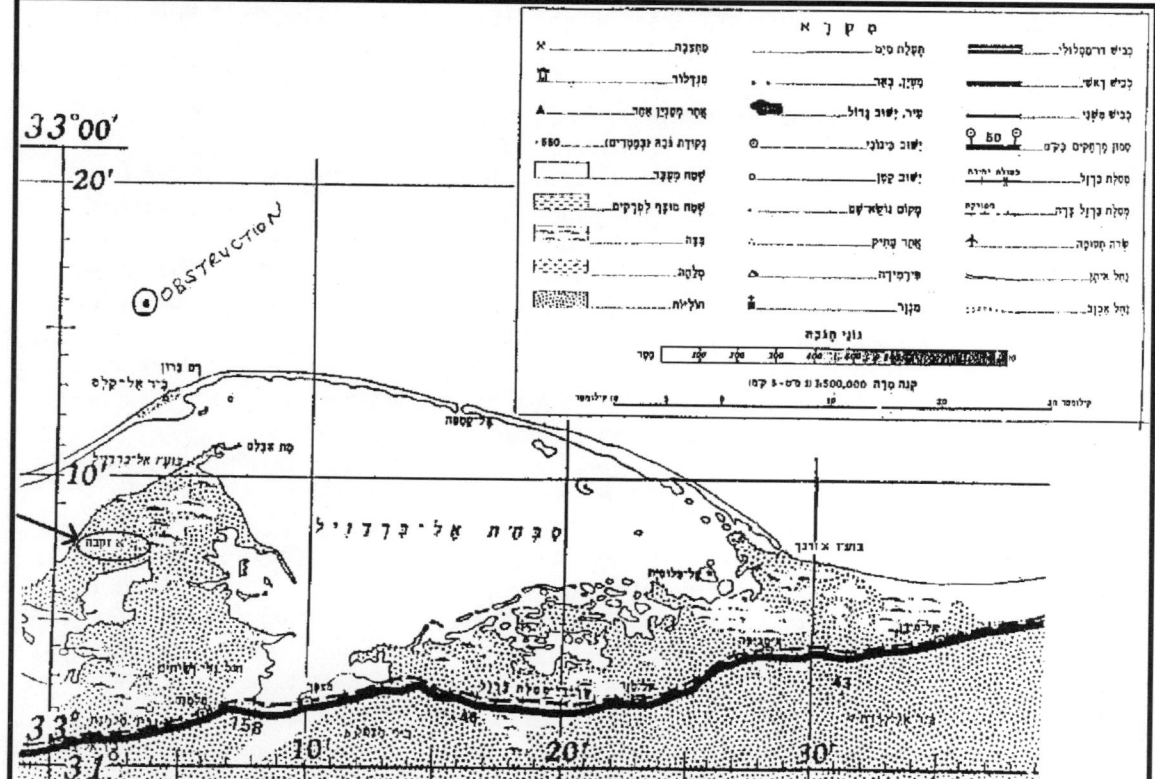

Sunday morning, May 30th, with a good chunk of my best finds temporarily sunk by the *q* in Zuqba, I went to the Northern Sinai Government office. The task was to concentrate on Figure 1I that had a Zuqba transliteration, to focus on Baal Zephon, and the Treasures in the Sand Plot (Figure 18). I also had to show them why it was in their interest to either cooperate with me or to check out the site on their own.

I almost didn't get into the building because I forgot to carry my passport, but my U.S. military reserve ID card did the trick. After four hours of meetings with Mahmoud Ayyad Alatrash, Gammal Mohammed, and Khalid Hassan, I left with the clear impression they would see to it that the prime site would be checked by the Egyptian military.

Mahmoud and Gammal both spoke good English and repeatedly stated their fascination with what they saw of my materials. They made copies of the news articles and asked good questions. Gammal told me he was a geologist and he stated his belief that something supernatural was afoot at Bir El Qals. His reasoning was that the barrier island was surrounded on both sides by salt water (the

Mediterranean and Lake Bardawil), but as the name implied, it was a *Well of Sweet Water*. He knew that saltwater intrusion should have ruined the taste, but this hadn't happened. "As a geologist, I'm unable to explain it," he marveled. What he told me was matched in the Codes as indicated on Figure 38.

Crossing Katib El Qals is the phrase *He threw it into the water and the water became sweet* (וישלך אל המים וימתקו המים). This is the only time in the Torah that sweet water is mentioned. Further, *Katib El Qals* is directly above Ark of the Covenant's non-wrapped occurrence at Numbers 10:33. This corresponds to a course of 180 degrees from the fort to 31° 9' North, 33° 4' East. It matches what's seen on a map, thus it can be considered an ELS map figure. Indeed, this same exact encoding of Katib El Qals has already been labeled as ELS Map Figure 7 in Chapter One, but there the row split function was enabled to show Jerusalem. In Figure 38 this function is disabled.

**Figure 38
Sweet Water at Katib El Qals**

Terms	Translation	Symbol	Skip	Start	End
קתב אל כלש	Katib El Qals	◯	-10560	Leviticus 9 V17 L3	Exodus 2 V15 L23
ארון ברית	Ark of the Covenant	▢	1	Numbers 10 V33 L25	Numbers 10 V33 L32
וישלך אל-המים וימתקו המים	He threw it into the water and the water became sweet	◯	1	Exodus 15 V25 L24	Exodus 15 V25 L44

For Figure 38 the ELS reference is 10560 characters between rows. There are 3 displayed terms in the matrix. The matrix starts at Exodus 2 V15 L19 and ends at Numbers 10 V33 L45. The matrix spans 126741 characters of the surface text. The matrix has 13 rows, is 21 columns wide and contains a total of 273 characters.

Both men confirmed that Bir El Qals has the Katib El Qals military fortress. As there are only camel trails leading to the area, it wasn't too surprising when they informed me that Egyptian helicopters operated from the site. This was particularly interesting to me because of the aircraft explosion encoded with the Ark site (shown earlier on Figure 19). We then discussed the importance of *not* loading the Ark onto an aircraft if it is found at the site.

My emphasis then was on the obstruction 2.9 nautical miles north of Katib El Qals. Mahmoud and Gammal both appeared afraid to personally go near the site for a swim or "fishing expedition" without direction from Cairo, but both also seemed somewhat ambitious. "Would either of you like to be Prime Minister or President one day?" I asked. "To be a leader sometimes you have to be proactive. I'm putting a lot of opportunity in your hands now," I said as I put the Experimental Report in Mahmoud's hands. "Use it wisely."

After accepting the report (with my warning about the *Zuqba* name problem), the men tried to introduce me to the regional governor. He wasn't in so I was next shown into the Minister of Tourism's office. There Minister Hassan was most interested in the atomic holocaust plots (Figures 24 to 29).

Hassan didn't speak much English. He required an interpreter, but the man summoned had English skills only a shade better than his. "How many people believe in your idea in America?" he wanted to know. I wasn't sure if he wanted a big number to see if I was sane, or because it meant more tourist dollars coming into the area.

"My ideas are just being published now," I told him. Then, to give him the large numbers that he seemed to demand, I added, "But there are many millions of Christian Americans who believe something awesome is about to happen within the next year or so. An Ark find would go a long way towards fulfilling their hopes."

"What is the name of this war that is predicted?" Hassan demanded next.

"World War Three, Nuclear War," I responded after he wouldn't accept the idea that I had no other name for it. He didn't seem to understand the word *nuclear* until a picture of an atomic explosion was drawn for him.

"Islam is a religion of peace!" he declared. "Why should we start a nuclear war?" I explained that Drosnin spoke of Libya starting the war with Syria joining in. "My findings suggested an Israeli retaliation that could involve Egypt. None of my findings, however, mean anything unless you find the Ark. If you can't find it or at least a wall at the site indicated, you can rip up my report and forget about the threat."

"Who else will be in this war?" he asked angrily. "The United States, Lebanon, Hezbollah, who?" He was less than satisfied when told that I had only seen encoding pertinent to Israel, Libya, Syria, Ramallah in the West Bank, and Egypt.

There seemed to also be rage in his response towards those Arabs that might draw Egypt into such a conflict.

"Did the Israelis give you permission to come here?" he wanted to know.

"Why should I ask them for permission? I'm an American citizen. I don't have to ask the Israelis for anything," I replied. It wasn't likely that the Israeli military would listen to me anyway, but they might listen to Rips and he had seen the nuclear plots shown in this book (and another, more sensitive one that might be dangerous to publish). I felt that I could count on him to relay the essential data to Mossad, the Israeli spy network *if* the quality of physical data uncovered in Egypt would be good enough. Without such evidence, there was no sense in alarming them anyway.

"Why didn't you go to our embassy in Washington? Why did you go in Tel Aviv?" the Minister asked suspiciously. I told him that Egypt's embassy in the U.S. was a thousand miles from my home, but that their embassy in Tel Aviv was a five-minute walk from my hotel.

Hassan then tried to stress that the war I warned of was a war between Judaism and Islam. I could have argued the point, but chose to focus on the idea that Allah had provided a way to prevent the war, that it would not, according to the Codes, actually be executed.

While Hassan's final response was that he could not provide any assistance without instructions from Cairo, he dragged out the interview for as long as he could to allow his secretary time to copy every single page of Drosnin's Bible Code book. He also made many enlarged photocopies of my maps and charts, personally labeling each of the suspect coordinates in order of my preference.

"You must get the backing of your State Department or your embassy," he insisted. It took a while to get across the concept that this would probably not be forthcoming without the kind of evidence that only he or his military could obtain with a simple dive at the area in question.

It was apparent that Hassan eventually understood that the Baal Zephon suspect site *did* need to be checked by Egyptian security forces. Finding either a submerged fortress wall, or the gold box that I had told him about could prevent the war.

Before departing from America I had been warned by Douglas Haldane at the Alexandria, Egypt Institute of Underwater Archeology that, "You can't just come to Egypt and expect to work here. It takes six months to get any project approved." The man is obviously correct.

I didn't reach my desired coordinates in 1999. If I were a single man, I would have toughed it out; but I'm a married man and at the time I was saddled with a six-year old son. Decent hotel rooms there cost three to four times what they do in the United States and there is little available to eat that's kosher. I had to resign my teaching job to launch my expedition when the Santaluces High School principal in my school denied my requested two-month leave of absence without pay. I was told by the Palm Beach County School Board that if I called in my intention to return by June 1, 1999, for reinstatement on August 9th of the same year, I would be rehired at my old salary (though with a loss of tenure and job location). Anytime after that,

I was warned that they would cut my salary by $10,000 (language that the CTA *union* had agreed to in contract talks). Having piled up so much credit card debt, there was little choice but to return to America to reclaim my job before running out of room on those cards.

While the above wasn't my first choice, it was the only sane one at the time. "I will hide My Face," God wrote in Deuteronomy 31, the prime latitude chapter. The area indicated by the Code is truly remote with access strictly controlled by Egyptian military forces that usually don't speak English very well (if at all).

The 1999 trip was never intended to be more than presentation of my Report in Jerusalem and a brief site survey. With respect to the survey, much was accomplished. Returning home didn't mean failure, it only meant "to be continued based on a more complete set of data." The Qatia map led to nearly all the ELS map figures. Further, the suspect coordinates had been published widely with the current primary site first printed on page 6A in the *Palm Beach Jewish Journal North* edition on April 7, 1998. All suspect coordinates including 31° 9' North, 33° 4' East were put into the hands of the Egyptian government. Amin Mohsen, Yasser Abed, Mahmoud Ayyad Alatrash, Gammal Mohammed and Khalid Hassan all knew the consequences of failure on the part of their government to investigate the site. I was also debriefed by a major serving as Assistant Naval Attaché at the U. S. Embassy in Tel Aviv upon my arrival there.

Others who read my findings will eventually travel to the site even if it's risky to do so. There will always be treasure hunters and there is surely no greater treasure than the Ark. The Egyptian government, I hope, has been pushed into investigating the sites before others do so for motives very different than mine.

Did I prevent a war on the 1999 trip? Who can say? If the Egyptians did investigate the site and found the Ark or Baal Zephon underwater at 31° 16' North, 33° 3.5' East, they may well have acted to prevent the war in 2000, but opted to keep it their secret.

The Ninth of Av – August 10, 2000

As the Ninth of Av (August 10) approached in 2000, there was great anxiety for Codes buffs. The summit between Yassir Arafat and Ehud Barak failed over the difficult issues of Jerusalem and refugees. On that day religious Jews fasted around the world as they do ever year at that time. But by 5 PM, I didn't mind the hunger. Though the fast still had almost four hours to go in my Florida home, in Israel it was already over. In Israel it was the 10th of Av and there were then six more years of breathing room before another potential Ninth of Av war date would be upon us. Drosnin found a plot that called for *Armageddon Asad Holocaust* (Figure 28). But, Hafez Asad died a few months before the Ninth of Av in 2000 and there was no holocaust. So what do we know now and what don't we know?

It's possible that the Egyptians found the Ark, took the Codes seriously, and then acted to short circuit a joint Syrian-Libyan attack plan. However, I have no evidence or indication that Asad's death was *sponsored* at this time. Nor can I say for certain that the Egyptians have ever even checked my prime suspect sites for the Ark. I had shown them all the suspect locations along the 33° 4' East line including the one at 31° 9' North, but my emphasis was on the underwater obstruction at 31° 16' North.

Although Hafez Asad is dead, we still aren't out of the woods with respect to the Armageddon plot, because another Asad (Bashar) rules Syria in his place. Bashar Adad rejected all attempts at a settlement by the Barak government too. Barak offered him return of the Golan Heights with Israel retaining only the northeastern corner of Lake Kinneret (the Sea of Galilee). Bashar refused to compromise. His demands threatened Israel's fresh water supply and thus its survival. Further, Bashar is probably just as paranoid as his father was when it comes to the personal consequences of making concessions. Cautious Syrian leaders like his father can rule for a very long time. Reckless ones face America and our allies. They can wind up caught like a rat in a hole as was the case with Saddam Hussein.

While Egypt may elect to closely guard the secret of the Ark, it would do well to let the world know what they have found (if anything). Today Egypt is wall to wall guns in tourist areas. Their fear isn't of Israel, but of Islamic extremism. One good thing *can* be said of religious extremists; they at least claim to believe in God. If the Ark is in Egypt at the suggested coordinates, the discovery might lead the Bin Laden types to a new and less threatening understanding of Allah. This would allow everyone to breathe a lot easier.

First Temple depiction.

Chapter 18

LOOKING AHEAD AFTER EGYPT

I didn't know about the fortress of Katib El Qals, or about the aircraft stationed there until I found the Qatia map (Map 3) while in Cairo. When I learned about the aircraft, I rationalized that the warning about an aircraft explosion in Figure 19 pertained to them. As such I felt confident enough about flying again to see a travel agent in Tel Aviv on Wednesday June 2, 1999, to buy tickets for a return home. The trip included an American Airlines, 2-engine jet across the Atlantic and a train back to Florida from New York. What I didn't know while I was buying the plane tickets was that at the same instant a 2-engine American Airlines jet (flight 1040) was suffering a fatal crash in Arkansas. Life is full of interesting, sometimes fortunate and sometimes unfortunate coincidences.

The flight home gave me time to reflect on all that had just transpired. There was a great deal of mathematical and computer talent at the First International Congress of Torah Codes (of the ITCS). It was unfortunate that the group chose to be limited by halacha. The Code can be investigated only in accordance with the unrestricted demands of the scientific method, and the study must be done dispassionately. While the Society certainly possesses men with the talent to participate in such a study, with the notable exception of Dr. Haralick, most aren't inclined to sidestep the rabbinate to do so properly. Their findings, without change in the Society's constitution, can never fully validate the Code. A mixed-faith investigative body (that includes atheists) would be more appropriate for an unbiased study.

If you're wondering why an atheist might be interested in the Codes, it's because investigation of the Codes is really a two-phase process. Phase One, the phase we're all still involved with in investigative circles, is to determine *if* the Code really exists at all. As has been made clear throughout this book, it is conceivable that the Code exists, but that its author was *not* God. Phase Two identifies the Author. If we find a star gate, a UFO base, or evidence of time travel in El Zuqba, we shall be inclined to arrive at a non-religious conclusion as the Codes source. But if we find the Ark along with angels; or if its return to Jerusalem (with the consent of Egypt) leads not only to a Third Temple, but to the return of God's Presence there and something like the resurrection of the dead, then we shall reach a religious conclusion.

Who would I recommend to lead or at least fund any future expedition? A university or an organization like National Geographic would be ideal; but if the backer is religious, it should be Christian. Why? While in Cairo we watched the light show at the Sphinx. It spoke of the monument as having seen the rise of Christianity and Islam, but overlooked Judaism. Egyptians still can't bring themselves to even mention the faith. As such, I would encourage a Christian group to finance and lead the next attempt. Their pockets are certainly far deeper than my checking account and they wouldn't be as suspect as a Jewish group coming into Muslim Egypt.

We often learn a lot from our mistakes. Three times during the course of my investigation, I drew apparently inaccurate or dubious conclusions from wrong words chosen to plot. The first time was when I used the verb *coordinate* when I really wanted the noun *coordinate*. The second mistake involved the Zuqba vs. Zuaba problem. The third mistake was made upon my return from Egypt to Tel Aviv.

I wanted to see if *helicopter* was encoded at the Bir El Qals site. I remembered the Hebrew for the word for helicopter was *masok* (מסוק), but couldn't recall its spelling, so I asked the receptionist in my hotel. She didn't understand me so I had to use a combination of words and gestures to indicate what I was talking about. Finally she indicated that she understood and insisted that the desired word was *m'avrer* (מאוורר). To my delight, I found it encoded between Deuteronomy 31:13 and 31:15. If chapter and verse correspond to degrees and minutes of latitude, the fortress is at 31°13' North, and the helicopter would have to fly from there to any of the suspect sites. *M'avrer* touched all kinds of marvelous *a priori* words, but before leaving for the U.S. Embassy on June 1st, I checked the word *m'avrer* with someone who spoke better English. It turned out that my initial memory was more accurate than the understanding of the Romanian immigrant to Israel. *M'avrer* means *ventilator or fan,* and not *helicopter*.

If interesting, even seemingly amazing results can be obtained in this fashion, then the legitimacy of other finds remains suspect.

Who else knew enough about the Codes to present their papers at the conference? Alphabetically, the list of other speakers was follows:

>Nachum Bombach
>Professor Paul Eidelberg
>Harold Gans
>Dr. Robert Haralick
>Dr. Moshe Katz
>Art Levitt
>Professor Ilya (Eliyahu) Rips
>Dr. Alex Rotenberg
>Dr. Leib Schwartzman
>Doron Witztum

In all, eleven of us presented experimental results or papers, and at least six held earned doctorates. Despite their talent, they were still struggling to come up with a common way to evaluate the statistical significance of their finds. I left the conference with no doubt that my method (covered in Appendix A), though crude, was both appropriately conservative enough and at the same time accurate enough to head the list of methods to be used. In fact, after the conference we found that probabilities obtained by the permutation technique (scrambling control texts) employed by Rips and Haralick were indeed in the ballpark with respect to what I was finding via my formula method. The only alteration I would later make would be to downgrade plot values by dividing the value of what had been found by the value of what had *not* been found. This was alluded to with Figure 8 (the Tunguska Asteroid). Dr. Haralick disputed the wisdom of the downgrade, but has yet to come up with a satisfactory alternate. That I did not so degrade all my Ark figures is again reason why I must insist on physical evidence to accept the value of my own findings.

Do I think the Code is real? I went to Egypt looking for the fort of Baal Zephon along the 33° 4' longitude line in the Bir El Qals area, and found Katib El Qals there. It wasn't submerged, but I feel confident that Baal Zephon will be submerged just north of the modern fortress. Today the Egyptians see the logic in having a fortress at the northernmost projection of the Sinai coast. They probably employed similar logic when Baal Zephon (which again means "Master of the North") was built over 3,000 years ago and the coastline was about 2.5 to 3 miles further north than it is today. Alternately, the photos that I have seen of the ark site area itself indicate the presence of a structure at the suspect longitude that might be ruins of Baal Zephon. These are the same images that show something resembling UFOs, but (again) I have reason to doubt the legitimacy of the images and the agent in question wishes to remain anonymous.

The fortress that certainly does exist at Bir El Qals wasn't the only physical evidence encountered on this trip. I expressed fear that there I would be killed in a plane crash or that there would be an aircraft explosion at the Ark coordinates, and I learned that aircraft are in fact stationed in the area at Katib El Qals. I learned that *Bir El Qals* means *Well of Sweet Water*, and found Katib El Qals (which means *Citadel of Sweet Water*) located there encoded and crossed by the Torah's only reference to sweet water in the open text. These are small, but nonetheless tangible bits of physical evidence. The ELS map figures cited in Chapter One also speak volumes that there is at least some form of Ark Code inserted into the text. I have seen too many dramatic *coincidences* and breathtaking finds by other researchers to blow off the Codes. Though the Codes are not yet fully proven to be real to me, sufficient funding and cooperation from the Egyptian government should produce more significant positive results in locating the ark.

It is wise to use the Codes now to predict the future? Not on an individual basis. Authors have been selective in their presentations, I have yet to acquire the quality of physical evidence required to authenticate the Codes, and even if this occurs we will still need careful studies to determine if deliberate encoding extends down to the level of every human conceived. This book is named *ARK CODE* because I believe there is massive Ark-related encoding in the Torah, but my impression is that other than events of world-shaking importance, much more extensive encoding is still questionable. This is because as software improved I began to produce many interesting word pairs *in permuted control (non-religious) texts*.

Rabbi Silman feared my study because he thinks making predictions based on Torah is a violation of Jewish Law. However the thrust of my work is to physically test the significance of the close appearance of terms or phrases. It is in the nature of science that such tests must from time to time involve highly specific, publicly made predictions. Any other approach is fatally flawed because the experimenter can choose to show only the successes.

The Ark, if not melted down for its gold, still exists somewhere in the world *today*. I am attempting to find something here *now*, not in the future. Further, if God went to the trouble of encoding His plan, important information, or warnings in a manner that He knew could be decoded by computer, we *must* assume that He intended for us to do just that.

It's also important to prove the Codes false if they are in fact bogus. People will make wrong life choices if they trust in meaningless data, and they will make incorrect (and possibly dangerous) interpretations of the scriptures if false Codes are not debunked. Since 1998 (due to the Codes) we have spent thousands of extra dollars on vacations, and we've driven many thousands of miles that would normally have been flown. I was fortunate to receive free passage to Spain for the 1999 trip, but could never have afforded the voyage if Royal Caribbean Cruise Lines had not been so generous. Although I will fly to and from the Middle East again if required for my research (and for the military when ordered to do so) it would be nice to go back to the skies without a Codes-based anxiety.

Chapter 19

SHOCKING SURPRISES

After my return to America there were astonishing improvements in software (and computer speed) that allowed me to find in a few seconds what would previously have required months to locate. All of the map plots previously shown were produced on the CodeFinder software developed by Kevin Acres. Many have tried to match his genius for Code software. None have succeeded. However, it was actually an odd error that I encountered while using an earlier version of his product that caused me to first contact him on February 27, 2000.

I found the phrase *Ark in Water* (ארון במים) in a 75-letter matrix with *Bardawil* (ברדויל) at its single skip +1 appearance in the Torah (Figure 39). This plot, which shall be referred to as the *Bardawil Ghost Plot*, is based on a wrapped plot, but that issue is irrelevant. That's because the plot was due to an apparent procedural, computer, or software failure. I was unable to reproduce the plot that is composed of two segments with an ELS of +21,632. Luckily, I preserved the initial findings as a gif file before realizing the matrix was bogus.

Why even mention the plot if it's bogus? At times I have felt that the Torah Codes was something akin to a form of artificial intelligence. As a virus comes alive for reproductive purposes when it enters a host cell, the Code seems to come alive when it enters a computer. Over and over again the Code links Bardawil with the Ark. An ELS Code should be limited to what is encoded at an ELS. But real artificial intelligence might be sentient, or at the least capable of breaking out of an ELS mode. A mistake appeared on my computer screen. It should have been gibberish, but it wasn't. It told me what I *wanted* to see – that the Ark is near Bardawil. As for being in water, orbital photos reveal that the suspect site is sometimes underwater (in the winter).

I contacted Kevin and told him that the string was correct with respect to *Ark in Water* and the next two letters only. But the ghost plot shows the next letter in sequence as *lamed* while a *caf* popped up on the *Torah Codes 1.0* crosschecks. The first letter of disagreement is actually at Deuteronomy 4:6, 6th word, 6th letter. This turned out to be *before* the program makes its second pass through the Torah. The string at skip +21,632 that connects with Bardawil *is* a real string with the letters *lamed ayin mem vav resh*. The last *resh* (of *Bardawil)* is at Exodus 10:15, 19th word, 3rd letter. So what we have are two strings at skip +21,632 that are real. Yet they don't belong together.

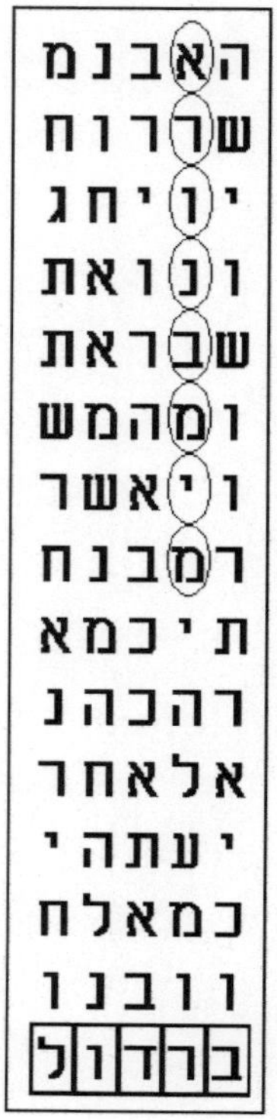

ה א ב נ מ
ש ר ר ו ח
י י ח ג
ו נ ו א ת
ש ב ר א ת
ו מ ה מ ש
ו י א ש ר
ר מ ב נ ח
ת י כ מ א
ר ה כ ה נ
א ל א ח ר
י ע ת ה י
כ מ א ל ח
ו נ ב ו נ
ב ר ד ו ל

Figure 39
The Bardawil Ghost Plot

Terms	Translation	Symbol	Skip	Start	End
ארון במים	Ark in Water	◯	21,632	Genesis 29 V10 L62	Numbers 3 V34 L18
ברדול	Bardawil	☐	1	Exodus 10 V15 L61	Exodus 10 V15 L65

For Figure 39 the ELS reference is 21632 characters between rows. There are 2 displayed terms in the matrix. The matrix starts at Genesis 29 V10 L61 and ends at Exodus 10 V15 L65. The matrix has 15 rows, is 5 columns wide and contains a total of 75 characters.

THIS MATRIX WAS GENERATED BY COMPUTER ERROR.

Kevin made several attempts to explain why the ghost plot appeared, but none of them held water. In the end, on February 29, 2000 he wrote the following:

Barry,

Although not into kabbalah, I have sufficient experience in the 'not-quite-normal' to recognize that the Torah is a power unto itself. There are many people that tried to write a Bible Code program and failed. The fabric of the universe seems to be a little tenuous where the Torah is concerned and that can expose some people to a certain degree of uncomfortable phenomena. What I do know though, is that your ghost plot will have a perfectly sensible and logical answer, even if the reason is difficult to determine. It will most likely be something that you did prior to the search, even if you don't consciously remember doing it, or, of course, it could be a bug that I left in version 1.19.

CodeFinder is up to Version 1.23 now, but there was one minor bug that I discovered in Version 1.21. In searching for *Ugret Selima* I found that the encoding at skip +37,187 showed up again at skip –267,618. The absolute value of these two numbers totals 304,805. This is the number of letters in the Torah. The plot produced resulted in the mirror image of a triangle shown on ELS Map Figure 6 with the letters of Ugret Selima in reverse order. Kevin's advice here was to limit search range to -152,402 to +152,403 to avoid getting what he calls "aliases."

Kevin isn't Jewish, so I felt a bit uneasy about suggesting that he remove the New Testament from his software. Still, on March 1, 2000, I transmitted the following message:

> *Kevin,*
>
> *Certainly English and Greek translations of Tenach or New Testament should be labeled as being there for control purposes. A King James Version of the Bible differs quite radically from a Revised Standard Version. Ancient New Testament fragments and texts like the Sinaticus or Vaticanus manuscripts also differ significantly from the King James Version in content and meaning. Inclusion of New Testament scriptures makes the product somewhat "traif," that is, nonkosher to Jews who have the greatest ability to use the program for research purposes.*
>
> *Barry*

I believed it was impossible for encoding based on Equidistant Letter Spacing to carry over from one language to another. For example, my first name requires five letters in English, but only three in Hebrew. So why alienate the Jewish market that was most able to use Hebrew and thus get something meaningful out of the Torah Codes? I wasn't yet aware that Kevin's new software had a truly superb Hebrew-English dictionary that almost leveled the playing field between those who can read Hebrew and those that can't.

Kevin and I traded a few other e-mails. He had a new and vastly improved version of his software. I had a manuscript that might give him some good ideas too. We decided to do a swap – my manuscript for his new CodeFinder. What Kevin found with his software after he received my manuscript was by far the most unexpected find then in nearly three years of research. On March 17, 2000 I received the following:

> *Barry*
>
> *I checked out a Space Shuttle photograph site and found out that Bardawil is a salt marsh rather than a lake. Although it probably means nothing to you, I enclose an English matrix that has a few interesting terms. These are THE ARK OF THE COVENANT, BARDAWIL, SALT, MARSH and IN THE LAND OF EGYPT. Although not shown in the GIF, three letters above the "A" of COVENANT running diagonally down and to the right is the term, "HO HO HO."*
>
> *Best Regards, Kevin*

Kevin made only one mistake. He assumed that I'd try to discount his *New Testament* find because it implies encoding there too, something that I had previously thought impossible and something that Judaism will be uncomfortable with because the New Testament is *not* part of a Jewish Bible. But as should be clear by now, I put my religion on the shelf with respect to Bible Codes research. My own beliefs and emotions are irrelevant. All that matters is, *What do the facts support?* Other religious people may not approve of such an attitude, but if it turns out that I do find evidence to clearly prove the existence of God, why taint it with bias?

We begin with an examination of Figure 40. This expands up by one row what Kevin originally sent me as the smallest cropped matrix.

Figure 40 – New Testament (KJV) Pairing of Bardawil with the Ark of the Covenant

F	O	O	L	I	S	H	N	E	S	S	O	F	G	O	D	I	S	W	I	S	E
L	F	N	O	T	D	I	S	C	E	R	N	I	N	G	T	H	E	L	O	R	D
I	L	S	T	W	E	A	R	E	A	T	H	O	M	E	I	N	T	H	E	B	O
W	O	R	K	S	O	F	T	H	E	L	A	W	O	R	B	Y	T	H	E	H	E
A	N	C	E	O	F	T	H	E	G	O	S	P	E	L	S	O	T	H	A	T	M
D	R	O	S	E	A	G	A	I	N	E	V	E	N	S	O	T	H	E	M	A	L
R	R	E	P	R	O	O	F	F	O	R	C	O	R	R	E	C	T	I	O	N	F
A	N	D	T	H	E	A	R	K	O	F	T	H	E	C	O	V	E	N	A	N	T
B	L	E	S	U	B	M	I	T	Y	O	U	R	S	E	L	V	E	S	T	H	E

Terms	Skip	Start	End
BARDAWIL	-21829	James 4 V6 L81	1 Corinthians 11 V29 L70
AND THE ARK OF THE COVENANT	1	Hebrews 9 V4 L24	Hebrews 9 V4 L45
PROOF FOR CORRECTION	1	2 Timothy 3 V16 L69	2 Timothy 3 V16 L86
SOFT	1	Galatians 3 V5 L85	Galatians 3 V5 L88
WEAR	1	2 Corinthians 5 V6 L47	2 Corinthians 5 V6 L50
FOOLISHNESS OF GOD	1	1 Corinthians 1 V25 L11	1 Corinthians 1 V25 L26

For Figure 40 the ELS reference is 21829 characters between rows. There are 4 displayed terms in the matrix. The matrix starts at 1 Corinthians 1 V25 L11 and ends at James 4 V7 L19. The matrix spans 174654 characters of the surface text. The matrix has 9 rows, is 22 columns wide and contains a total of 198 characters.

Dr. Haralick stated in an e-mail on March 19, 2000 that,

> *"It is not clear what is a priori and what the experimental protocol was that Kevin used. How many different spellings were tried and so on?*

Kevin's response to Dr. Haralick's concerns on March 23rd included this:

> *Robert,*
>
> *In this instance, having received Barry's manuscript, I put in the two terms BARDAWIL (from both Barry's spelling and from the map) and THE ARK OF THE COVENANT. You can imagine my surprise, then, when the only embedded instance of BARDAWIL crosses next to the only surface text occurrence of THE ARK OF THE COVENANT. By my (basic) maths, I calculate that the odds against both terms occurring in that size of matrix is just over 10,000:1. This is enough to make me sit up and take notice.*
>
> *Another search, subsequent to finding some space shuttle pictures of the area, used the terms SALT and MARSH. These terms do appear in the matrix, with the H of MARSH coinciding with the H of THE in the surface phrase IN THE LAND OF EGYPT.*
>
> *Best Regards, Kevin*

Haralick was most anxious to find some way to shoot down Kevin's findings; but while all the Christological material seen by both of us before was easy to dismiss mathematically, it was evident that Kevin's find was in another league. The New Testament is a much larger document than the Torah. It has (in the King James Version or KJV) 739,167 letters while the Torah has 304,805. I checked for *all* encodings of Bardawil in the Torah and found the five-letter spelling (ברדול) present 11,930 times. With the six-letter spelling (ברדויל) there are another 971 hits. We know there are six uses of the term Ark of the Covenant in the Torah, plus seven encodings of the term. The word *Ark* comes up at skip +1 some 25 times and *the Ark* arises another 21 times in the Torah. But, again, there is only one eight-letter English spelling of *Bardawil* encoded in the New Testament and only one direct mention of the *Ark of the Covenant* there (though the *ark of his testament* is mentioned in Revelations 11:19). Whatever the correct odds are for these terms meeting in the New Testament, they are obviously far more remote than in the Torah.

For the record, I have not spent much time looking for other items in the KJV English Bible. Codes researcher Roy Reinhold has investigated the English texts for codes, and he is of the opinion that the KJV is not a source of much other encoding. The terms *salt*, *marsh* and *Ho Ho Ho* cited by Kevin aren't significant because the matrix must be expanded from 198 letters to 1,440 letters to see them. Having said that, while there doesn't appear to be a general *Bible Code* in the KJV, there does seem to be a very limited *Ark Code*. Our analysis for Figure 40 begins with *Proof for Correction*. The phrase is precisely paired with the beginning of *The Ark of the Covenant* one row below. It clings to *The Ark of the Covenant* until one letter from the end of *The Ark of the Covenant* only because it has one less letter than *The Ark of the Covenant*. Placement of words is probably just as important as presence of words on an encoded plot, so the question must be asked, *"Proof for correction of what?"*

My hope, obviously, is that the Ark will be found in the Bardawil area. Then all that will be corrected will be our understanding of where the Ark wound up and that the Torah is a computer database as well as a spiritual book. The latter idea will *not* be a surprise to studious Orthodox Jews, but it will be for most other people.

Some Christians will hope that Kevin's New Testament find, if validated near Bardawil, will lead the Jews to some sort of acceptance of the Nazarene. Given the Jewish understanding of the term *Messiah*, I'd be shocked if they accepted him in that capacity. However, I do hope that Jews and Christians will ally to find the Ark and help bring on the messianic age. As to whether time will reveal a first time successful messiah as Orthodox Judaism teaches, or a returned messiah that Christianity longs for, let the chips fall where they may.

It's obvious that the closeness of Bardawil and the Ark are to be unexpected. If this and the phrase *Proof for Correction* was all there was, I would understand the wide grins that break out on the faces of my Christian friends when I show them the plot. But there's more of interest here and its implication, if deliberately placed with Bardawil, is not what either Christians or Jews would expect. The phrases *Foolishness of God, Soft + Wear, Proof For Correction* (and *Ho Ho Ho*) all smack of mocking, whether by a human or an alien from the future.

When I attempted to look for similar encoding in the KJV Old Testament, the results were mixed. Neither *Bir El Qals, El Zuqba, nor Katib El Qals* popped up at all. *Bardawil* was there four times, but only once with any interesting material nearby. On Figure 41 we see that the word *fort* touches Bardawil (we are looking for the *fort* of *Baal Zephon* and we know that the fort of *Katib El Qals* is on the northern side of Bardawil). The word *waters* appears twice on the 135-letter matrix and *Bardawil* is a lake (or salt marsh). Running through the letter *B* of *Bardawil* is *Place Blessed*, an appropriate description of the area if it is or surrounds the current resting place of the Ark. *Baal* touches the *W* of *Bardawil*, but there is no *Zephon* or *North* present to complete the name sought, *Baal Zephon* (If *VEPUN* under Baal read *ZEPUN*, it would have been another matter – as in Hebrew the same character is used for *P* and *F*).

Figure 41 – Bardawil in KJV Old Testament

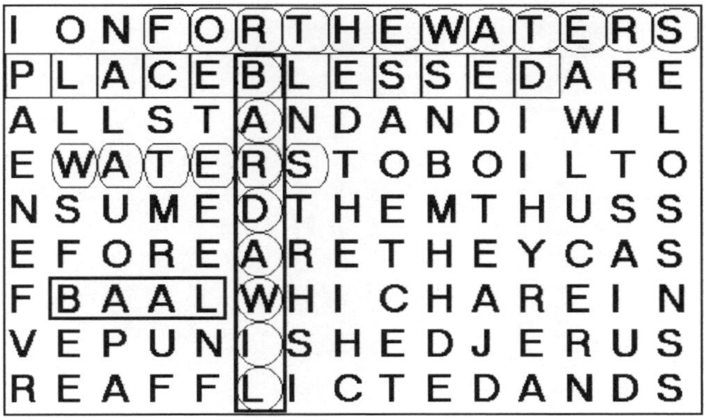

```
I  O N F O R T H E W A T E R S
P  L A C E B L E S S E D A R E
A  L L S T A N D A N D I W I L
E  W A T E R S T O B O I L T O
N  S U M E D T H E M T H U S S
E  F O R E A R E T H E Y C A S
F  B A A L W H I C H A R E I N
V  E P U N I S H E D J E R U S
R  E A F F L I C T E D A N D S
```

Terms	Skip	Start	End
BARDAWIL	36474	Isaiah 32 V20 L1	Lamentations 1 V4 L105
PLACE BLESSED	1	Isaiah 32 V19 L63	Isaiah 32 V20 L7
WATERS	1	Isaiah 64 V2 L45	Isaiah 64 V2 L50
FORT	1	Isaiah 15 V6 L1	Isaiah 15 V6 L4
WATERS	1	Isaiah 15 V6 L7	Isaiah 15 V6 L12
BAAL	1	Jeremiah 32 V35 L28	Jeremiah 32 V35 L31

For Figure 41 the ELS reference is 36474 characters between rows. There are 6 displayed terms in the matrix. The matrix starts at Isaiah 15 V5 L181 and ends at Lamentations 1 V4 L114. The matrix spans 291807 characters of the surface text. The matrix has 9 rows, is 15 columns wide and contains a total of 135 characters.

Figure 42 was by far the best Old Testament KJV find. I wondered whether Ugret Selima would be there. It wasn't at the full spelling, but when I dropped back to Ugret Slma as a 9-letter transliteration - it came up once. The phrase from Daniel 5:3, *Golden vessels that were taken out of the Temple of the House of God which was at Jerusalem* crosses *Ugret Slma* with the word *Temple* at the intersection. The partial phrase *taken out of the Temple* occurs only twice in the Old Testament. As cherubim were on the Ark cover, the phrase, *Gone up from the cherub* that crosses *Ugret Slma* is also of interest. These items are *a posteriori*, but I think they are potentially significant.

Figure 42 – Ugret Selima (UGRET SLMA)
in the KJV Old Testament

```
F I S R A E L W A S G O N E U P F R O M T H E C H E R U B W H E R E
U S S A I T H T H E L O R D G O D W O E T O T H E B L O O D Y C I T
D M E A S U R E D T H E T H R E S H O L D O F T H E G A T E W H I C
T A K E N O U T O F T H E T E M P L E O F T H E H O U S E O F G O D
E T A L L T H E I N H A B I T A N T S O F T H E L A N D T R E M B L
H E C U P O F T H E L O R D S R I G H T H A N D S H A L L B E T U R
N D T H E L O R D G O D C A L L E D U N T O A D A M A N D S A I D U
I S C A M E L S A N D T H E M A N W O N D E R I N G A T H E R H E L
O R E H I S N A M E W A S C A L L E D P H A R E Z A N D A F T E R W
```

Terms	Skip	Start	End
UGRET SLMA	52817	Ezekiel 9 V3 L35	Genesis 38 V29 L134
TAKEN OUT OF THE TEMPLE OF THE HOUSE OF GOD	1	Daniel 5 V3 L40	Daniel 5 V3 L73
UP FROM THE CHERUB	1	Ezekiel 9 V3 L35	Ezekiel 9 V3 L49

For Figure 42 the ELS reference is 52817 characters between rows. There are 3 displayed terms in the matrix. The matrix starts at Ezekiel 9 V3 L21 and ends at Genesis 38 V30 L9. The matrix spans 422570 characters of the surface text. The matrix has 9 rows, is 34 columns wide and contains a total of 306 characters.

When Figure 42 is expanded to 74 columns, the following report applies:

Terms on Figure 42 (expanded)	Skip	Start	End
UGRET SLMA	52817	Ezekiel 9 V3 L35	Genesis 38 V29 L134
GOLDEN VESSELS THAT WERE TAKEN OUT OF THE TEMPLE OF THE HOUSE OF GOD WHICH WAS AT JERUSALEM	1	Daniel 5 V3 L19	Daniel 5 V3 L92
UP FROM THE CHERUB	1	Ezekiel 9 V3 L35	Ezekiel 9 V3 L49

For Figure 42 when expanded the ELS reference is 52817 characters between rows. There are 3 displayed terms in the matrix. The matrix starts at Ezekiel 9 V2 L210 and ends at Genesis 38 V30 L28. The matrix spans 422610 characters of the surface text. The matrix has 9 rows, is 74 columns wide and contains a total of 666 characters.

If I had only seen Kevin's New Testament *Bardawil* find, I would have been tempted to blow off its pairing with *Ark of the Covenant* as a lucky accident. But the *Ugret Slma* pairing with gold taken from the Temple in Jerusalem raises an interesting possibility – that of ongoing manipulation of scriptural texts to ensure that the Ark will be found when the technology to do so is ready (i.e. in our age). This possibility has broader implications with respect to the accuracy of the Torah text itself.

Code critics argue that the Torah has been altered over time, and that such alterations would naturally destroy any ELS Code. Their point is well taken if the introduction of the Code was a onetime event – when God (or some other author) presented Moses with the Torah. But if the Code was given as a strand of 304,805 letters to Moses by God, angels, a human from the future, or aliens, what is to prevent any of these agents from returning from time to time to correct the text when it was distorted?

Initially, I believed that under the above scenario, alterations to the text could even have been deliberately introduced into the Torah *after* the Ark was hidden and the position was known. If that were the case, latitude could be calculated at an early date, but knowledge of the location of the prime meridian would still be needed and that wasn't set until 1884 CE. The King James Version could also have been written in 1611 CE to ensure an overlap in position-related data there and in the Torah. While I'm uncomfortable suggesting alterations to Torah, according to the Talmud (Shabbos 115b-116a), verses found at Numbers 10:35 to 10:36 constitute a separate (out of place) book of Torah. The verses are offset in an actual Torah with an inverted letter *nun* (‫נ‬) before and after the section in question. I have heard that there is some belief the section will be moved when the Messiah arrives.

There is still much more to the issue of alteration of Scriptures by the issuing Authority. Recall that Dr. Moshe Katz told me, "We can only accept papers based on Torah Codes, and your paper adds the concept of chapters and verses rather than limiting its scope to just the 304,805 letters of the Torah." My first response was to spit back his own COMPUTORAH book words, "Moses was like a scribe, copying what he had seen onto parchment, while God's voice taught him the spacing of words, *verses,* and paragraphs…" But what if the agent of encoding was also an agent of maintenance and repair of various scriptures, Torah and otherwise throughout the ages? Would that same agent not also have the power and/or ability to supervise the division of Torah into chapters and verses? What is difficult to prove, is that encoding has occurred. Once this is shown, other lesser modifications and spelling corrections would not only be easier to accept, but might actually be expected.

After further research, especially into the career of the prophet Jeremiah, I've come to believe that God's original plan was to have him take the Ark to the site of His most obvious (witnessed) miracle, splitting the sea. If this turns out to be the case, then the coordinates could easily have been accurately encoded without need for alteration when the Torah was given. All that would be necessary would be foreknowledge of the coordinate system as established in 1884 CE.

So who wrote the Code if it's real? It would surprise me if aliens would deliberately encode a bit of humor like Kevin's *Ho Ho Ho* find. Alleged alien encounters documented by Budd Hopkins (*Witnessed, Intruders,* and *Missing Time*) focus on genetic experiments aimed at producing a hybrid human/alien race. But there are hints of humor from time to time in some of these incidents (occasionally intended; at other times due to slip-ups like returning abductees to the wrong cars or beds, or with incorrect clothes put back on when multiple abductions supposedly occurred).

A human from the future might also be a source of mocking humor. In July of 2000, an article appeared in the journal *Nature* in which it was claimed that scientists at the NEC Research Institute at Princeton had sent a brief pulse of laser light 310 times faster than normal light speed. They were still arguing about sending a *signal* faster than light. Part of the problem seems to be with the definition of the term *signal*. Though Gunter Nimtz had sent Mozart's symphony faster than light, to be a signal one must get around the issues of causality and smoothly varying functions. An article (*Superluminal Motion: Fact or Fiction?*) by Ryan Frewin, Renee George, and Deborah Paulson states, "If a wave packet's shape upon incidence is smooth and well-defined, it is a straightforward calculation to determine its shape after transmission. Because the final shape can be mathematically determined, the causality principle does not restrict the travel speed of the packet. Basically, since no useful information is being transmitted, it would not be possible to use the wave packet as a signal to shut off the original signal. Because of this, most scientists would not consider a smoothly varying function to be a signal." I believe, however, that this line of reasoning leaves out the possibility that a signal that travels into the past will reach a different universe. Ask Gunter Nimtz about whether or not Mozart's symphony was useful information, and he will argue that it is. The question then, it seems, is which (of an infinite number of parallel universes) will receive such information in the past?

I think it will be eventually proven feasible to send a signal into the past. But could the entire Torah have been transmitted in such fashion? It was stated earlier that (at least) the Torah Code seems to anticipate questions and to get down to a very personal level. Given this observation, if it can be validated through something like an Ark find, it seems most reasonable to conclude that the Code is someone's successful effort to produce an artificial intelligence (complete with sense of humor) or that it is the work of God Himself. The first of these possibilities in no way precludes the second. The focus of an enormous amount of encoding appears to be the whereabouts of a religious artifact that is so meaningful to the world's great monotheistic faiths. As such it would seem almost certain that if we find the Ark through the Codes, we shall at the same time find God.

APPENDIX A

Appendix A

THE ARK OF THE COVENANT IN THE TORAH CODES, EXPERIMENTAL REPORT EXTRACT AND UPDATE

METHODS PRESENTED BY BARRY STEVEN ROFFMAN TO THE FIRST INTERNATIONAL CONGRESS OF TORAH CODES, JERUSALEM, MAY 10, 1999

PURPOSE: To determine if the so called *Torah Code* contains useful, empirically testable data or whether the phenomenon is merely due to the chance pairing of letter combinations.

HYPOTHESIS: Based on the 1994 Witztum, Rips, Rosenberg study published in Statistical Sciences (showing 66 specific rabbis predicted in Torah), it is hypothesized that the Torah Code would contain the specific location of that which was most central to the worship of God during the existence of the Temple in Jerusalem: the Ark of the Covenant. Recovery of the actual physical Ark (believed to have disappeared between 925 and 586 BCE) would be sufficient to prove the computer-compatible encoding of the Torah if the Torah Codes computer software (and area charts) are the sole sources of data used to find it.
NOTE: It is implicit in this experiment that there are two tests to be met to support the hypothesis: (1) Statistically significant data collection worthy of actual field investigation, and (2) Recovery of the Ark by means of actual expedition should the first test be met. The hypothesis is to be rejected unless both conditions are met.

MATERIALS: Torah Codes 1.0 (Torah codes Software, Inc.) was used initially. After two years there was a switch to infinitely more powerful CodeFinder 1.21 software developed by Kevin Acres. BA Chart 56100, several Biblical atlases and other maps were also employed.

OBSERVATIONS: Short words (up to four letters) can be found almost wherever one desires to find them. Multiple related short words have to appear relatively close to the plot *conditional axis words* sought (usually Ark of the Covenant) to be of any value. The larger a *matrix* (that is, plot area of given number of columns and rows), the larger the number of intervals that can theoretically yield a hit when searching for a key word. An example of how to calculate the number of possible intervals for a matrix follows:

Determine the number of possible intervals that could yield a four-letter word if the plot matrix contains eleven columns and eight rows. First, let's examine the plot area in terms of boxes with a box for each letter in the plot:

FIGURE 1-A

```
COLUMN->  1   2   3   4   5   6   7   8   9  10  11
ROW
  1   | | | | | | | | | | | |
  2   | | | | | | | | | | | |
  3   | | | | | | | | | | | |
  4   | | | | | | | | | | | |
  5   | | | | | | | | | | | |
  6   | | | | | | | | | | | |
  7   | | | | | | | | | | | |
  8   | | | | | | | | | | | |
```

Since Hebrew is read right to left, let's spell out the English 4-letter word *four* from right to left on the first row. We will only show the first row for the next few plots. If a skip (interval) of 1 is used, then the plot looks like this:

FIGURE 1-B

```
COLUMN->  1    2    3    4    5    6    7    8    9   10   11
ROW
  1    |    |    |    |    |    |    |  R |  U |  O |  F |
```

But if a skip of 2 is used, the plot looks like this:

FIGURE 1-C

```
COLUMN->  1    2    3    4    5    6    7    8    9   10   11
ROW
  1    |    |    |    |  R |    |  U |    |  O |    |  F |
```

And if a skip of 3 is used, the plot looks like this:

FIGURE 1-D

```
COLUMN->  1    2    3    4    5    6    7    8    9   10   11
ROW
  1    |  R |    |    |  U |    |    |  O |    |    |  F |
```

Finally if a skip of 4 is attempted, the plot fails:

FIGURE 1-E

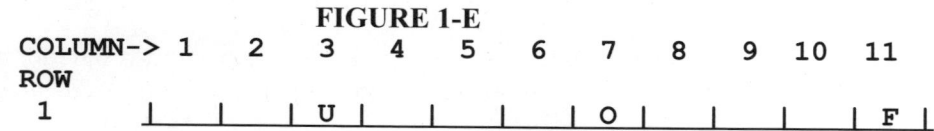

```
COLUMN->  1    2    3    4    5    6    7    8    9   10   11
ROW
  1    |    |  U |    |    |    |  O |    |    |    |  F |
```

The previous plot failed because we ran out of room for the letter "R." So, on the first row in a forward direction skips of 1 to 3 work (three skips). What about vertically? Let's assume that a plot is based on a skip of 306, that is, 306 letters on each row, but that we still use a matrix of 11 columns and eight rows. How many vertical encodings are possible? Certainly N (306) works:

FIGURE 1-F

COLUMN->	1	2	3	4	5	6	7	8	9	10	11
ROW											
1											F
2											O
3											U
4											R
5											
6											
7											
8											

We can see that 2N also works:

FIGURE 1-G

COLUMN->	1	2	3	4	5	6	7	8	9	10	11
ROW											
1											F
2											
3											O
4											
5											U
6											
7											R
8											

But at 3N we can not fit all the letters of the key word in:

FIGURE 1-H

COLUMN->	1	2	3	4	5	6	7	8	9	10	11
ROW											
1											F
2											
3											
4											O
5											
6											
7											U
8											

Working vertically our matrix is restricted to N and 2N. These two intervals, when added to our previous three intervals shown on Figures 1B, 1C, and 1D take our subtotal to 5 intervals. Next consider diagonal intervals possible. The first example slants down to the left (N+1):

FIGURE 1-I

COLUMN->	1	2	3	4	5	6	7	8	9	10	11
ROW											
1											F
2										O	
3									U		
4								R			
5											
6											
7											
8											

The second example will be N+2:

FIGURE 1-J

COLUMN->	1	2	3	4	5	6	7	8	9	10	11
ROW											
1											F
2									O		
3							U				
4					R						
5											
6											
7											
8											

The third example will be N+3:

FIGURE 1-K

COLUMN->	1	2	3	4	5	6	7	8	9	10	11
ROW											
1											F
2								O			
3					U						
4		R									
5											
6											
7											
8											

The fourth example, N+4, fails:

FIGURE 1-L

COLUMN->	1	2	3	4	5	6	7	8	9	10	11
ROW											
1											F
2							O				
3			U								
4											
5											
6											
7											
8											

So we have skips N+1, N+2, and N+3 that work. These three intervals take our subtotal up to 8. What happens when the encoded word slants down and to the right? The first example, which slants down to the right, will be N-1:

FIGURE 1-M

COLUMN->	1	2	3	4	5	6	7	8	9	10	11
ROW											
1	F										
2		O									
3			U								
4				R							
5											
6											
7											
8											

The second example will be N-2:

FIGURE 1-N

COLUMN->	1	2	3	4	5	6	7	8	9	10	11
ROW											
1	F										
2			O								
3					U						
4							R				
5											
6											
7											
8											

The third example will be N-3:

FIGURE 1-O

COLUMN->	1	2	3	4	5	6	7	8	9	10	11
ROW											
1	F										
2				O							
3							U				
4										R	
5											
6											
7											
8											

The fourth example, N-4, fails:

FIGURE 1-P

COLUMN->	1	2	3	4	5	6	7	8	9	10	11
ROW											
1	F										
2					O						
3									U		
4											
5											
6											
7											
8											

So intervals N-1, N-2, and N-3 work. These three new intervals take our subtotal to 11. Intervals 2N-1, 2N-2, 2N-3, 2N+1, 2N+2 and 2N+3 will also work. These six intervals take our subtotal up to 17. Of these, only 2N-3 will be shown below:

FIGURE 1-Q: 2N-3

COLUMN->	1	2	3	4	5	6	7	8	9	10	11
ROW											
1	F										
2											
3				O							
4											
5							U				
6											
7										R	
8											

So for a 4-letter word *in a forward direction only*, there are 17 intervals that work for a matrix that measures 11 columns by eight rows. Now we must double this number of intervals to account for *reverse* encodings of the same word. In-other-words, the previous plot backwards might look like this (it could also be shifted up one row, but the interval would remain the same):

FIGURE 1-R: 2N-3 Backwards

COLUMN->	1	2	3	4	5	6	7	8	9	10	11
ROW											
1											
2		R									
3											
4					U						
5											
6								O			
7											
8											F

There are thus a total of 34 intervals that would work to encode the word *four* (2 X the 17 intervals in a forward direction).

SUMMARY OF THE METHOD USED TO DETERMINE POSSIBLE SKIPS

Rather than grind through the logic of the skips used to search for each word over and over again throughout this report we will simply state the method used to obtain skip numbers through a combinations of Tables and formula given below:

STEP 1: Determine the number of skips possible in a forward direction through use of the Tables offered below:

A. FOR THREE-LETTER WORDS. Because three-letter words are so easy to find, do not accept any three-letter word for plotting purposes unless the letters are within three letters of each other.

Table 1A
HORIZONTAL/VERTICAL SKIPS POSSIBLE FOR A THREE-LETTER WORD

COLUMNS (C) OR ROWS (R)	SKIPS POSSIBLE FOR A 3-LETTER WORD	
1	0	
2	0	
3	1	
4	1	
5	2	
6	2	
7	3	
8	3	
9	4	NOTE: NORMALLY
10	4	INTERVALS OF 4
11	5	OR MORE ARE
12	5	REJECTED AS TOO
13	6	FAR APART.

Table 1B – HORIZONTAL/VERTICAL SKIPS FOR A 4-LETTER WORD

COLUMNS (C) OR ROWS (R)	SKIPS POSSIBLE 4-LETTER WORDS	COLUMNS OR ROWS	SKIPS POSSIBLE FOR 4-LETTER WORDS
1	0	50	16
2	0	51	16
3	0	52	17
4	1	53	17
5	1	54	17
6	1	55	18
7	2	56	18
8	2	57	18
9	2	58	19
10	3	59	19
11	3	60	19
12	3	61	20
13	4	62	20
14	4	63	20
15	4	64	21
16	5	65	21
17	5	66	21
18	5	67	22
19	6	68	22
20	6	69	22
21	6	70	23
22	7	71	23
23	7	72	23
24	7	73	24
25	8	74	24
26	8	75	24
27	8	76	25
28	9	77	25
29	9	78	25
30	9	79	26
31	10	80	26
32	10	81	26
33	10	82	27
34	11	83	27
35	11	84	27
36	11	85	28
37	12	86	28
38	12	87	28
39	12	88	29
40	13	89	29
41	13	90	29
42	13	91	30
43	14	92	30
44	14	93	30
45	14	94	31
46	15	95	31
47	15	96	31
48	15	97	32
49	16	98	32

A set of Tables similar to those just presented may be found in Appendix B. There skips possible for words from three to eight letters long are listed. ELS terms of nine letters or greater length are rarely found to be encoded more than once in the Torah.

STEP 2: THE FORMULA FOR TOTAL SKIPS.

(1) Let the number of skips possible in a forward direction on one row of length (R), where R = the number of columns in the matrix be equal to **Sr**.

(2) Let the number of skips possible in a vertical direction on one column of length (C), where C = the number of rows in the matrix be equal to **Sc**.

(3) The formula for total skips is as follows:

$$\text{Skips} = 2(Sr + Sc + 2[Sr][Sc]) = 2Sr + 2Sc + 4SrSc.$$

An example of skip value determined through use of the above tables and formula follows: Determine the number of skips possible for a 4-letter word in a matrix 28 columns by 11 rows (as with Figure 1).

Solution: For a 4-letter word use Table 1B. On it find that 28 columns = nine possible skips forward. Thus Sr = 9. Now note that 11 rows = three possible skips vertically. Thus Sc = 3. Now apply the formula which is Skips = 2Sr + 2Sc + 4SrSc.

$$2Sr + 2Sc + 4SrSc = 2(9) + 2(3) + 4(9)(3) = 18 + 6 + 108 = 132 \text{ SKIPS}$$

ASSUMPTIONS

(1) The greater the number of workable skips in a matrix, the greater the probability of finding the key word sought.

(2) A sense of how likely a word is to be found with a given number of intervals possible can be gleaned from a Control text. Usually this is the 304,805 letters of the Torah. We search the Control for a key word at number of intervals equal to the number of intervals possible to find the key word in a matrix at an Equidistant Letter Spacing (ELS). *It is important to search the Control at intervals similar to the interval/s plotted in the matrix.* For example, if one searches for the word חשמל (electricity) at skips 1 to 100 in the Book of Numbers, it will occur much more often than it will at skips 201 to 300. This is because at a skip of 2 the frequently occurring number "50" (חמשים) will share 3 letters with חשמל. Thus, for the Control to better represent expected frequencies, for words plotted at low intervals, search low intervals in the Control (like intervals 1 to 100 for four or longer lettered words or generally 1 to 28 for 3-letter words). Employ higher skips (like 101 to 200 for longer words or 101 to 128 for 3-letter words) in the Control to assist in calculating the probability

of plotting words at high skips in a matrix.

This number of hits in the Control is divided by the letters in the Control. This gives us a "Word Frequency Per Letter." This quotient is then multiplied by the number of letters in a matrix to produce an "Expected Word Frequency in the Matrix." Finally, the expected frequency may be converted to a probability by the Poisson Equation. These probabilities are often conservative for the specific size and shape matrix because they ignore reduced number of encodings possible due to space taken up by words without common letters. However, as a measure of how likely the key words are to be in a matrix of the same number of letters, they may be somewhat liberal due to the fact that a 100-letter matrix could be 10 rows by ten columns, or it could be 100 * 1, 2 * 50, 4 * 25, 5 * 20, etc. Different combinations of rows and columns will yield different combinations of Sr and Sc.

(3) Each plot will contain one **conditional axis word** or **conditional axis term**. For most plots this word will be ברית ארון (Ark of the Covenant), but the probabilities offered throughout this paper will always be conditional on the axis term being present. As such, all axis words are automatically assigned probabilities of 1.0 even if there is less than a 100% certainty that such words would be encoded at least once in the Torah.

(4) Words encoded would normally be considered independent of each other unless it can be shown that they were deliberately encoded. Such a demonstration would validate the Torah Codes.

(5) If there is no deliberate encoding, words not in the open text will tend to be found at similar Equidistant Letter Spacing (ELS) frequencies throughout the Torah. This assumption was employed in the construction of a Control and was checked through a statistical test known as *Chi-Square* (Table 4 and Appendix B, 221).

(6) Only a concrete and highly improbable find based solely on the Code can clearly answer the question of whether or not the Code is a useful source of data. Recovery of the Ark of the Covenant would clearly qualify as such a find if the Codes (and existing area charts) were all that were used in the recovery.

(7) The initial assumption was made that Ark's position would be based on at least one encoding of *Ark of the Covenant* (ברית ארון). The encoding would be within a restricted space of not more than three chapters with spacing under 3,000 letters. This was because words like *Ark of the Covenant* with eight letters could occur with an interval of up to 43,543 letters in a single non-toroidal pass through the Torah. Intervals this large overtaxed the 3,000-letter per line print memory capabilities of the Torah Codes 1.0 software program. It was assumed that any deliberate encoding would employ lower skip numbers to facilitate the search. The certainty of this assumption was shaken when Ark data and other significant information popped up at much larger skips. Only one Ark encoding was found with an interval less than 3,000 letters. This is shown on Table One as are six additional encodings discovered in searches conducted out to 43,544 skips forward and 43,544 skips backward (all skips possible):

TABLE ONE -ENCODINGS OF ARK OF THE COVENANT (ארון ברית)

Letter	Book	Chapter	Verse	Word	Letter	Skip	Letter	Book	Ch.	Vr.	Word	Letter	Skip
א	Numbers 34	8	4	3		-306	א	Numbers	22	35	10	1	9698
ר	Numbers 34	2	11	3		-306	ר	Numbers	29	8	1	4	9698
ו	Numbers 33	53	4	1		-306	ו	Numbers	34	12	5	7	9698
נ	Numbers 33	46	4	4		-306	נ	Deuteronomy	4	1	23	1	9698
ב	Numbers 33	37	6	1		-306	ב	Deuteronomy	9	10	9	1	9698
ר	Numbers 33	24	2	3		-306	ר	Deuteronomy	15	10	5	2	9698
י	Numbers 33	11	4	2		-306	י	Deuteronomy	22	28	3	2	9698
ת	Numbers 33	4	3	2		-306	ת	Deuteronomy	28	67	4	2	9698

Letter	Book	Chapter	Verse	Word	Letter	Skip	Letter	Book	Ch.	Vr.	Word	Letter	Skip
א	Exodus	15	8	2	1	3,102	א	Numbers	17	11	1	3	-15,677
ר	Exodus	17	2	5	5	3,102	ר	Numbers	7	84	13	3	-15,677
ו	Exodus	19	14	1	1	3,102	ו	Leviticus	27	33	13	1	-15,677
נ	Exodus	21	33	12	2	3,102	נ	Leviticus	19	10	12	2	-15,677
ב	Exodus	24	3	1	3	3,102	ב	Leviticus	10	14	11	2	-15,677
ר	Exodus	26	8	14	3	3,102	ר	Exodus	39	30	4	3	-15,677
י	Exodus	28	10	9	6	3,102	י	Exodus	30	12	12	2	-15,677
ת	Exodus	29	24	11	1	3,102	ת	Exodus	20	20	9	1	-15,677

Letter	Book	Chapter	Verse	Word	Letter	Skip	Letter	Book	Ch.	Vr.	Word	Letter	Skip
א	Genesis	27	24	7	1	3,621	א	Numbers	17	14	4	1	-24,926
ר	Genesis	29	25	2	4	3,621	ר	Numbers	4	7	10	4	-24,926
ו	Genesis	31	19	6	1	3,621	ו	Leviticus	17	2	4	1	-24,926
נ	Genesis	32	33	23	2	3,621	נ	Leviticus	2	12	1	4	-24,926
ב	Genesis	35	20	7	3	3,621	ב	Exodus	27	21	1	1	-24,926
ר	Genesis	37	25	18	4	3,621	ר	Exodus	10	28	6	4	-24,926

י	Genesis	40	5	8	2	3,621	|	י	Genesis	44	26	11	2	-24,926
ת	Genesis	41	51	13	3	3,621	|	ת	Genesis	30	40	4	3	-24,926

Letter	Book	Chapter	Verse	Word	Letter	Skip
א	Leviticus	5	12	16	3	-8,752
ד	Exodus	39	8	14	4	-8,752
ו	Exodus	34	10	1	1	-8,752
נ	Exodus	29	5	6	4	-8,752
ב	Exodus	23	24	14	3	-8,752
ך	Exodus	17	2	10	5	-8,752
י	Exodus	12	12	3	4	-8,752
ת	Exodus	6	19	6	5	-8,752

The encoding at a skip of -306 was covered fully throughout Chapter One of this book with respect to Figures 1A through 1I. All of those figures were originally combined in Figure 1 shown below:

Figure 1: Combined Findings of Figure 1A Through Figure 1I

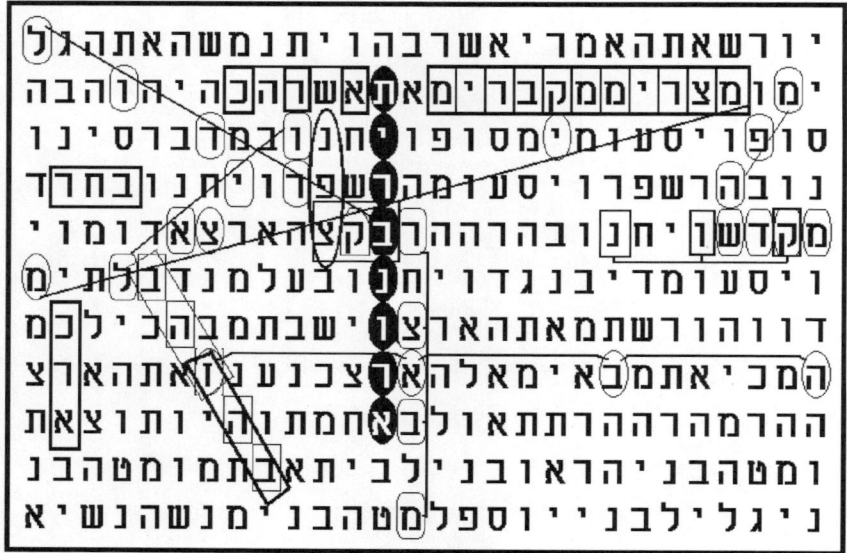

Terms on Figure 1	Translation	Skip	Start	End
ארון ברית	Ark of Covenant	-306	Numbers 34 V8 L13	Numbers 33 V4 L14
מצרים מקברים את	Egyptians were burying	1	Numbers 33 V4 L2	Numbers 33 V4 L12
ברדול	Bardawil	-303	Numbers 33 V37 L21	Numbers 32 V40 L12
ים סוף	Yam Suf	1	Numbers 33 V11 L7	Numbers 33 V11 L11
מבצר	Fortress	-612	Numbers 34 V23 L10	Numbers 33 V37 L20
בעל	Baal	1	Numbers 33 V46 L18	Numbers 33 V46 L20
צפן	Zephon	-306	Numbers 33 V37 L23	Numbers 33 V11 L15
מפה	Chart	307	Numbers 33 V3 L81	Numbers 33 V23 L18
נוק	56100	-3	Numbers 33 V37 L13	Numbers 33 V37 L7
זהב	Gold	305	Numbers 34 V2 L41	Numbers 34 V14 L25
זהב	Gold	-305	Numbers 34 V2 L41	Numbers 33 V46 L24
מצרים	Egypt	-312	Numbers 33 V46 L28	Numbers 33 V4 L2
מקום	Position	-310	Numbers 33 V46 L21	Numbers 33 V11 L6
צקב	Zuqba	-1	Numbers 33 V37 L23	Numbers 33 V37 L21
ארכ	Longitude	2	Numbers 33 V4 L15	Numbers 33 V4 L19
ארכ	Longitude	-306	Numbers 34 V8 L24	Numbers 33 V53 L25
רחב	Latitude	-1	Numbers 33 V24 L19	Numbers 33 V24 L17
לא-י ו	31-16	-308	Numbers 33 V46 L25	Numbers 33 V11 L16
מקדש	Temple/Sanctuary	1	Numbers 33 V37 L6	Numbers 33 V37 L9

For Figure 1 the ELS reference is 306 characters between rows. There are 19 displayed terms in the matrix. The matrix starts at Numbers 32 V39 Letter 31 and ends at Numbers 34 V23 Letter 23. The matrix spans 3088 characters of the surface text. The matrix has 11 rows, is 28 columns wide and contains a total of 308 characters. **(Note there are more terms here than are highlighted in Figures 1A through 1I)**

(8) *A-posteriori data will be plotted, but not included in probabilities.* The words "Egyptians were burying" are "interesting," but they were found *a posteriori*. While they served as cause to continue the hunt, they can not be used in a probability study because I did not predict that they would be there.

(9) Three-letter words are so easy to find, especially if one has the entire Torah to search, that

(with the exception of one word – *latitude* found on Figure 2 on the first night of the study), they are not plotted unless the letters are within three letters of each other.

SPELLING: The Hebrew transliteration of the Arabic name *Zuqba* was searched for in the Control with 3 different spellings. Figure 1 had *tsadeh kof bet* (צקב) at an ELS of –1 intersecting *Ark of the Covenant*. Figure 17B used this spelling plus a *hey* (ה) at the end. At other times the search was for *Zayin Kof Bet Hey* (זקבה), a spelling found on a map used to get from Israel into Egypt in 1999. The latter spelling at its third shortest ELS (skip -13) in Figure 43 connects two open text references to *the Ark of the Covenant*:

Figure 43 – Zuqba at Skip -13 and the Ark of the Covenant

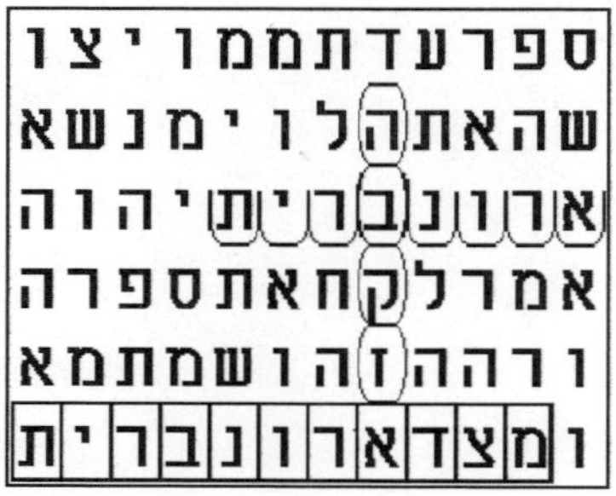

Terms on Figure 43	Translation	Symbol	Skip	Start	End
זקבה	Zuqba	◯	-13	Deuteronomy 31 V26 L15	Deuteronomy 31 V25 L10
ארון ברית	Ark of Covenant	⊔	1	Deuteronomy 31 V25 L19	Deuteronomy 31 V25 L26
מצד ארון ברית	Fortress of the Ark of the Covenant	▢	1	Deuteronomy 31 V26 L25	Deuteronomy 31 V26 L35

For Figure 43 the ELS reference is 13 characters between rows. There are 5 displayed terms in the matrix. The matrix starts at Deuteronomy 31 V25 L6 and ends at Deuteronomy 31 V26 L35. The matrix spans 64 characters of the surface text. The matrix has 5 rows, is 12 columns wide and contains a total of 60 characters.

Iblis was usually spelled with a final *sin,* but an end *samech* was also checked. For Latitude (קו רחב, line of width) only the short form (רחב) was used. A similar procedure was usually used for longitude (ארך rather than קו ארך) but Figure 18 used the longer form twice. Where target *a priori* words had alternate spellings, or where synonyms existed that would fill the search bill, the control was searched for all such spellings and synonyms and the value of the plot was downgraded in accordance with the larger word frequencies obtained.

RESULTS FOR THE LONGITUDE SEARCH:

Figure 1 contained the initial longitude data. This figure is based on a skip of 306 (306 letters per column on a full plot) with anchor letter (1st letter) set at Numbers 32:39, 7th word, 6th letter (ה). Table 2 identifies the words found on Figure 1, whether found *a priori* or *a posteriori*, and the significance of the material:

Table 2 – Explanation of Figure 1 Findings

Words	Found *a priori* or *a posteriori*	Significance
Ark of the Covenant	N/A	Initial object of the experiment
Egyptians were	A-posteriori	The Ark may be buried in Egypt.
Longitude	A-priori	The Ark ends its encoding at a chapter & verse that equals an Egyptian longitude.
Egypt (encoded)	A-priori	"Egypt" passes through Ark of the Covenant
Bardawil	A-priori	This lake surrounds the Zuqba Peninsula. "Bardawil" originates in Ark of the Covenant.
Baal + Zephon	A-priori	This Biblical fortress site is often placed in the area of Zuqba.
Zuqba	A-priori	This site name corresponds to what is on the map at the intersection of the coordinates based upon chapter and verse placements of Ark of the Covenant – encoded in Numbers, and open text in Deuteronomy.
Gold	A-posteriori	The Ark is made of gold; *a posteriori* forward at skip 305, but *a priori* backward.
Yam Suf (Sea of Reeds)	A-posteriori	Some authors believe that this body of water was the Bardawil Lake.
Position	A-priori	We want the Ark's position.
Latitude	A-posteriori	At a skip of -1, this word is close to 31-16, a suspect Ark or Baal Zephon latitude
Fortress	A-priori @ skip 612 backward	There are fortresses and fortress ruins along the coastal area in question.
31-16 spelled *lamed alef yud vav*	A-priori	British Admiralty Chart 56100 shows an underwater obstruction at 31-16 North, 33-4 East. This might be a fortress that holds the Ark or it may be Baal Zephon.
Chart	A-priori	BA Chart 56100 covers the suspect area.
56100	A-priori	BA Chart 56100 covers the suspected area. 56100 touches "chart."
Temple	A-priori	The angle from Temple to Ark of the Covenant equals the course angle from Jerusalem to the prime suspect site at Zuqba.

197

CONTROL DEVELOPMENT

In a December, 1997 BR article criticizing the Code, Charles Bryant-Abraham of the Jerusalem Center for Biblical Studies and Research remarks, "Of the other high-frequency letters cited above, at least one combination is impressively ubiquitous in every context and spacing interval conjurable, shin qoph and resh (שקר), which spell *sheqer* (*falsehood*)." I took him at his word and found *falsehood* in a few embarrassing places. At this point, the decision was made to stop and do a frequency check of words employed throughout the Ark search.

As a control for Ark-related encodings, Genesis, Exodus and Leviticus were initially employed, since none of the initial plots centered on those texts. For large plots the Control was searched at the standard 28 skips searched for each 3-letter word. On one matrix containing 1,664 letters it was found there was an 88.7% chance for *falsehood* to appear. The same was not true of most key words found on Ark plots, but even when word probabilities were that high, the words were only used if consistent with **many** related words on the plot.

Part I of Table 3 below sums up the numbers of verses, words, and letters in the five books of the Torah. Part II of Table 3 shows the frequency of some key words in all Torah Books. Table 4 shows the frequency of key words per letter in the Control when those words are searched for in the Control at skips similar to those plotted. A Chi-square test shows that with 40 degrees of freedom and a chi-square sum of 56.1, at the .01 level of significance we cannot reject the null hypothesis that there is no significant difference between the first three books of the Torah and the last two books. Whereas no significant differences between the initial Control and the last two books of Torah were seen, it was generally assumed that all five books of Torah would also give a fair picture of letter and word frequencies. As Table 4 indicates with the word מפה (chart) that shares two letters with משה Moses, who is not discussed in Genesis, there are occasional exceptions. However, the exceptions to using the five books of Torah were few and far between. Eventually the full five books were adopted as the standard.

Table 3 – Part I – Statistical Comparison of Torah Books

BOOK:	GEN	EX	LEV	NUM	DEUT
VERSES	1533	1210	859	1288	956
WORDS	20612	16713	11950	16408	14293
LETTERS	78064	63529	44790	63530	54892

Table 3 – Part II – Word Frequencies in 5 Torah Books (Skips +1 to +100)

	GEN	EX	LEV	NUM	DEUT
ARK OF THE COVENANT	0	0	0	0	0
UNDER WATER	2	1	1	1	0
Baal Zephon with *vav*	0	0	0	1	0
Baal Zephon, no *vav*	0	2	0	0	0
RAS BURUN	0	0	0	0	0
AIRPLANE	3	1	3	3	2
ROFFMAN (3)	3	0	2	5	3

ZUABA AT SKIP -1	1	0	1	0	3
BARDAWIL	4	4	4	2	2
TEMPLE, Skips 2 to 101	4	18	4	11	7
TEMPLE, Skip of 1	0	9	34	13	3
PARALLEL	4	5	0	1	0
JEREMIAH with *vav*	5	3	0	2	2
EGYPT (AT A SKIP 2+)	6	5	0	4	2
CHERUBIM	9	20	2	10	9
IBLIS with letter *samech*	15	14	8	12	14
ZUABA	20	16	9	15	17
ITAMAR	24	24	13	16	21
JEREMIAH (no *vav*)	34	39	17	25	26
BURY, UNENCODED	39	1	0	9	5
ELECTRICITY	48	55	20	113	28
MESSIAH	83	87	46	84	66
EGYPT,UNENCODED	94	176	11	33	51
33-4	95	60	45	64	75
EXPLOSION	109	65	28	70	38
POSITION,UNENCODED	43	7	25	19	32
POSITION(INTERVALS 1 TO 100)	133	72	72	80	73
IBLIS with letter *sin*	138	102	74	123	83
31-9	180	102	74	123	83
ARK	223	146	133	183	128
COAST	324	235	200	334	108
GOLD	212	344	266	225	198
BURY	451	254	234	334	234
LATITUDE	616	469	356	527	342
31-11	619	327	264	343	336
FINDS (SKIP = 1)	58	24	7	11	30
LONGITUDE	1749	1211	897	896	1616
31-16 *lamed alef tet zayin*	0	1	4	2	1
31-16 *lamed alef yud vav*	554	364	270	355	371
OBSTRUCTION *(ayin kaf vav vet)*	59	49	38	27	62
FORTRESS *(mem tsadeh dalet* at interval = 1)	5	9	0	0	5
FORTRESS *(mem vet tsadeh resh)*	33	21	11	19	22
MY GLORY *(Kaf vet vav dalet)*	40	24	13	19	30
THE SEAS (at int. = 1)	45	36	37	29	42
FALSEHOOD	356	314	219	328	216

While Table 3 is based upon skips 1 to 100, actual searches for material used seldom employ this arbitrary limit. The actual skips chosen for search in the Control were dictated by the Roffman Skip Formula and considerations shown earlier in this report (see also the Chi-Square Data and Computations on Table 4 of the following page).

For skips employed for three-letter words, except for *latitude* on Figure 2 (skip +6) found on the first day of the experimental search for *Ark of the Covenant*, all intervals employed on a single line were 1 to 3 (three skips). Vertical intervals of N, 2N and 3N were allowed (another three skips). Finally, for up to two lines separation, skips of N (or 2N) +1, N (or 2N) +2, N (or 2N) -1, and N (or 2N) -2 were accepted. These additional eight intervals takes the subtotal to fourteen intervals (3 + 3 + 8) which must be doubled to account for backwards encodings. Thus, with the exception of Figure 2 we normally use 28 intervals as the appropriate number of intervals to be searched in the Control to establish expected frequencies for 3-letter words at three or less letters separation, not the 100 employed on Table 3.

The first step for each matrix was to list its words found. In general, only those words that pertain to position or a description of the Ark were entered into the calculations. No a-posteriori data was included.

Next we establish the frequency of a word per letter. To do this the frequency of each 4+ letter word as found at the number of skips designated in accordance with Tables 1B to 1F and the Skip Formula, or for three-letter words at 28 skips employed in the Control was divided by letters in the Control. The quotient is the **Word Frequency Per Letter**. This is multiplied by the number of letters on each plot (matrix) to reveal **Word Expectancy Per Plot**. It is inherent in this procedure that the larger the number of letters in the matrix, the larger the number of placements possible for any given key word at any ELS.

In general, when chi-square values for key words were too high the decision was made to look carefully for and weed out variables that might affect the quality of the Control. *It was found that chi-square values were lowest when words were searched for in the Control at skips <u>and direction</u> similar to those in the matrices.*

After determining Word Frequency Per Plot we apply the Poisson Equation to see the probability that they are present at least once. This is necessary to determine a true probability for each word. Just because a word is likely to appear once per plot does not imply it will always be there. Words may average out to many times per plot area without actually being in a given plot of that area. Of course, if the expected frequency is sufficiently high we eventually reach a probability like 0.9999999 which we simply round off as 1.0.

TABLE 4
CONTROL WORD LIST AND
CHI-SQUARE CALCULATIONS:
WORDS WITH
EXPECTANCIES >5
(SKIPS AFTER @)

A	B SKIPS USED IN PLOTS AND DEUT.	C HITS FOUND IN NUM.EXOD. AND LEV.	D HITS FOUND IN GEN.THE AND IN THE CONTROL	E DIVIDE BY LETTERS PER LETTER	F QUOTIENT EQUALS FREQUENCY DEUT. WORD	G E QUOTIENT X 118422 = NUMBERS+ EXPECTANCY EXPECTED	H OBSERVED MINUS EXPECTED	I DIFFERENCE SQUARED (CHI-SQUARE)	J PREVIOUS DIVIDED BY EXPECTED
TACHSHIM @ 901 - 1000	918	10	11	186383	5.9018E-05	6.989060161	3.010939839	9.065758714	1.2971356
TEMPLE @ 101 - 200	183	20	38	186383	0.00020388	24.14402601	-4.144026011	17.17295158	0.711 27125
CHERUBIM @ 2 TO 101	45	16	17	186383	9.121E-05	10.80127479	5.198725206	27.02674376	2.50218093
IBLIS WITH SAMECH @ 301 - 400	310	17	26	186383	0.0001395	16.51959674	0.480403256	0.230787288	0.01397052
ZUABA Z)BH @ 101-200	147	43	55	186383	0.00029509	34.94530081	8.054699195	64.87817912	1.856556376
ZUABA C)BH @ -4069 TO -4168	-4069	66	107	186383	0.00057409	67.98449429	-1.984494294	3.938217603	0.05792817
ITAMAR @ 101 - 200	121	24	37	186383	0.00019852	23.50865691	0.491343095	0.241418037	0.01026932
JEREMIAH - NO VAV @ 151 - 250	184, 202	54	79	186383	0.00042386	50.19415934	3.805840661	14.48442314	0.2885679
ELECTRICITY @ 201 - 300	253	90	126	186383	0.00067603	80.0565073	9.943492701	98.87304709	1.23504073
MESSIAH @ 1 - 100	2	150	216	186383	0.0011589	137.2397268	12.7602732	162.8245722	1.18442448
33-4 @ 2 - 29	-2	38	54	186383	0.00028973	34.3099317	3.6900683	13.61660406	0.39687063
EXPLOSION @ 301 - 328	306	21	51	186383	0.00027363	32.40382438	-11.40382438	130.0472106	4.01332908
POSITION - OPEN TEXT	1	51	75	186383	0.0004024	47.65268292	3.347317084	11.20453166	0.23512908
POSITION @ 101 - 200	104	99	180	186383	0.00096575	114.366439	-15.366439	236.1274475	2.06465681
SHABTAI @ 101 - 200	90, 205	195	307	186383	0.00164715	195.0583154	-0.058315404	0.003400686	1.7434E-05
IBLIS WITH END SIN @ 11 - 110	12, 147	214	303	186383	0.00162568	192.516839	21.48316102	461.5262073	2.397322903
31-9 @ 51 - 150	63, 147	418	715	186383	0.00383619	454.2889105	-36.28891047	1316.885023	2.89878312
ARK @ 101 - 200	102	267	453	186383	0.00243048	287.8220048	-20.8220481	433.5642134	1.50636124
COAST SKIPS 1 - 28	10	138	209	186383	0.00112135	132.7921431	5.207856694	27.1217739	0.20424231
BURY SKIPS 61 - 88	63	183	268	186383	0.0014379	170.2789203	12.72107971	161.825869	0.950357562
LATITUDE SKIPS 1 - 100	6, 63, -1	869	1441	186383	0.00773139	915.5668811	-46.5668811	2168.474415	2.368445004
31-11 SKIPS 1 - 50 AND 119 - 168	4,4,168	697	1194	186383	0.00640616	758.630712	-61.63071203	3798.344665	5.00684273
LONGITUDE SKIPS 1 - 100	2	2510	3855	186383	0.02068322	2449.347902	60.6520981	3678.677004	1.50190057

TABLE 4 CONTINUED
CONTROL, WORD LIST AND
CH-SQUARE CALC.:
WORDS WITH
EXPECTANCIES >5

(SKIPS AFTER @)	SKIPS USED IN PLOTS DEUT. LEV.	HITS FOUND GEN AND DEUT. AND	HITS GEN AND LEV. IN THE CONTROL	DIVIDE BY THE FREQUENCY PER LETTER DEUT. WORD CONTROL	QUOTIENT EQUALS X 118422 =	E QUOTIENT X 118422 = NUMBERS+ WORD EXPECT.	OBSERVED MINUS EXPECTED	DIFFERENCE SQUARED	PREVIOUS EXPECTED DIVIDED BY (CH-SQUARE)
31-16 LAMED ALEF YUD VAV	63, -308, -2'	726	1188	186383	0.006373972	754.8184974	-28.8184974	830.5057921	1.100272178
OBSTRUCTION @ 51 - 150	127, -88	86	134	186383	0.00071895	85.13946014	0.8605398856	0.740528844	0.008697833
FORTRESS MBCR 601 - 700	-612	43	68	186383	0.00036484	43.20509918	-0.20509918	0.042065673	0.000973627
MY GLORY @ 1 - 100	68	49	77	186383	0.000413128	48.92342113	0.07657887873	0.005864324	0.000119867
THE SEAS SKIP = 1	1	71	118	186383	0.000633105	74.97355446	-3.973554455	15.78913501	0.210596058
LIAR (SHEKER) @ 101 - 128	N/A	146	258	186383	0.001384246	163.9252292	-17.9252923	321.313843	1.960124409
GOLD @ 301 - 328	305, -305	103	165	186383	0.000885274	104.8359024	-1.835902416	3.370537681	0.032150605
JEREMIAH WITH VAV 274 - 373	274	6	12	186383	6.43836E-05	7.624429267	-1.624429267	2.638770442	0.34609416
ROFFMAN @ 51 - 150	99	6	8	186383	4.29224E-05	5.082952844	0.917047156	0.840975486	0.165450184
EGYPT @ 301 - 400	303	3	8	186383	4.29224E-05	5.082952844	-2.082952844	4.338692562	0.85357179
FORTRESS (METSAD), SKIP = 1	1	5	14	186383	7.511415E-05	8.895167478	-3.895167478	15.17232968	1.705682295
BARDAWIL @ 250 - 349	303	7	9	186383	4.82877E-05	5.71832195	1.28167805	1.642698624	0.287269349
56-100 @ -1 TO -28	-3	220	383	186383	0.002054908	243.3463674	-23.3463674	545.052872	2.239823334
BAAL SKIP = 1	1	54	75	186383	0.000402397	47.65268292	6.347317084	40.28843416	0.845459934
ZEPHON 3 LET. -301 TO -326	-306	19	50	186383	0.000268265	31.76845528	-12.76845528	163.0334502	5.131928788
ZEPHON 4 LET. -301 TO -400	N/A	7	11	186383	5.90183E-05	6.989060161	0.010939839	0.00011968	1.71239E-05
CHART @ 307 TO 334 **	307	424	372	108319	0.003434301	406.6967383	17.30326166	299.4028642	0.736182113
WORDS WITH EXPECTANCY < 5 BELOW		27	25	186383	0.000134132	15.88422764	11.11577236	123.5603952	7.778810402
TOTALS		8165	12767			8297.981029			56.10685178 TOTAL CH-SQUARE
WORDS WITH EXPECTANCY < 5		27	25						

8 TERMS WITH EXPECTANCY <5: "I WILL HIDE" BAAL ZEPHON (VAV + NO VAV), RAS BURUN, AIRPLANE, ZUABA @ SKIP=1, UNDERWATER, + PARALLEL

TOTAL FOR ABOVE "BUCKET"	27	25

** NOTE: Due to the similarity of the Hebrew mapah (mem peh hey) with Moshe (mem shin hey) and due to the fact that Moshe (Moshe) "is not mentioned in Genesis, the Control here includes only 2 books - Exodus and Leviticus.

STEPS TO CALCULATE THE PROBABILITY OF <u>A WORD APPEARING AT LEAST ONCE</u>

1. FIND PROBABILITY IT DOES NOT OCCUR BY POISSON EQUATION.

$$f(x) = \frac{\text{Lambda } e^{x \, (-\text{lambda})}}{x!} \quad x = 0 \qquad \text{lambda} = \text{expected frequency per matrix}$$

2. $1 - f(0) =$ THE PROBABILITY OF OCCURRING AT LEAST ONCE.
   (where $f(0) =$ the probability it will not occur)

3. On the figure spreadsheets, head column G as $= 1\text{-EXP(-F\#)}$ where # equals the row number of the spreadsheet.

Once individual encoding probabilities are established, combined probabilities may be obtained for each plot by multiplying together all individual probabilities on a plot so long as the words used are independent of each other. It is assumed that all encoded words would be independent. The combined probabilities on the spreadsheet yields an approximation of how good our Figure 1 data really is for the above a-priori material being in a plot area of this size with Ark of the Covenant is the product of the above individual probabilities occurring at least once. It works out to be one chance in 304,997,615.

Some of the words on Figure 1 are "special case." For a-priori words at skip +1, search the Control only at skip +1. For those terms at skips N (column width), -N, and –1, the Control is searched only at skips N, -N, -1 and +1 to see how likely the more obvious hits are to be there. On Figure 1, these special cases include *Baal* at skip +1, *Zephon* at N (skip -306), and *Zuqba* at skip -1. Special case considerations alter the odds to one chance in 39,565,398,602.

SPREADSHEET FOR FIGURE 1

ROFFMAN SKIP FORMULA APPLIED THROUGHOUT

A	B	C	D	E	F	G
FIGURE 1	SKIPS	NUMBER	DIVIDE	QUOTIENT	EQUOTIENT	POISSON
A-PRIORI, NON-RELIGIOUS WORDS	PLOTTED	IN	BY	EQUALS	X 308	PROBABILITY
ON THE PLOT, STANDARD ROFFMAN	FIGURE	CONTROL	LETTERS	FREQUENCY	EQUALS	FOR EACH
SKIP FORMULA APPLIED. CONTROL	TWO		IN THE	PER LETTER	WORD	WORD
SEARCH AT SKIPS INDICATED BELOW	PLOTS		CONTROL		EXPECTANCY	APPEARING
						ONCE
ZUQBA @ SKIPS -1 TO -2 - TWO SPELLINGS	-1	149	304805	0.000488837	0.150561835	0.139775463
ZUQBA(TSADEH KOF BET) @ -1 TO -28	-1	97				
ZUQBA (ZAYIN KOF BET) @ -1 TO -28	N/A	52				
POSITION @ SKIPS -301 TO -432	-310	394	304805	0.00129263	0.398129962	0.32842525
LATITUDE @ SKIP -1 TO -28	-1	667	304805	0.002188284	0.673991568	0.490329871
LONGITUDE @ SKIP 2 TO 29	2	1853	304805	0.006079297	1.872423353	0.846249382
31-16 - BOTH SPELLINGS @ -308 TO -439	-308	2572	304805	0.008438182	2.598959991	0.925649136
31-16 LAMED ALEF TET ZAYIN	-308	13				
31-16 @ -308 TO -439 LAMED ALEF YUD VAV	-308	2559				
FORTRESS - BOTH SPELLINGS	-612	377	304804	0.00123686	0.380953006	0.316790004
FORTRESS (MEVTSAR) @ SKIPS -612 TO -743	-612	145				
FORTRESS (METSAD) @ SKIPS -601 TO -628	N/A	232				
GOLD @ SKIPS 301 TO 328	305	268	304805	0.000879251	0.270809206	0.237237987
BARDAWIL @ SKIPS -303 TO -366	303	10	304805	3.28079E-05	0.010104821	0.010053939
BAAL @ SKIPS 1 TO 28	1	1249	304805	0.004097702	1.262092157	0.716938802
ZEPHON - BOTH SPELLINGS	-306	98	304805	0.000321517	0.099027247	0.09428197
ZEPHON @ SKIP -301 TO -328 (3 LETTER)		72				
ZEPHON @ SKIP -301 TO -432 (4 LETTER)		26				
EGYPT @ SKIPS -312 TO -375	312	12	304805	3.93694E-05	0.012125785	0.012052564
CHART @ SKIPS 307 TO 334*	307	797	226741	0.003515024	1.082627315	0.661295528
56-100 @ SKIPS -1 TO -28	-3	604	304805	0.001981595	0.610331195	0.456829056
						COMBINED
*NOTE: THE CONTROL HERE DON'T INCLUDE						PROB. =
GENESIS FOR CHI-SQUARE REASONS						3.27893E-09
RELATED "TO THE LACK OF MOSHE (MOSES)						THE ABOVE =
IN GENESIS. "MOSHE AND MAPAH(CHART)						1 CHANCE IN
DIFFER BY ONLY ONE "LETTER.						304977615.2

SPREADSHEET FOR FIGURE 1: SPECIAL CASE RULES APPLIED

A	B	C	D	E	F	G
FIGURE 1	SKIPS	NUMBER	DIVIDE BY	THE QUOTIENT	E QUOTIENT	POISSON
A-PRIORI, NON-RELIGIOUS	PLOTTED	IN	LETTERS	EQUALS	X 308	PROBABILITY
WORDS ON THE PLOT (SPECIAL CASE	ON	CONTROL	IN THE	FREQUENCY	EQUALS	FOR EACH
SKIP RULES APPLIED) CONTROL	FIGURE		CONTROL	PER LETTER	WORD	WORD
SEARCH AT SKIPS INDICATED BELOW	TWO				EXPECTANCY	APPEARING
ZUQBA @ -1 TO -2 - TWO SPELLINGS	-1	15	304805	4.92118E-05	0.015157232	0.015042939
ZUQBA(TSADEH KOF BET) @ -1 ONLY	-1	15				
ZUQBA (ZAYIN KOF BET) @ -1 ONLY	N/A	0				
POSITION @ SKIPS -301 TO -432	-310	394	304805	0.00129263	0.398129952	0.32842525
LATITUDE @ SKIP -1 TO -28	-1	667	304805	0.002188284	0.673991568	0.490329871
LONGITUDE @ SKIP 2 TO 29	2	1853	304805	0.006079297	1.872423353	0.846249382
31-16 BOTH SPELLINGS	-308	2572	304805	0.008438182	2.598959991	0.925649136
31-16 @ -308 TO -439 L)+Z		13				
31-16 @ SKIPS -308 TO -439 L)HW	-308	2559	304805	0.008395532	2.585823723	0.924666
FORTRESS - BOTH SPELLINGS	-612	377	304804	0.00123686	0.380953006	0.316790004
FORTRESS (MEVTSAR) @ -612 TO -743	-612	145				
FORTRESS (METSAD) @ -601 TO -628	N/A	232				
GOLD @ SKIPS 301 TO 328	305	268	304805	0.000879251	0.270809206	0.237237987
BARDAWIL @ SKIPS -303 TO -366	303	10	304805	3.28079E-05	0.010104821	0.010053939
BAAL @ SKIPS 1 ONLY	1	129	304805	0.000423221	0.130352192	0.122213773
ZEPHON - TWO SPELLINGS @ N, -1, +1, -1	-306	40	304805	0.000131231	0.040419284	0.03961332
ZEPHON @ N, -N, +1, -1 (3 LETTER)	-306	26				
ZEPHON @ N, -N, +1, -1 (4 LETTER)	N/A	14				
EGYPT @ SKIPS -312 TO -375	312	12	304805	3.93694E-05	0.012125785	0.012052564
CHART @ SKIPS 307 TO 334*	307	797	226741	0.003515024	1.082627315	0.661295528
56-100 @ SKIPS -1 TO -28	-3	604	304805	0.001981595	0.610331195	0.456829056
*NOTE: CONTROL HERE DOSEN'T						COMBINED
INCLUDE GENESIS FOR						PROB. =
CHI-SQUARE REASONS DUE						2.52746E-11
TO THE LACK OF MOSHE (MOSES) IN						THE ABOVE =
GENESIS. "MOSHE AND MAPAH (CHART)						1 CHANCE IN
DIFFER BY ONLY ONE "LETTER.						39565398602

What words were left out of the Figure 1 calculations but were seen on the plot?

Word	Reason left out of the calculation
Temple	Initially thought to be only religious, a separate analysis of this word's map figure location will be offered on the next page.
Egyptians were burying	Found *a posteriori*
Barry	Personal & found *a posteriori*

Fire	Too short & found *a posteriori*
Explosion	Found when developing another plot
Coast	**Skip (10) too large + requires a 385-letter matrix**

Probability Calculation for the Possible Placements for מקדש (Temple) to yield a course of 251.565 Degrees to the Ark of the Covenant (ארון ברית) on ELS Map 1. Actual Location of מקדש shown and included below:

Figure 44 – Key Word Placements for ELS Map 1

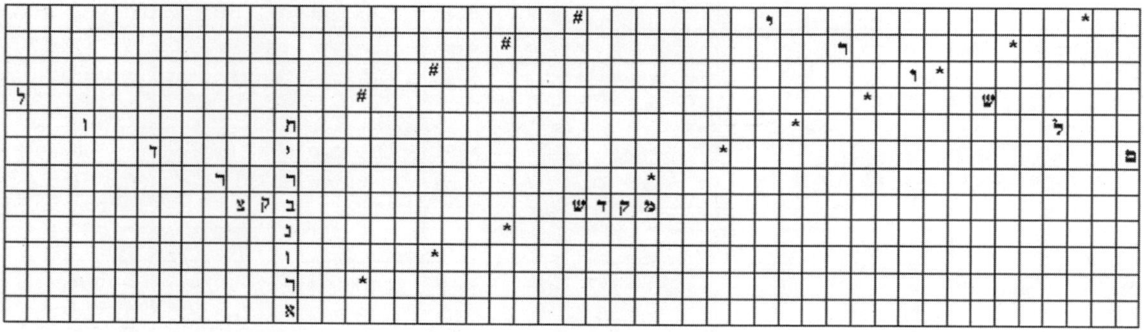

Stars and ש reveal 11 positions that will yield a proper course with the start of ארון ברית. **# reveals 4 positions that will yield a proper course with the end of ארון ברית.**

Probability calculation #1: What is the chance that מקדש will be at skip +1 somewhere on the 48 column by 12-row matrix of ELS Map Figure 1?

Given: מקדש occurs at skip +1 a total of 59 times in Torah. The matrix has 576 characters. There is no interference from Bardawil (ברדול), Zuqba (צקב), or Jerusalem (ירושלם).

TEMPLE AT THE PROPER ANGLE FROM ARK OF THE COVENANT ON ELS MAP FIGURE 1	SKIPS USED ON MAP PLOT	C NUMBER IN SKIP RANGE	D DIVIDE BY 304805 LETTERS IN TORAH	E THE QUOTIENT EQUALS FREQUENCY PER LETTER	F E QUOTIENT x 576 EQUALS WORD EXPECTANCY	G POISSON EQUATION PROBABILITY FOR TEMPLE APPEARING AT LEAST ONCE	H CHANCE FOR TEMPLE TO BE IN THE BOX
TEMPLE @ SKIP 1 ONLY	1	59	304805	0.000193566	0.111494234	0.105503451	9.478362943

The above spreadsheet reveals a probability of 0.105503451 or about one chance in 9.5 that Temple (מקדש) would be somewhere on the matrix at skip +1 (which is why it was originally ignored). However, Figure 44, shows what happens when a course of exactly 251.565 degrees is required (meaning a ratio of 3 columns to 1 row change in the proper direction). Then only 15 of the 576 cells on the matrix are suitable for placement of מקדש. Whereas 15/576 = 0.026041667, it is argued that the probability of having מקדש on the matrix and having it at the mandatory angle seen on five other map plots (including one developed by Dr. Haralick) is the product of 0.105503451 and 0.02604166. This equals 0.002747486 (about **one chance in 363).**

The above calculation for ELS Map Figure 1 is based upon a larger matrix than that originally found on Figure 1. The map plot in question includes display of both Jerusalem and Bardawil. The original matrix (presented at the ITCS in 1999) was 11 rows by 28 columns for a total of 308 letters. Since מקדש is on that plot too, let's see what the chance was for it to be there at the correct angle on what was the very first matrix produced in my Ark search in October, 1997. We are still working with 59 occurrences of מקדש at skip +1.

THE PROPER	USED	NUMBER	DIVIDE BY	THE QUOTIENT	E QUOTIENT	POISSON EQUATION	CHANCE FOR
ANGLE FROM	ON	IN	304805	EQUALS	x 308	PROBABILITY FOR	TEMPLE
ARK OF THE	MAP	SKIP	LETTERS	FREQUENCY	EQUALS	TEMPLE	TO BE IN
COVENANT	PLOT	RANGE	IN	PER LETTER	WORD	APPEARING	THE BOX
ON FIGURE 1;			TORAH		EXPECTANCY	AT LEAST ONCE	
TEMPLE @							
SKIP 1 ONLY	1	59	304805	0.000193566	0.059618445	0.057876062	17.27830051

So the chance for מקדש to be somewhere on that plot was only about one in 17. However, when we consider possible working placements, the picture looks like Figure 45:

Figure 45: Placement of מקדש at the Proper Angle on Figure 1

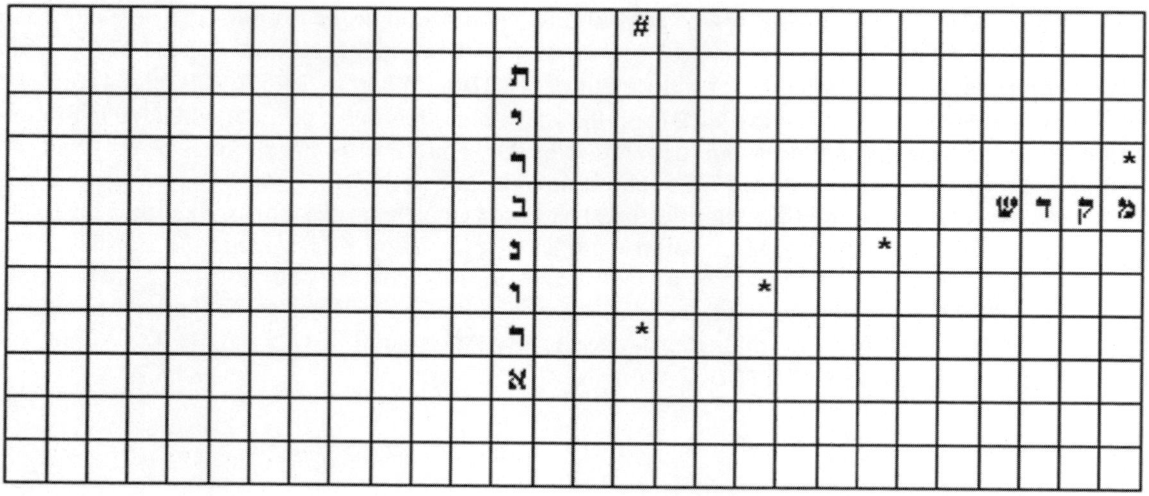

Stars and ש reveal 5 positions that will yield a proper course with the start of ארון ברית**.**
 # reveals 1 position that will yield a proper course with the end of ארון ברית**.**

Thus there are 6 positions out of 308 on the matrix that will produce the desired angle. 6/308 = 0.0196078431. Multiply this by the chance that מקדש would be somewhere on the matrix (0.057876062), and the product is 0.001134825 or about one chance in 881. And this is, of course, only one small part of the Figure 1 series of matrices.

LATITUDE PROBABILITY CALCULATIONS

Figure 2 was the first latitude plot. It initially encompassed only three rows and 24 columns. The plot was based around the open-text finding of Ark of the Covenant at Deuteronomy 31:9. There were two key words sought for this plot: *latitude* and *31:9*. The encoding of 31-9 fit the normal standard that requires all letters of a three-letter word to be within three letters of each other, as this word appears at an interval equal to "N" (which is 63). But *latitude* appears on one line at an ELS of +6 which does *not* fit the standards developed later in the experiment. There are other good encodings of *latitude* that were found later near *Ark of the Covenant*'s Deuteronomy 31:9 appearance. But, they were not immediately found on the first day of the experiment and, in all honesty, they did not serve as the initial cause of looking at a map to see where 31° 9' North intersected 33° 4' East.

For this figure we can not use the normal parameter of 28 skips. The plot has only three rows so vertically only "N" is possible, not 2N or 3N. Although it was earlier stated that 3-letter words would not normally be printed if beyond three letters apart on the first line, I did not form this restriction until later in my experiment. Since a 3-letter word may be seen across 24 columns at skips 1 through 11, we will use the more honest figure of 11 possible skips (1 to 11) on one line in a forward direction. These 11 skips, when added to the one vertical skip possible = 12 skips in a forward direction. I would like to say that skips for the "N" line would be limited to N +/- 1 to 2 as I did earlier in this Report, but again that was not my search parameter when I started the latitude search, so we will go with N +/- 1 to 11 intervals. As such we must now add another 22 possible skips to the previous total of 12. This brings our total so far to 34 skips. Now we must double this to account for the reverse direction. Thus the number of intervals searched here (in a forward direction only) is 68.

Next we must determine by raw computer search how many times *latitude* (רחב) and *31-9* (ל-א) occur in the five Torah books of our Control.

WORD	NUMBER OF HITS IN TORAH AT SKIPS +1 TO +68
LATITUDE	1,562
31-9	791

Now we divide each of the above figures by the 304,805 letters in the Control to obtain Word Frequency per Letter.

WORD FREQUENCY PER LETTER

WORD	
LATITUDE	1,562/304,805 = 0.005124588
31.9	791/304,805 = 0.002595107

Next we multiply the word frequency per letter times the number of letters on the plot. Three rows times 24 columns = 72 letters.

WORD EXPECTANCY PER PLOT

WORD	
LATITUDE AT 68 SKIPS	0.005124588 * 72 = .368970336
31-9 AT 68 SKIPS	0.002595107 * 72 = .18684704

Now we employ the Poisson equation to convert word expectancy per plot to probability.

WORD PROBABILITY PER PLOT

WORD	WORD EXPECTANCY	POISSON PROBABILITY
LATITUDE AT 68 SKIPS	0.368970336	0.308554079
31-9 AT 68 SKIPS	0.18684704	0.170429382

COMBINED PROBABILITY = 0.052586681

This represents one chance in 19.01. These odds aren't astounding, but were cause for the initial continuation of the experiment.

Much of the material in my original Experimental Report is described in this book before the current Appendix. Some of the most important spreadsheets are included in chapter 9. With regard to the spreadsheets for Figure 8 (Tunguska), the crude process by which the value of the find was downgraded is still an uncertain one. What is seen on the second spreadsheet is what happens when we divide the value of what was found by the value of what was not found. While this procedure is questionable, I believe that it is also questionable to proclaim the statistical value of plots that show what was found while overlooking what was not found. For now I will leave it to other mathematically inclined researchers to further tackle the problem. In the end what concerns me is not the statistic, but the presence or absence of predicted physical evidence at the site in question. Only such evidence can, in the end, put the question of Code reality to a rest.

FIGURE 8 TUNGUSKA ASTEROID

A	B	C	D	E	F	G
CALCULATION #1						
WITHOUT CONSIDERATION						
OF KEY WORDS SOUGHT						
BUT NOT FOUND	B	C	D	E	F	G
A	SKIP	NUMBER	DIVIDE	QUOTIENT	E QUOTIENT	POISSON
TUNGUSKA IS CONDITIONAL	USED	IN	304805	EQUALS	X 375	EQUATION
AXIS TERM @ SKIP 9551	ON	TORAH	LETTERS	FREQUENCY	EQUALS	PROBABILITY
There are 15 lower ELS finds for	PLOT		IN THE	PER LETTER	WORD	WORD
this Tunguska spelling, but there			TORAH		EXPECTANCY	APPEARING
are other transliterations.						AT LEAST ONCE
1 TAMMUZ @ SKIPS 4976-5065	**4976**	**7**	**304805**	**2.29655E-05**	**0.008612063**	**0.008575086**
ASTEROID @ SKIP +1 ONLY	**1**	**10**	**304805**	**3.28079E-05**	**0.012302948**	**0.012227576**
STARS OF HEAVEN @ +1 ONLY	**1**	**6**	**304805**	**1.96847E-05**	**0.007381769**	**0.00735459**
SINCE THE PHRASE STARS OF HEAVEN						combined
BEGINS WITH THE SAME WORD AS						probability =
ASTEROID, IT COULD BE ARGUED THAT						7.71147E-07
THIS PLOT IS NO BETTER THAN THE						The above =
INTERSECTION OF TUNGUSKA WITH						1 chance in
STARS OF HEAVEN + 1 TAMMUZ ON						1296769.142
PLOT. IF SO, THEN THE COMBINED						Divide above by
PROBABILITY IS READJUSTED TO						16 because there
0.000104853						are 15 lower ELS
						finds for this
THIS IS ONE CHANCE IN						spelling. This
9537.205798						is 1 chance in
THE CHANCE TO GET THIS PLOT						81048.07139
IS READJUSTED TO						for this spelling.
596.0753624						There were 39
DUE TO 15 LOWER ELS FINDS FOR						additional hits for
THE CONDITIONAL AXIS TERM AT						15 other
THIS SPELLING.						transliterations
WHEN 39 OTHER ADDITIONAL HITS						of Tunguska.
AT A LOWER ELS THAN THIS						If we consider
TUNGUSKA WERE FOUND AT						the total of 54
ALTERNATE SPELLINGS FOR						lower ELS
TUNGUSKA, THE FINAL VALUE OF						findings of
THE PLOT WAS DOWNGRADED TO						Tunguska, the
ONE CHANCE IN						adjusted chance =
173.4037418						1 in chance in
WHAT KEY WORDS WERE NOT FOUND						15040.83619
ON PLOT? RUSSIA, SIBERIA, AND						
HEBREW YEAR 5668. ALL THESE						
HAVE 5 LETTERS, THE SAME AS						
DATE 1 TAMMUZ. IF WE SEACH						
TORAH AT THE SAME FORMULA						
SKIP RANGE AS 1 TAMMUZ, THERE						
WERE 10 HITS FOR RUSSIA,3						
FOR SIBERIA, AND 1 FOR THE YEAR.						
ADD THESE TO THE HITS FOR 1						
TAMMUZ. READJUSTED DATA IS						
IS AS FOLLOWS ON THE NEXT SPREADSHEET						

Figure 8 – Tunguska Asteroid Calculation (Downgraded for Words Sought but Not Found).

FIGURE 8 TUNGUSKA ASTEROID	SKIPS	NUMBER	DIVIDE BY	QUOTIENT	E QUOTIENT	POISSON
CALCULATION #2	USED	IN	304805	EQUALS	X 375	EQUATION
WITH CONSIDERATION OF	ON	TORAH	LETTERS	FREQUENCY	EQUALS	PROBABILITY
KEY WORDS SOUGHT BUT NOT	PLOT		IN THE	PER LETTER	WORD	FOR WORD
FOUND AXIS TERM. There are 15 lower			TORAH		EXPECTANCY	APPEARING
ELS finds for						AT LEAST
this spelling of Tunguska, but there						ONCE
are several other transliterations.						
1 TAMMUZ @ SKIPS 4976 TO 5065	4976	7				
RUSSIA, SIBERIA + 5669 @ SAME SKIPS	**N/A**	**14**				
1 TAMMUZ + RUSSIA + SIBERIA + 5668		**21**	304805	6.88965E-05	0.02583619	0.025505292
ASTEROID @ SKIP+1 ONLY	1	10	304805	3.28079E-05	0.012302948	0.012227576
STARS OF HEAVEN @ SKIP +1 ONLY	1	6	304805	1.96847E-05	0.007381769	0.00735459
						combined
SINCE THE PHRASE STARS OF HEAVEN						probability =
BEGINS WITH THE SAME WORD AS						2.29366E-06
ASTEROID, IT COULD BE ARGUED THAT						The above =
THIS PLOT IS NO BETTER THAN THE						1 chance in
INTERSECTION OF TUNGUSKA WITH						435984.2973
STARS OF HEAVEN + 1 TAMMUZ ON						Divide above by
PLOT. IF SO, THEN THE COMBINED						16 as there are
PROBABILITY IS READJUSTED TO						15 lower ELS
0.000187581						finds for this
THIS IS ONE CHANCE IN						spelling. This
5331.031103						equals 1
THE CHANCE TO GET THIS PLOT						chance in
IS READJUSTED TO						27249.01858
333.1894439						for this spelling.
DUE TO 15 LOWER ELS FINDS FOR						There were 39
THE CONDITIONAL AXIS TERM AT						additional hits
THIS SPELLING.						for 15 other
WHEN 39 OTHER ADDITIONAL HITS						transliterations
AT A LOWER ELS THAN THIS						of Tunguska.
TUNGUSKA WERE FOUND AT						If we consider
ALTERNATE SPELLINGS FOR						the total of 54
TUNGUSKA, THE FINAL VALUE OF						lower ELS
THE PLOT WAS DOWNGRADED TO						findings of
ONE CHANCE IN						Tunguska, the
96.92783824						adjusted prob. =
						in chance in
						7926.987224

APPENDIX B

Appendix B

SKIP TABLES TO BE EMPLOYED WITH THE ROFFMAN SKIP FORMULA

Table 1A - HORIZONTAL/VERTICAL SKIPS POSSIBLE FOR A 3-LETTER WORD

COLUMNS (C) OR ROWS(R)	SKIPS POSSIBLE FOR 3-LETTER WORDS	
1	0	
2	0	
3	1	
4	1	
5	2	
6	2	
7	3	
8	3	
9	4	NOTE: NORMALLY
10	4	INTERVALS OF 4
11	5	OR MORE ARE
12	5	REJECTED AS TOO
13	6	FAR APART.

TABLE 1B – HORIZONTAL/VERTICAL SKIPS FOR A 4-LETTER WORD

COLUMNS (C) OR ROWS (R)	SKIPS POSSIBLE FOR 4-LETTER WORDS	COLUMNS OR ROWS	SKIPS POSSIBLE FOR 4-LETTER WORDS
1	0	50	16
2	0	51	16
3	0	52	17
4	1	53	17
5	1	54	17
6	1	55	18
7	2	56	18
8	2	57	18
9	2	58	19
10	3	59	19
11	3	60	19
12	3	61	20
13	4	62	20
14	4	63	20
15	4	64	21
16	5	65	21
17	5	66	21
18	5	67	22
19	6	68	22
20	6	69	22
21	6	70	23
22	7	71	23
23	7	72	23
24	7	73	24
25	8	74	24
26	8	75	24
27	8	76	25
28	9	77	25
29	9	78	25
30	9	79	26
31	10	80	26
32	10	81	26
33	10	82	27
34	11	83	27
35	11	84	27
36	11	85	28
37	12	86	28
38	12	87	28
39	12	88	29
40	13	89	29
41	13	90	29
42	13	91	30
43	14	92	30
44	14	93	30
45	14	94	31
46	15	95	31
47	15	96	31
48	15	97	32
49	16	98	32

TABLE 1C – HORIZONTAL/VERTICAL SKIPS FOR A 5-LETTER WORD

COLUMNS (C) OR ROWS (R)	SKIPS POSSIBLE FOR 5-LETTER WORDS	COLUMNS OR ROWS	SKIPS POSSIBLE FOR 5-LETTER WORDS
1	0	50	12
2	0	51	12
3	0	52	12
4	0	53	13
5	1	54	13
6	1	55	13
7	1	56	13
8	1	57	14
9	2	58	14
10	2	59	14
11	2	60	14
12	2	61	15
13	3	62	15
14	3	63	15
15	3	64	15
16	3	65	16
17	4	66	16
18	4	67	16
19	4	68	16
20	4	69	17
21	5	70	17
22	5	71	17
23	5	72	17
24	5	73	18
25	6	74	18
26	6	75	18
27	6	76	18
28	6	77	19
29	7	78	19
30	7	79	19
31	7	80	19
32	7	81	20
33	8	82	20
34	8	83	20
35	8	84	20
36	8	85	21
37	9	86	21
38	9	87	21
39	9	88	21
40	9	89	22
41	10	90	22
42	10	91	22
43	10	92	22
44	10	93	23
45	11	94	23
46	11	95	23
47	11	96	23
48	11	97	24
49	12	98	24

217

TABLE 1D – HORIZONTAL/VERTICAL SKIPS FOR A 6-LETTER WORD

COLUMNS (C) OR ROWS (R)	SKIPS POSSIBLE FOR 6-LETTER WORDS	COLUMNS OR ROWS	SKIPS POSSIBLE FOR 6-LETTER WORDS
1	0	50	9
2	0	51	10
3	0	52	10
4	0	53	10
5	0	54	10
6	1	55	10
7	1	56	11
8	1	57	11
9	1	58	11
10	1	59	11
11	2	60	11
12	2	61	12
13	2	62	12
14	2	63	12
15	2	64	12
16	3	65	12
17	3	66	13
18	3	67	13
19	3	68	13
20	3	69	13
21	4	70	13
22	4	71	14
23	4	72	14
24	4	73	14
25	4	74	14
26	5	75	14
27	5	76	15
28	5	77	15
29	5	78	15
30	5	79	15
31	6	80	15
32	6	81	16
33	6	82	16
34	6	83	16
35	6	84	16
36	7	85	16
37	7	86	17
38	7	87	17
39	7	88	17
40	7	89	17
41	8	90	17
42	8	91	18
43	8	92	18
44	8	93	18
45	8	94	18
46	9	95	18
47	9	96	19
48	9	97	19
49	9	98	19

TABLE 1E – HORIZONTAL/VERTICAL SKIPS FOR A 7-LETTER WORD

COLUMNS (C) OR ROWS (R)	SKIPS POSSIBLE FOR 7-LETTER WORDS	COLUMNS OR ROWS	SKIPS POSSIBLE FOR 7-LETTER WORDS
1	0	50	8
2	0	51	8
3	0	52	8
4	0	53	8
5	0	54	8
6	0	55	9
7	1	56	9
8	1	57	9
9	1	58	9
10	1	59	9
11	1	60	9
12	1	61	10
13	2	62	10
14	2	63	10
15	2	64	10
16	2	65	10
17	2	66	10
18	2	67	11
19	3	68	11
20	3	69	11
21	3	70	11
22	3	71	11
23	3	72	11
24	3	73	12
25	4	74	12
26	4	75	12
27	4	76	12
28	4	77	12
29	4	78	12
30	4	79	13
31	5	80	13
32	5	81	13
33	5	82	13
34	5	83	13
35	5	84	13
36	5	85	14
37	6	86	14
38	6	87	14
39	6	88	14
40	6	89	14
41	6	90	14
42	6	91	15
43	7	92	15
44	7	93	15
45	7	94	15
46	7	95	15
47	7	96	15
48	7	97	16
49	8	98	16

TABLE 1F – HORIZONTAL/VERTICAL SKIPS FOR AN 8-LETTER WORD

COLUMNS (C) OR ROWS (R)	SKIPS POSSIBLE FOR 8-LETTER WORDS	COLUMNS OR ROWS	SKIPS POSSIBLE FOR 8-LETTER WORDS
1	0	50	7
2	0	51	7
3	0	52	7
4	0	53	7
5	0	54	7
6	0	55	7
7	0	56	8
8	1	57	8
9	1	58	8
10	1	59	8
11	1	60	8
12	1	61	8
13	1	62	8
14	1	63	9
15	2	64	9
16	2	65	9
17	2	66	9
18	2	67	9
19	2	68	9
20	2	69	9
21	2	70	10
22	3	71	10
23	3	72	10
24	3	73	10
25	3	74	10
26	3	75	10
27	3	76	10
28	4	77	11
29	4	78	11
30	4	79	11
31	4	80	11
32	4	81	11
33	4	82	11
34	4	83	11
35	5	84	12
36	5	85	12
37	5	86	12
38	5	87	12
39	5	88	12
40	5	89	12
41	5	90	12
42	6	91	13
43	6	92	13
44	6	93	13
45	6	94	13
46	6	95	13
47	6	96	13
48	6	97	13
49	7	98	14

CHI SQUARE TABLES
Percentile Values
For the Chi-Square Distribution
With degrees of freedom shown at left side.

Deg free	X^2 .995	X^2 .99	X^2 .975	X^2 .95	X^2 .90	X^2 .75	X^2 .50	X^2 .25	X^2 .10	X^2 .05	X^2 .025	X^2 .01	X^2 .005
1	7.88	6.63	5.02	3.84	2.71	1.32	.455	.102	.0158	.0039	.0010	.0002	.0000
2	10.6	9.21	7.38	5.99	4.61	2.77	1.39	.575	.211	.103	.0506	.0201	.0100
3	12.8	11.3	9.35	7.81	6.25	4.11	2.37	1.21	.584	.352	.216	.115	.072
4	14.9	13.3	11.1	8.49	7.78	5.39	3.36	1.92	1.06	.711	.484	.297	.207
5	16.7	15.1	12.8	11.1	9.24	6.63	4.35	2.67	1.61	1.15	.831	.554	.412
6	18.5	16.8	14.4	12.6	10.6	7.84	5.35	3.45	2.20	1.64	1.24	.872	.676
7	20.3	18.5	16.0	14.1	12.0	9.04	6.35	4.25	2.83	2.17	1.69	1.24	.989
8	22.0	20.1	17.5	15.5	13.4	10.2	7.34	5.07	3.49	2.73	2.18	1.65	1.34
9	23.6	21.7	19.0	16.9	14.7	11.4	8.34	5.90	4.17	3.33	2.70	2.09	1.73
10	25.2	23.2	20.5	18.3	16.0	12.5	9.34	6.74	4.87	3.94	3.25	2.56	2.16
11	26.8	24.7	21.9	19.7	17.3	13.7	10.3	7.58	5.58	4.57	3.82	3.05	2.60
12	28.3	26.2	23.3	21.0	18.5	14.8	11.3	8.44	6.30	5.23	4.40	3.57	3.07
13	29.8	27.7	24.7	22.4	19.8	16.0	12.3	9.30	7.04	5.89	5.01	4.11	3.57
14	31.3	29.1	26.1	23.7	21.1	17.1	13.3	10.2	7.79	6.57	5.63	4.66	4.07
15	32.8	30.6	27.5	25.0	22.3	18.2	14.3	11.0	8.55	7.26	6.26	5.23	4.60
16	34.3	32.0	28.8	26.3	23.5	19.4	15.3	11.9	9.31	7.96	6.91	5.81	5.14
17	35.7	33.4	30.2	27.6	24.8	20.5	16.3	12.8	10.1	8.67	7.56	6.41	5.70
18	37.2	34.8	31.5	28.9	26.0	21.6	17.3	13.7	10.9	9.39	8.23	7.01	6.26
19	38.6	36.2	32.9	30.1	27.2	22.7	18.3	14.6	11.7	10.1	8.91	7.63	6.84
20	40.0	37.6	34.2	31.4	28.4	23.8	19.3	15.5	12.4	10.9	9.59	8.26	7.43
21	41.4	38.9	35.5	32.7	29.6	24.9	20.3	16.3	13.2	11.6	10.3	8.90	8.03
22	42.8	40.3	36.8	33.9	30.8	26.0	21.3	17.2	14.0	12.3	11.0	9.54	8.64
23	44.2	41.6	38.1	35.2	32.0	27.1	22.3	18.1	14.8	13.1	11.7	10.2	9.26
24	45.6	43.0	39.4	36.4	33.2	28.2	23.3	19.0	15.7	13.8	12.4	10.9	9.89
25	46.9	44.3	40.6	37.7	34.4	29.3	24.3	19.9	16.5	14.6	13.1	11.5	10.5
26	48.3	45.6	41.9	38.9	35.6	30.4	25.3	20.8	17.3	15.4	13.8	12.2	11.2
27	49.6	47.0	43.2	40.1	36.7	31.5	26.3	21.7	18.1	16.2	14.6	12.9	11.8
28	51.0	48.3	44.5	41.3	37.9	32.6	27.3	22.7	18.9	16.9	15.3	13.6	12.5
29	52.3	49.6	45.7	42.6	39.1	33.7	28.3	23.6	19.8	17.7	16.0	14.3	13.1
30	53.7	50.9	47.0	43.8	40.3	34.8	29.3	24.5	20.6	18.5	16.8	15.0	13.8
40	66.8	63.7	59.3	55.8	51.8	45.6	39.3	33.7	29.1	26.5	24.4	22.2	20.7
50	79.5	76.2	71.4	67.5	63.2	56.3	49.3	42.9	37.7	34.8	32.4	29.7	28.0
60	92.0	88.4	83.3	79.1	74.4	67.0	59.3	52.3	46.5	43.2	40.5	37.5	35.5

2

Source: Catherine M. Thompson, Table of percentage points of the *X* distribution, Biometrica, Vol. 32 (1941)

BIBLIOGRAPHY

BIBLIOGRAPHY

Aharoni, Yohanan, and Avi-Yonah, Michael, *THE MACMILLAN BIBLE ATLAS*, Prepared by Carta, Jerusalem, The MacMillan Company, New York, 1968.

Alcalay, Reuben, *THE COMPLETE ENGLISH-HEBREW DICTIONARY*, Massada Publishing Company, Tel Aviv – Ramat Gan, Israel.

Bowditch, Nathaniel, LL.D., *AMERICAN PRACTICAL NAVIGATOR*, U.S. Naval Hydrographic Office, U.S. Government Printing Office, Washington, D.C. 1966.

Chase, Scott I., *TACHYONS*, Physics, 22 March 1993. http://math.ucr.edu/home/baez/physics/ParticleAndNuclear/tachyons.html

Clarke, Arthur C. and Stephen Baxter, THE *LIGHT OF OTHER DAYS*, Tor Books, New York, NY, 2000.

Cohen, Rev. Dr. A., Editor, *THE SONCINO BOOKS OF THE BIBLE*: Joshua and Judges; Jeremiah, Chronicles, Samuel, the Twelve Prophets; The Soncino Press, London, U.K., 1977.

Chronicle Encyclopedia of History, High School Excelerator CD, World History, Topics Entertainment, Renton, Washington, 2001.

Croce, C.M. 2001, *HOW CAN WE PREVENT CANCER*? Proceedings of the National Academy of Sciences, 98 (Sept. 25):10986-10988.

Crotser, Tom, *ARK OF THE COVENANT, IT IS FOUND!*, Prophecy Publications, 1993, pp. 13-15. published by Church, R.H. http://www.thefutureevent.com/Ark.htm

Drosnin, Michael, *THE BIBLE CODE*, Simon and Schuster, New York, New York, 1997.

Drosnin, Michael, *BIBLE CODE II*, Viking, New York, New York, 2002.

Frewin, Ryan; George, Rene; Paulson, Deborah, *SUPERLUMINAL MOTION: FACT OR FICTION*, http://www.math.utexas.edu/~clong/newlumin1.html

García Martínez, Florentino, *THE DEAD SEA SCROLLS TRANSLATED: THE QUMRAN TEXTS IN ENGLISH*. 2nd ed. New York/Grand Rapids: Brill/Eerdmans, 1996.

Hancock, Graham, *THE SIGN AND THE SEAL*, Touchstone Books, Westport, Connecticut, 1993. Also *THE SIGN AND THE SEAL: QUEST FOR THE LOST ARK OF THE COVENANT,* Crown Publishers, 1992.

Hertz, Rabbi Naftali ben Elchanan, *EMEK HAMELEK*, Amsterdam, Holland, 1648.

Horn, Seigfried, Biblical Archeology Review , page 69 , May/June 1983.

Katz, Dr. Moshe, *COMPUTORAH*, The Kest-Lebovits Jewish Heritage and Roots Library, Jerusalem, Israel.

Lerman, Matthew, *MARINE BIOLOGY, ENVIRONMENT, DIVERSITY, AND ECOLOGY*, The Benjamin/Cummings Publishing Company, Inc., Menlo Park, California, 1986.

McKay, Brendan D.; Bar-Natan, Dror; Bar-Hillel, Maya, and Kalai, Gil, *SOLVING THE BIBLE CODE PUZZLE*, Statistical Science, Vol 14, pp150-173 (1999).

National Geographic, *ATLAS OF THE WORLD, REVISED SIXTH EDITION*, National Geographic, Washington, D.C. 1992

Potok, Chaim, *WANDERINGS, HISTORY OF THE JEWS*, Fawcett Crest, New York, NY, 1978.

Price, Randall, *IN SEARCH OF TEMPLE TREASURES*, Harvest House Publishers, Eugene, Oregon 97402, 1994.

Pritchard, James, Editor, *COLLINS ATLAS OF THE BIBLE*, Border Press in association with HarperCollins, Ann Arbor, Michigan, 2003.

Pritchard, James B., Editor, *THE HARPER ATLAS OF THE BIBLE*, Times Books Limited, Harper and Row, New York, New York, 1987.

Robins, Gerald, *VENDYL JONES AND THE ARK OF THE COVENANT*, An article serialized in the Jewish Herald Voice Newspaper, Houston, TX in May 2000, http://www.rense.com/general2/ark.htm (posted 6 June 2000).

Scherman, Rabbi Nosson and Zlotowitz, Rabbi Meir, *THE STONE EDITION THE CHUMASH*, Artscroll Series, Mesorah Publishers, Ltd., Brooklyn, N.Y., 1994.

Sharpe, Captain Richard OBE Royal Navy, *JANE'S FIGHTING SHIPS*, Jane's Information Group, Sentinel House, Coulsdon, Surrey, United Kingdom, 1997.

Shorrosh, Dr. Anis A., Quotation from the Wichita Eagle-Beacon, cited in the Longview Morning Journal, July 11, 1982. Also see the Shorrosh book, THE EXCITING DISCOVERY OF THE ARK OF THE COVENANT, Winona, Minnesota, 1984.

Stafford, Peter, *PSYCHEDELICS ENCYCLOPEDIA,* And/Or Press, Berkeley, CA. 1977.

Times Books, *THE TIMES ATLAS OF THE WORLD, COMPREHENSIVE EDITION*, Times Books London in collaboration with John Bartholomew & Son Limited, 1981.

Thompson, Catherine M., Table of percentage points of the X^2 distribution, Biometrica, Vol. 32 (1941).

Van Biema, David, *DECIPHERING GOD'S PLAN*, Time Magazine, Jun 9, 1997.

Wallace, Debra L., *LOCAL TEACHER PROPOSES ACID TEST FOR TORAH CODES*, Palm Beach Jewish Journal North, Page 6A, April 7, 1998.

Wang, Lijun; Kuzmich, A.; and Dogairiu, A., *GAIN-ASSISTED SUPERLUMINAL LIGHT PROPAGATION*, Nature 406, 277 - 279 (2000). See also http://physicsweb.org/article/news/4/7/8

Wead, Doug; Lewis, David; and Donaldson, Hal, *WHERE IS THE LOST ARK?,* Bethany House Publishers, Minneapolis, Minnesota 55438, 1982.

Wise, Michael O., *THE DEAD SEA SCROLLS, A NEW TRANSLATION*, HarperCollins, San Francisco, CA 1996.

Witztum, Doron; Rips, Eliyahu; and Rosenberg, Yoav; *EQUIDISTANT LETTER SEQUENCES IN THE BOOK OF GENESIS*, Statistical Sciences.

Wohlgelernter, Elli, *ALL THAT WAS, IS AND WILL BE IS IN THE TORAH*, an article in the Jerusalem Post, May 20, 1999.

INDEX OF MATRICES, ELS MAPS,
AND GEOGRAPHIC MAPS

INDEX OF MATRICES, ELS MAPS, AND GEOGRAPHIC MAPS

Table 1 – Index of Matrices

Table 2 – Index of ELS Maps and Geographic Maps

ELS Maps	Page	Geographic Maps	Page
1 Zuqba, Bardawil, Jerusalem, and Temple	9	**1** Pre-Expedition Map of Bardawil	3
2 Dr. Haralick's Find	11	**2** Course from Jerusalem to Bardawil	10
3 Jerusalem to Position of Ark	13	**3** Qatia	15
4 Position of the Ark and Jerusalem	14	**4** Bir El Abd	23
5 Ugret Selima and Jerusalem	16	**5** Zuabatiya	24
6 Ugret Selima to Ark	18	Labeled Satellite photo of Bardawil	28
7 Katib El Qals and Jerusalem	19	**6** Migdol and Baal Zephon	36 & 75
8 Katib El Qals and Jerusalem	21	**7** Baal Zephon in Harper Atlas	76
9 Jerusalem to Bir El Abd	22	**8** Chart BA 56100	80
10 Zuaba, Jerusalem and Ark	25	**9** Hebrew map of Sinai	160

INDEX